VCs

OF THE FIRST WORLD WAR

THE SIDESHOWS

VCs OF THE FIRST WORLD WAR

THE SIDESHOWS

GERALD GLIDDON

First published 1996
This edition published 2014

The History Press
The Mill, Brimscombe Port
Stroud, Gloucestershire, GL5 2QG
www.thehistorypress.co.uk

British Library Cataloguing in Publication Data.
A catalogue record for this book is available from the British Library.

ISBN 978 0 7509 5378 8

Typesetting and origination by The History Press
Printed in Great Britain

Contents

In memory of Leo Cooper, publisher
(1934–2013)

ACKNOWLEDGEMENTS

As always I would like to thank the staff of the following institutions for their assistance during the research for this book: the Commonwealth War Graves Commission, the Imperial War Museum, the National Army Museum and the National Archives at Kew. In addition, I would like to thank the archivists and curators of the many county archives, regimental museums and libraries who have replied to my request for information.

As with my previous books in the *VCs of the First World War* series, Donald C. Jennings of Florida has been extremely kind in allowing me to reproduce many of his photographs of both graves and memorials. In addition, David Harvey, before his untimely death in 2004, gave me permission to use some of the illustrations from his book, *Monuments to Courage*. Where other photographs have been used, their owners have been acknowledged within the picture's caption.

Most of the maps used have been taken from the *Official History of the Great War Military Operations: Other Theatres, 1914–19*, which the Naval & Military Press has kindly allowed me to use.

I am grateful to the late George Sassoon for his kind permission to reproduce the extract from *Siegfried Sassoon Diaries, 1915–1918*, edited and introduced by Rupert Hart-Davis (Faber & Faber, 1983, © Siegfried Sassoon).

Other individuals who have been of great help in many ways include: first and foremost, Peter Batchelor and Dr Graham Keech; John Bolton, Steve Brown, Roger Chapman, Andrew England, Winifred Gliddon, the late Miles Hudson, Walter Ireland, the late Philip Lewis, Chris Matson, Dennis Pillinger, Steve Snelling, Anthony Staunton and Iain Stewart. Those whose names are not mentioned here have been acknowledged in the list of sources at the end of the book.

PREFATORY NOTE

This book is the thirteenth and last volume in the *VCs of the First World War* series and requires a note of explanation. Its purpose is to cover the lives and careers of those men who won the Victoria Cross while serving in the Army in what were sometimes called 'sideshows' or 'other theatres'. However, Gallipoli, the biggest of these sideshows, has already been written about by Steve Snelling. The title chosen for this book is not meant in any way to denigrate the role of men involved in these theatres, but it does appear to be the most appropriate solution in the circumstances and was a term that was used during the war itself. In addition, and owing to the way the series developed, fourteen VCs have now been written up twice in the series, namely, E.C. Boyle, J.P.F. Butler, N.G. Chavasse, R. Bell Davies, G.L. Drewry, N.D. Holbrook, W. St A. Malleson, M.E. Nasmith, H.P. Ritchie, E.G. Robinson, G. McKenzie Samson, A.W. St C. Tisdall, E. Unwin and W.C. Williams. However, with the publication of this final volume, all 628 VCs awarded during the First World War have been finally covered.

This volume also excludes both the Naval and Aviation VCs and sets out to tell the stories of the military men who gained the Victoria Cross in other theatres apart from Gallipoli and the Western Front in France and Belgium; hence the territories covered include East and West Africa, the North-West Frontier of India, Italy, Mesopotamia, Palestine and Salonika. Although the names of most of these regions have changed, together with their geographical boundaries, I have chosen to retain the nomenclature of the period.

I have not set out to tell the complete histories of these six campaigns, so readers will look in vain for mentions of T.E. Lawrence's leadership of the Arab Revolt, during which time 12,000 Turkish troops were tied down, or of the Duke of Westminster in March 1916 rescuing a group of seamen captured by members of the Senussi tribe. Although it was mooted that both of these men might be awarded the VC, in the end they weren't and had to make do with the award of the Distinguished Service Order (DSO) instead. What I have attempted to do is to place each of the forty-six soldiers who won the nation's highest military honour in the historical background to which they belonged at the time of gaining the VC.

Finally, a note about decorations: most of the men written about in this book shared certain medals, although differences and variations do occur. The 1914 Star (or Mons Star) covers active military service for the period August–November 1914. The 1914 Star was awarded to men who actively served up to 31 December 1915, and who had not already been awarded the 1914 Star. The British War Medal (BWM) was given to servicemen who served overseas in the period 1914–18. The Victory Medal (VM) was awarded to men who served in an overseas theatre of war. Any VC holder mentioned in this book who survived the First World War and was still alive in 1937 would have been entitled to a King George VI Coronation Medal, as he would also have been if he survived until 1953 when Queen Elizabeth II was crowned.

Instead of writing an introduction to the book in the opening pages, I have decided to place a brief note of explanation at the beginning of each of the six main sections.

The History Press has decided to re-issue the *VCs of the First World War* series in new editions and I have taken advantage of this decision by revising and updating the text of the current volume. Since the initial research for this book was carried out ten years ago there has been an increasing interest in and awareness of the stories and lives of the men who were awarded the nation's and the Commonwealth's highest military honour. Evidence of this can be found in the amount of interest in the subject by the media, new books being published on the subject, the issuing of servicemen's records by the National Archives and the accessibility of other records of family history, which are now available via *Ancestry*, the family history magazine, and from other sources. The Internet has also played a major part, although information received using this method should always be verified by cross-checking. Finally, the founding of the Victoria Cross Society in 2002 by Brian Best has encouraged further research and publication of informative articles on the holders of the Victoria Cross.

While this book was in preparation, the British government announced plans for commemorating the First World War centenary from 2014 to 2018. One of the ideas is directly linked with the commemoration of men who had won a Victoria Cross during the Great War. It is proposed that towns or regions most associated with each serviceman will commemorate their 'local hero' with a paving stone set in a prominent place. The men born outside the United Kingdom will hopefully also be remembered, but this is being negotiated. In addition, all the names of the 628 VC holders will be commemorated on a central paving stone surrounded by panels, which would also include regimental names and date of the award. This would be set up at the National Memorial Arboretum, Cannock Chase, Staffordshire.

Gerald Gliddon, July 2014

AFRICA

J.F.P. BUTLER

The Cameroons, West Africa, 17 November 1914

In August 1914 Germany's African colonies consisted of German East Africa, German South-West Africa and, in the west, the Cameroons and Togoland. It was naturally the aim of the British and French armies to drive Germany out of these territories. It was obvious from the beginning of the war that the Germans would eventually be defeated and pushed out of Africa, if only by the sheer weight of troop numbers.

The wily German Commander Gen. von Lettow-Vorbeck was military commander in German East Africa in August 1914 and never had more than 15,000 troops under his command during the war. On the other hand, the Allies had command of the sea and were able to muster up to 100,000 men from India and many parts of Africa itself. The German aim was to tie up this Allied force for as long as possible and prevent the soldiers from being used on the Western Front. It is an odd, but very well-known fact, that the enemy in East Africa was never defeated and had to be instructed to cease fire only several days after the Armistice had been agreed in Europe.

In Togoland in West Africa on 12 August 1914, in what must have been one of the very first actions of the war (even the BEF had not yet set foot in France), a single native regiment of the Gold Coast Regiment, together with French troops, conducted a successful mounted attack against the German forces to the east of Gold Coast. On 25 August Tepe was taken by the Allies and, by the following day, Togoland had been conquered.

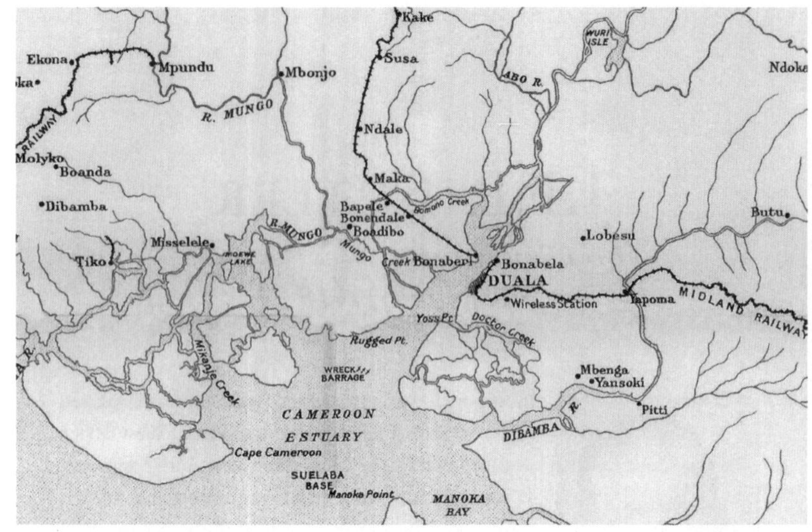

North of Duala, Cameroons, 17 November 1914.

Three days later, however, the British were defeated at Garua and also suffered another reverse near Nsanakong (Nsana Kang). But also on 26 October the Allies captured Duala, the capital of the Cameroons. During the Cameroons Campaign much of the fighting took place around the important railways that ran to the north and east of Duala.

Three weeks later, on 17 November, Capt. J.F.P. Butler of the King's Royal Rifle Corps (KRRC), attached to Pioneer Company, Gold Coast Regiment, West African Forces, became the first man to win the VC in Africa during the First World War when he won the decoration for conspicuous bravery in the Cameroons fighting. He was with a party of thirteen men in thick bush when they attacked a force of about 100 troops, including several Europeans. Butler's party defeated them and captured their machine-gun, as well as a great quantity of ammunition. Nearly six weeks later, on 27 December, when an advance was held up, Butler was on patrol with a small group and swam across the River Ekam, which was in enemy hands. Alone and in the face of brisk fire he carried out reconnaissance on the far bank before swimming back to safety.

The New Year began with an Allied thrust into the bush-filled interior when their German adversary was making considerable use of native troops. In March, Butler was made a captain before returning to England. His VC was gazetted on 23 August 1915 and it was presented to him by the King at Buckingham Palace the following day. J.F.P. Butler's citation appeared in the *London Gazette* on 23 August 1915 as follows:

> John Fitzhardinge Paul Butler, Capt., King's Royal Rifle Corps, attached Pioneer Coy [Company] Z, Gold Coast Regt., West African Frontier Force. For most conspicuous bravery in the Cameroons, West Africa on 17 Nov. 1914. With a party of 13 men he went into the thick bush, and at once attacked the enemy, in strength about 100, including several Europeans; defeated them, and captured their machine gun and many loads of ammunition. On 27 Dec. 1914, when on patrol duty with a few men, he swam the Ekam River, which was held by the enemy, alone and in face of a brisk fire; completed his reconnaissance on the further bank and returned in safety. Two of his men were wounded while he was actually in the water.

Despite the capture of Duala, the Germans were still well entrenched and used a number of mountain strongholds from which they were able to conduct raids into neighbouring countries. Although they made considerable use of native troops, they did not treat them well; a factor that later in the war was to tell against them.

Capt. Butler was involved again in the Cameroons Campaign in December 1915 when fighting with the Gold Coast Regiment, which managed to get behind the German lines and capture a village, together with a machine-gun and the papers of the local German commander before establishing a base there. Two weeks later, Dschang Mangas, between Wum Biagas and Jaunde, a German base on the fringe of the Jaunde district, was also captured by them. By this time most of the forestry region was behind them, and before them lay a cultivated area which would be much easier to operate in. By 30 December they were entirely clear of the bush and a small party marched into Jaunde on New Year's Day 1916. Seven weeks after the enemy had been slowly squeezed out of the country, the German Army surrendered. The citation for Butler's DSO was published in the *London Gazette* on 5 June.

On 6 July the Gold Coast Regiment left the West African capital of Accra and sailed to East Africa, landing at Kilindini on the 26th. When they reached the firing line, the enemy was pushed back across the central railway. In German East Africa, the first firm contact with the enemy occurred on 4 September near the main highway to the east of the Matombo mission station. This was south of the railway in the Uluguru Mountains, which the Germans were preparing to strongly defend. The Allied positions were overlooked by the Kikirunga Hill, which was about 3,000ft high and covered with trees and undergrowth; this was a landmark that had to be captured. The action lasted two and a half days and duly ended with the capture of the hill, but the day was marred by the death of Capt. Butler. The full details of the incident are recorded in the history of the Gold Coast Regiment by Sir Hugh Clifford:

> At 7 a.m. on the 4th September the Regiment moved out of camp, and about two hours later the enemy opened fire with a couple of howitzers upon the road a little ahead of the marching troops. No casualties were inflicted but the Regiment was halted, moved off the road and took up a sheltered position on the right side of it, in a gut between two hills.
>
> Captain Butler was then sent forward with a Pioneer Company to reconnoitre the enemy positions and the small party climbed towards the head of the pass that led to the Uluguru Mountains, that had Kikirunga as its culminating point. The Pioneer Company reached a point where they could overlook the enemy positions but they must have been spotted as a German machine gun opened up from the right and another gun about 100ft higher also opened up on the small party.
>
> It was not until about 5 o'clock in the afternoon that the Pioneer Company became seriously threatened and it was when Butler had gone forward to check his picket on the bend of the road that he and several of his party were wounded by a sudden burst from one of the machine guns. They had been lying down, close to the road and the enemy machine gunners were either aware of them, or just fired off a round or two at random. Twelve men were wounded during the afternoon but the party still managed to stand firm. Later 'B' Company under a Captain Shaw was sent up to reinforce the Pioneers, and to make the ground won, good. They settled down for the night after attending to the wounded.

Butler had been wounded in the shoulder, but more seriously a bullet had penetrated one of his lungs and, according to a witness, Maj. G.H. Parker MC, RA, he lay dying by his side all through the night. The Regimental History noted the following of Butler:

> A young officer, possessed at once with a charming and forceful personality, of an absolutely fearless disposition, and of more than ordinary ability, he has won for himself a conspicuous place in the Gold Coast Regiment, and had earned the devotion and affection of the men in a very special degree. His death, in this first action in which the Regiment had been engaged since its arrival in East Africa, was felt to be a specially malignant stroke of ill-fortune and he was mourned as a personal loss by his comrades of all ranks.

Unofficially, Butler died of his wounds on 5 September 1916 near Matombo (later Tanzania). He was buried in the Morogoro Cemetery, Tanganyika (Tanzania), Plot III, Row C, Grave 3. He was Mentioned in Despatches (MiD) three times.

John Fitzhardinge Paul Butler was the son of Lt Col Francis John Paul Butler of Wyck Hill, Gloucestershire, and his wife the Hon. Elspeth Fitzhardinge, daughter of the 2nd Lord Gifford. He was born at the Chantry, Berkeley, Gloucestershire, on 20 December 1888, and was a nephew of Maj. Lord Gifford VC, the 3rd baron, who had won the VC in the First Ashanti War (1823–31).

John Butler was educated at Mr Kempthorne's House at Wellington, and then the Royal Military Academy (RMA) at Sandhurst, where he won the Military History Prize. In February 1907, when he was 18, he was awarded a commission in the KRRC, and in August 1909 he was promoted to lieutenant, serving in India until 1913. On 1 October 1913 he was seconded to the Gold Coast Regiment in West Africa and during the war served in the Togoland and Cameroons Expeditions.

John Butler had married Alice Amelia of Apsley House, Portfield, Chichester, and after the war his name was commemorated on the war memorial at Cirencester Parish Church. He also has a pair of candlesticks in his name in St Lawrence's Church, Bourton-on-the-Water. His decorations are in the keeping of the Royal Green Jackets in the Peninsular Barracks, Winchester, Hampshire. Apart from the VC and DSO they include a 1914–15 Star, BWM, VM (1914–19) and MiD Oakleaf.

W.T. DARTNELL

Near Maktau, East Africa, 3 September 1915

By the end of the nineteenth century, most of East Africa was divided up and controlled by Great Britain (Kenya) and Germany (Tanganyika), with the two countries sharing a border which ran from Lake Victoria to the Indian Ocean via the base of Mount Kilimanjaro. The two colonial powers had also set up extensive railway building programmes in order to create an infrastructure for the country.

However, this coexistence was to end with the declaration of war in August 1914 when each side sought to take control of the whole region. On 16 October an 8,000-strong force under Maj. Gen. Aitken left Bombay for Mombasa, and as a preliminary strike against German forces the Allied troops arrived 80 miles south of Mombasa at the port of Tanga on 2 November. Soon after disembarking and having moved inland, the force came up against well-prepared strong enemy positions manned by African troops and was severely routed. In addition, there seemed to be little allowance for any necessity of evacuation procedures.

This defeat was a humiliation, although admittedly the Allied force was made up from a predominantly African and Indian force who had received little in the way of training and had just endured a debilitating voyage from India. In other words, they were in no fit state to face an efficient enemy lying in wait for them. Any plans for a future offensive were delayed until 1916.

Nearly ten months after Capt. John Butler won his VC in the Cameroons Campaign, Wilbur Taylor Dartnell became the second man to win the honour on African soil during the First World War when he won a posthumous award at Maktau, East Africa, on 3 September 1915.

The most important priority for the British was to defend against any German attacks on the Uganda railway, which began at the port of Mombasa. In the early part of the war, the enemy made at least fifty attacks against this key rail line, leading to the derailment of trains and the destruction of bridges. It seems that whole stretches of the line were left unguarded and the raiders were only pursued *after* making a raid. A note in the war diary of the 2nd Loyal North Lancashires suggests that it would have been much better to use blockhouse posts as a superior way of guarding the lines against attacks. An additional problem was manpower, as the continual presence of fever kept the defenders down to half strength.

Dartnell's battalion, the 25th (Service (S)) Royal Fusiliers (Frontiersmen), left Plymouth for British East Africa on 10 April 1915, arriving at Mombasa on 4 May. Their first duties were to take up positions on the section of the railway that led to Uganda at the military post Kajiado, and to defend it against possible enemy attacks, which would probably develop from the south-west in the German-held portion of East Africa. On 19 June a detachment from the 25th Royal Fusiliers detrained at Kisumu, the terminus for the Uganda railway. Three days later the 400-strong party sailed across Lake Victoria with the plan of making an attack from the north against German-held territory on the western shores of the lake. Initially, the troops were faced with the task of climbing a 'cliff-like incline' where they met no opposition. However, once they reached the rocky ground at the foot of the hill towards Bukoba, they were faced with vigorous German resistance.

As darkness fell the attack paused, to be resumed the following morning when a heavy thunderstorm further delayed proceedings. Despite this, a determined group of men, soaked to the skin and with rifles out of action, overcame the last of the German defensive resistance. The wireless station was destroyed together with ammunition and stores, and on 24 June the men re-embarked and returned to Kisumu.

During the battle at Bukoba, 2/Lt Dartnell distinguished himself during the successful raid when, on arriving at the enemy post leading the attack, he entered the enemy fort and pulled down the German Imperial flag from the roof, replacing it with a Union Jack. During the operation eight men were killed and twelve wounded, and Dartnell was recommended for the DSO and Mentioned in Despatches. As a consequence, he was also promoted to lieutenant at the end of July.

The battalion then moved to Voi, a town about 55 miles north of the frontier between Nairobi and Mombasa, from which the military rail line was being constructed towards Taveta on the border, a town which had been captured by the Germans on 14 August 1914 and used as a base for raids.

The 25th Royal Fusiliers were split up, with one half going to Nairobi for training and the other half moving to the small village of Maktau, about 35 miles from Voi and at that time an important railhead for the construction of a military railway to use in any future Allied invasion of German-held East Africa. The enemy was not far away, having established an outpost a day's ride away at Mbuyuni, from which they continued to harass groups of men working on the railway line construction. A small observation fort was put up by the British, which overlooked Maktau. At the same time, mounted patrols were sent out to cover the area.

At the end of August a Mounted Infantry Company (MIC) was formed to combat German attacks and the troops were to be drawn from a group of about seventy-five men from Dartnell's 25th Royal Fusiliers and an equal number from the 2nd Loyal North Lancashires (LNL). Initially under the command of Capt. J.S. Woodruffe (Royal Sussex Regiment, attached to the Loyal North Lancashires), the remaining officers in the company were drawn from the 25th Royal Fusiliers, South Lancashire Regiment and the Loyal North Lancashires.

A section of men supplied from the Royal Fusiliers, under Lts Ryan and Dartnell, together with fifty rifles, left Mile 56 on the Mogodi railway via Voi to Maktau and then joined up with the other section of the MIC which was then under the command of Capt. G.P. Atkinson (LNL).

On 3 September it was reported that the enemy had crossed the border and laid a mine on the Mombasa–Nairobi line, and on their return would pass as close as 5 miles from Maktau. A party of the MIC, four officers and sixty-three men supplemented by fifty Baluchi troops from the 130th Battalion, was sent out at 6.30 a.m. to intercept the enemy on their way back. The MIC was under the command of Capt. Woodruffe, who gave orders to dismount and to establish a firing line on a slight slope and to establish picquets. However, at about 10.15 a.m. the advance posts were suddenly ambushed and men forced back to the firing line 'where desperate fighting took place at very short range'. It was estimated that the enemy force was about 200 strong, and on hearing the sound of heavy firing the Baluchi troops took cover. Woodruffe gave orders to fix bayonets, but his men were completely overwhelmed and the German-controlled Askaris or native troops closed in on the small party. The fighting continued for about thirty minutes, during which time Woodruffe was badly wounded in the back and his force was in grave danger of becoming surrounded; he gave orders to withdraw and for the wounded to be evacuated promptly.

During the action Lt Dartnell was wounded in the leg below the knee and carried to safety. However, realising just what might happen to the badly wounded who could not be moved, and knowing full well that the Askaris were likely to hack the British wounded to pieces, he gave orders to be left, in the hope of being able somehow to save the lives of some of his comrades. He was twice asked to leave and finally gave an order to abandon him. When last seen alive the enemy was within 25yd of his position. He courageously fought on to the bitter end, trying to save life but losing his own in the process. When the dead were brought in a few hours later by Maj. Robinson with a force of stretcher-bearers, Dartnell's fears were confirmed as the bodies had been stripped and mutilated by the Askaris, who had shown no mercy.

On 14 September a similar action took place when a German patrol was ambushed south-west of Maktau, when the enemy had again been attempting to attack the railway line. The MIC, under the command of Capt. G.P. Atkinson, also employed Askaris. German casualties were one officer and twenty-eight Askaris.

Eight of the men who died as a result of the ambush on 3 September were initially buried in Maktau Military Cemetery and later reinterred in Voi Cemetery: five from the Loyal North Lancashires and three (including Dartnell) from the Royal Fusiliers. Dartnell was buried in Plot V, Row B, Grave 1, and his stone carried the inscription 'Greater love hath no man'. However, there were at least three other men from these battalions who died on that day as a result of the action;

the remains of two of them were never found and their names are commemorated on the panels of the Nairobi and Indian Memorial, together with a third man, L/Cpl S. Goddard (LNL), who was possibly taken prisoner and buried in a former German cemetery.

Wilbur Dartnell's VC citation was published on 23 December 1915 as follows:

> Wilbur Dartnell, Temporary Lieut., late 25th (Service) Battn. (Frontiersmen) The Royal Fusiliers (City of London Regt.). For most conspicuous bravery near Maktau (East Africa) on 3 Sept. 1915. During a mounted infantry engagement the enemy got within a few yards of our men, and it was found impossible to get the more severely wounded away. Lieut. Dartnell, who was himself being carried away wounded in the leg, seeing the situation, and knowing that the enemy's black troops murdered the wounded, insisted on being left behind in the hope of being able to save the lives of the other wounded men. He gave his own life in the gallant attempt to save others.

After the sale of his kit in October 1915, the proceeds being sent to a Mabel Evans of East London, Cape Province, the money was later claimed by his wife in a letter dated 27 October 1915. Her address was 9 Tranmere Avenue, Murrumbeena, Victoria, Australia. She later lived at 'Maktau', Phillips Avenue, Murrumbeena, Victoria. She was presented with her husband's VC by His Excellency Sir Ronald Munro Ferguson, Governor-General of Australia, at Federal Government House, Melbourne, on 7 October 1916. She was also invited to the VC centenary celebrations in London in June 1956.

Wilbur Dartnell is one of several men commemorated on a plaque in the foyer of the Theatre Royal, Drury Lane, as before the war he had been a professional actor. He is also remembered by Dartnell Street in Canberra. The German flag captured at Bukoba in June 1915 was returned to England and displayed in the corridor of the City of London Headquarters (HQ), the Royal Regiment of Fusiliers.

On 18 March 1981 Dartnell's VC, together with the Queen's South Africa Medal for his service in the Victorian Mounted Rifles in the Boer War (he was entitled to the Queen's South Africa Medal (3 Clasps)), King's South Afica Medal (2 Clasps), the Natal Rebellion Medal (1906), the 1914–15 Star, BWM, VM (1914–19) and MiD Oakleaf, were sold for $24,000 at Sothebys to Messrs Spinks on behalf of their Sydney office. Dartnell was one of only four men to win the VC in the East African Campaign. Two years later the VC and four other medals were put up for sale again, this time at the Wentworth Hotel in Sydney. They were bought for $36,000 by a Mr Berry, a private collector, who presented them to the Australian War Memorial in Canberra in 1984. His reason was that he was 'fed up' with the way that medals were being treated simply as financial investments and he was keen for them to be in public hands.

William Thomas Dartnell, son of Henry and Ros Ann (née Hanley), was born in Fitzroy, near Collingwood, Melbourne, Australia, on 6 April 1885 and went to school in Melbourne. At the age of 15 he joined the Australian Contingent and, from March 1901, served for a year in the South African Campaign, first with the Victorian Bushmen and then with the 5th Victorian Mounted Rifles, where his number was 1172 and with whom he served until March 1902. He later served in Royston's Horse during the 1906 Natal Rebellion. On his return from Natal he married Elizabeth Edith Smyth at Holt's Matrimonial Agency, 448 Queen Street, Melbourne, on 15 April 1907 and the couple lived in Fitzroy and were to have one daughter. It is not really clear how Dartnell survived between 1906 and 1912, but most accounts say the same thing, namely that he ran his own business until 1912–13, then he left once more for South Africa, settling in East London, Cape Province, where he took a job with the Standard Printing Company (Co.) and regularly submitted articles to the *Weekly Standard*, a Saturday evening newspaper. It is possible that he decided to seek his fortune in the new Continent and then send for his family later. Also when living in South Africa he changed his name to Wilbur Taylor Dartnell.

On the outbreak of war, Dartnell was determined to take part and called a meeting of Australians who lived locally and would be willing to serve. Chairing the proceedings he placed his name at the top of the list. He then contacted the War Office in London, offering the group's services and asking for their passage to England. The group left for England on 23 September 1914 and Dartnell enlisted with the Legion of Frontiersmen under the command of Col O.P. Driscoll

DSO on 12 February, the day that the Service battalion was formed as the 25th Royal Fusiliers (S) Battalion (Frontiersmen) (City of London Regiment). He was awarded a temporary commission. In his application to Col O.P. Driscoll, Dartnell stated that he had lived in Africa 'for a number of years and am well accustomed to handling natives. I have a fair knowledge of native tongues and dialects. I thoroughly understand horses and am a good rider.' He was initially stationed at Swaythling, close to Southampton, and from there he made several trips to Belgium when in charge of drafts of artillery horses destined for the front. A photograph of Dartnell and Col Driscoll outside the commandant's house at Bukoba was later published in vol. 10 of *The Times History of the War*.

It appears that when Dartnell returned to Africa he became engaged to another lady, Mabel Frances Katherine Evans from East London. It was in her favour that he made out a will dated 23 September 1914, and when his kit was put up for auction after his death, the sum of £52 9s was raised and sent to her.

Dartnell is commemorated in the Victoria Cross Memorial Park in Canberra and in the Victoria Cross Memorial in the Queen Victoria Building, Sydney.

W.A. Bloomfield

Mlali, East Africa, 24 August 1916

On the outbreak of war in August 1914, German-held territories in Africa included the section of East Africa bordered by Kenya and Uganda to the north, and Nyasaland and Northern Rhodesia to the south. In October, a weak Allied attempt had been made to land a force of Indian troops in order to occupy Tanga, north of German-held Dar es Salaam, which, owing to the lack of training and experience of the invading force, turned into a disaster. No serious attempt to oust the Germans was made again until 1916, after their other possessions in Africa had been wrested from them.

The Germans had adopted a policy of making raids into Uganda and, in particular, the area including Lake Victoria. However, by early 1916 a small British military presence had been reinforced and, in late August, was placed under the command of Gen. Smuts, who had successfully fought against the British in the Boer War, twenty years earlier. In February 1916 an attacking brigade was drawn from men selected from British and Indian troops, supported by a larger group of men from South Africa. Their first success was the capture of the area around Mount Kilimanjaro. On 23 August the brigade reached the railway line to the east of Mkata, south-west of Tanga, and captured three Askaris. The plan was to attack a large enemy force at Mlali, known to be led by Gen. von Lettow-Vorbeck.

The August war diary of the 2nd South African Mounted Brigade recorded on 24 August:

> Make attack on Mlali. Reinforcements from Morogoro arrive and Germans manage to escape on footpath to MGETA mission station but our force held the position which commands wagon road Morogoro–Kissaki via Mahalaka and to Kidodi. Germans unable to remove their guns and are therefore compelled to blow up two of their three 5-inch Naval guns.
>
> We captured 200 4.1 shells and 300 other shells and large quantity of supplies and cattle. Our losses 1 killed 7 wounded.

It was during actions on this day that Capt. William Bloomfield, formerly a captain in Van Deventer's Scouts, South African Scout Corps, 2nd South African Mounted Brigade, carried out the deeds which led to the award of the VC. After the enemy reinforcements arrived from Morogoro, they began to work round the flanks of Bloomfield's advance sector. In danger of becoming isolated, he withdrew his section to a new position ¼ mile away. It was at that point, when considering the positions of his new defences, that he discovered a wounded soldier, Cpl D.M.P. Bowker, had been left behind. He decided to return to fetch the non-commissioned officer (NCO) and, in full view of the enemy, who did not stop their machine-gun or rifle fire, he reached the wounded man and brought him in. The citation for his VC action at Mlali was published in the *London Gazette* four months later on 30 December as follows:

> William Anderson Bloomfield, Capt., Scout Corps, South African Mounted Brigade. For most conspicuous bravery. Finding that, after being heavily attacked in an advanced and isolated position, the enemy was working round his flanks, Capt. Bloomfield evacuated his wounded, and subsequently withdrew his command to a new position, he himself being amongst the last to retire. On arrival at the new position he found that one of the wounded – No. 2475. Corpl. D.M.P. Bowker – had been left behind. Owing to very heavy fire he experienced difficulties in having the wounded corporal brought in. Rescue meant passing over some 400yds of open ground, swept by heavy fire, in full view of the enemy. This task Capt. Bloomfield determined to face himself, and, unmindful of personal danger, he succeeded in reaching Corpl. Bowker and carrying him back, subjected throughout the double journey to heavy machine-gun and rifle fire. This act showed the highest degree of valour and endurance.

The war diary entry for the following day noted:

> Make attack to prevent Germans from escaping on footpath to Mgeta Station but unable to do so on account of their heavy maxim fire. Get information strength German forces 10 Coys. Von Lettow & Germans escape on footpath after which German forces to retreat to mountains.

Von Lettow-Vorbeck led the German Governor and ten companies of his men to safety. The war diary file also includes an extensive handwritten report on the actions signed by Brig. Gen. B. Enslin, officer commanding (OC) 2nd Mounted Brigade, who had this to say about Capt. Bloomfield's gallantry:

> In returning from the above advanced position to the main position and the magazine, Trooper Bowker who was badly wounded through the stomach was left behind. When Capt. Bloomfield of the Scouts discovered this he ran back under heavy cross maxim and rifle fire, picked Tr. Bowker up and carried him a distance of 500yds to our lines. By doing this Capt. B. saved Tr. Bowker's life for if he had not carried him out Bowker would have remained on the veldt during the night and following day and as a result of such exposure would have died, his wound being a severe and dangerous one. In view of the above I would strongly recommend that Capt. B's noble and gallant act be specially recognised.

Col G. Tylden sent notable VC historian Canon Lummis a letter about several of the South African VC holders he had known. Of Bloomfield he wrote:

> Bloomfield I knew slightly. He was down and out with the man he rescued when a young S.A. Dutchman rode back & got both men out. Bloomfield put the chap up for a V.C. & failed, so his (B's) father bought & stocked a farm in the Transvaal and gave it to the youngster title deeds & all.

Six months after he won his VC Bloomfield was Mentioned in Despatches, returned to South Africa and relinquished his commission. He then volunteered for active service in France and was awarded the rank of major. He served in France from 19 September 1917 until the end of the war in November 1918. On 20 October 1917 he received his VC from the King at Buckingham Palace.

On his return home he was demobilised at Rosebank on 23 July 1919.

William Anderson Bloomfield, an only son, was born in Edinburgh on 30 January 1873 (David Harvey, *Monuments to Courage*, notes that he was born 'Broomfield'), and his parents left for South Africa when he was 6 years old. Soon he was orphaned, having lost both parents. In the early 1890s, when in his late teens, he became a trooper in the Cape Mounted Police and served in Bechuanaland. In 1897 he settled in the Transvaal and joined the Ermelo Commando on the outbreak of the Boer War. When serving in Natal he was put in charge of the ambulance section. Thus he became the only man to fight for the Boer forces and also win the VC. In 1899 he served in the Cape Police at the same time as another VC recipient, John Sherwood-Kelly. They were both members of a mounted bodyguard to Sir Alfred Milner, Governor-General of the Cape Colony, when he was on a visit to Transkei.

Bloomfield took an active part in many military engagements, including the Battle of Spion Kop. Towards the end of the year he was captured at Ermelo Hospital, while he attended the wounded men in his charge. He remained in the town and took over a hotel.

On 14 December 1904 he married Maria Magdalena de Villiers and the couple were later to have two daughters, in 1906 and 1907. Bloomfield was a section leader of the local Ermelo Town Guard during the rebellion. In early 1915 he became a member of the 16th Intelligence Unit (Collins' Scouts) with the rank of private, but was commissioned two months later in March. He first fought in the campaign in South-West Africa (modern-day Namibia), before being released from service in August 1915.

Eight months later, on 1 April 1916, Bloomfield rejoined the army, this time as a captain in the 2nd Mounted Brigade Scout Corps. The unit departed for East Africa on 18 May and for three months it took part in the campaign to push the extremely wily and tactically brilliant Gen. von Lettow-Vorbeck, with his mixed force of German and African native troops, back across the border into the Portuguese-held part of East Africa. Later in the year, Bloomfield won his VC at Mlali on 24 August 1916.

After the end of the war Bloomfield served on various committees; he was a member of the town council and, in 1933, deputy mayor of Ermelo, where he had lived since the Boer War after purchasing the Phoenix Hotel together with a Mr Rust. Later he took over a cartage contract business with the South African Railways. He was to play a leading role in public life in the town and was offered the mayorship on three occasions, but declined the offer each time.

At the age of 91 William Anderson Bloomfield died on 12 May 1954 from heart failure at Ermelo. He was buried three days later with civic honours at the local cemetery in Ousthuizen Street. Ex-servicemen and local Freemasons took part. According to an account in the *Highveld Herald* of 21 May 1954:

> A traffic policeman on a motor cycle led the municipal fire engine carrying the coffin, which was covered by the Union flag with the late Major's decorations, medals, sword and helmet placed on top, after which came the procession of relatives, official representatives and many friends paying their last respects to an honoured Ermelo resident.
>
> On arrival at the Cemetery, Town Councillors acted as pallbearers for part of the way to the grave, subsequently being replaced by relatives and close friends of the deceased.

After various wreaths were laid, including one by Mrs Bloomfield, the local lodge of Freemasons carried out their own ceremony in honour 'of their departed brother'. The newspaper account wrote that Bloomfield 'will always be remembered for the keen interest he took in all public matters, especially ex-servicemen's affairs and the fact that he unveiled the Ermelo War Memorial in Joubert Park'. His widow died fifteen years later on 28 June 1969.

Bloomfield is one of the South African VCs commemorated at Delville Wood in Longueval on the Somme. His decorations include the Cape General Service Medal (1880–90) and clasp for Bechuanaland, BWM, VM (1914–19) and MiD Oakleaf, King George V Silver Jubilee Medal (1935), King George VI Coronation Medal (1937) and Queen

Elizabeth Coronation Medal (1953). They are in the Military History Museum in Johannesburg. The museum also holds other memorabilia, including his tunic, cap, Sam Browne belt, a diary, notebook and three portraits. His VC is held by his family.

F.C. BOOTH

Johannesbruck, near Songea, East Africa, 12 February 1917

Between 11 and 24 November 1916 the 1st Rhodesia Native Regiment, to which Frederick Booth was attached from the South African Police, was involved in a defence of the town of Songea, 80 miles east of Lake Nyasa. Further fighting also took place in the area three months later when, on 12 February 1917, the regiment took part in an attack on enemy positions at Johannesbruck, near Songea, on the eastern side of Lake Nyasa. Sgt Booth of the Rhodesia Native Infantry led his men against an enemy position in an attack through thick bush and under heavy rifle fire. He then went forward to rescue a seriously wounded colleague. Later he rallied and reorganised the native troops and led them back to the firing line. For this deed he was later to be awarded the VC.

Two weeks later, on 28 February, Booth was with Col Tomlinson when he received orders to pursue the German Gen. Wintgens and defeat him by surrounding his forces. The Rhodesian force had arrived by gunboat at Mwaya and was brigaded with the Southern Rhodesia Column. The Rhodesians travelled via New Langenburg, reaching the Igali Pass on 9 March. The plan was to attack the German force at Old Utengule, which the Rhodesians reached a week later to find that the enemy had moved back westwards to St Moritz Mission. Col Tomlinson advanced on the Mission from the south, while

Col Murray, as leader of the Rhodesian forces, made for Itaka with the intention of moving northwards, thus preventing the enemy moving further westwards. A battalion of King's African Rifles was instructed to move to Old Utengule to meet up with the enemy.

St Moritz Mission was on the south bank of the Songea River, which at the time was in flood and the only way the enemy could cross it was by using a bridge at St Moritz itself. The King's African Rifles planned to prevent this crossing from taking place, while Col Murray was to advance on the Mission from positions at Itaka and then join Col Tomlinson's force. However, owing to Col Tomlinson misunderstanding his instructions, he was faced with the German force on 20 March and as a result suffered many casualties and was forced to retire. Having made this initial error, he made an even worse decision when he dug-in on the plains instead of heading for the protection of the hills south of St Moritz. As a result his troops became surrounded.

It is at this point that Booth, who must have been aware of the situation, enters the story. Someone was required to move through enemy lines and make contact with Col Murray to ask him for urgent assistance, and Booth volunteered immediately. He set off at 7.30 p.m., accompanied by a single Askari, and the two men made a detour in order to avoid the enemy between them and Itaka.

Booth succeeded in his mission the following day and he was able to inform Col Tomlinson of his success by using lamp signals from a hill position. Three days later, using his knowledge of the country, Booth was able to lead the relief party on the morning of 27 March. However, by now the enemy force had made its escape and had retired across the Songea River in a northerly direction without firing a shot.

Booth was clearly a very distinguished and courageous NCO, and he was soon promoted to lieutenant and awarded the DCM for gallantry on 15 May (for rescuing two Askaris from a shark-infested stream under fire). A short while later, Booth was wounded and evacuated from East Africa.

The citation for his VC was published in the *London Gazette* on 8 June 1917 as follows:

> Frederick Charles Booth, No. 1630, Sergt., South African Forces, attached Rhodesia Native Regt. For most conspicuous bravery during an attack in thick bush on the enemy position. Under very heavy rifle fire Sergt.

> Booth went forward alone, and brought in a man who was dangerously wounded. Later he rallied native troops, who were badly organized, and brought them to the firing line. This N.C.O. has on many previous occasions displayed the greatest bravery, coolness and resource in action, and has set a splendid example of pluck, endurance and determination.

In October 1917 Booth was recommended for a permanent commission in the Regular Army and left for Britain in November 1917. He received his VC from the King at Buckingham Palace on 16 January 1918. A few weeks later, on 12 February, he officially left the Rhodesia Native Regiment on being appointed to a permanent commission in the Middlesex Regiment with the rank of captain.

Frederick Charles Booth, son of Charles Booth, was born at Bowes Park, Upper Holloway, London, on 6 March 1890 and educated at Cheltenham College where he was a boarder at Hazelwell.

After leaving college he emigrated to South Africa and joined the British South African Police (1912–18), and was attached to the Rhodesia Native Regiment. During one of the very first actions to take place in August 1914, Booth, then serving as a trooper, was involved in fighting at an outstation in Karonga, at the northern end and western shore of Lake Nyasa, Nyasaland Protectorate, German East Africa. The station included a small block of offices and residences, and was a depot for the Ross-Adam Trading Co. Having been alerted to the likelihood of an enemy attack, a British force made up of 500 troops together with 200 non-combatants left Fort Johnston by steamer, arriving at Karonga five days later on 22 August. After much confusion over where the enemy was actually deployed, the enemy was ejected with heavy casualties. It should perhaps be noted just how early in the war this fighting took place and that, had the enemy been successful at this early stage, then they would have been able to control the whole of Nyasaland.

Just over three weeks later on 16 September, Trooper Frederick Booth dived into the Zambesi at Kazungula in order to save the life of a troop horse which had broken loose and had become caught up in some thick reeds. This deed received a commendation in Police Orders on

3 November 1914. In 1916 Booth, by now a sergeant, was attached to the Rhodesia Native Regiment soon after it was formed and proceeded to East Africa where he won his VC on 12 February 1917.

John Sherwood-Kelly, also a member of the British South African Police, was attached to the 1st Rhodesia Native Regiment and was also to win a VC, during the Battle of Cambrai in November 1917.

In 1921, three years after the end of the war, Frederick Booth married Dolores, a widow since 1919 and a lady of substantial means with an income of about £10,000 to £12,000 a year from the will of her late husband, half of which went to the care of her two children. With hindsight the marriage was disastrous for both parties. She had known Booth for a number of years, but the marriage quickly ran into trouble and the two were clearly incompatible. Booth was moody and drank a fair amount, and on occasions struck his wife. Not surprisingly, Mrs Booth filed a petition for divorce on the grounds of cruelty, but it was dismissed. The couple did agree to separate, but in 1925 Booth planned to visit his wife's home, The Lodge, Effingham, Dorking, Surrey, and wrote informing her of his impending visit. He was told that, if he appeared, steps would be taken to restrain him.

On his arrival and finding the house open, Booth went into the sitting room and sat down. He was requested by three servants to leave the house, but refused unless he spoke to his wife first. A police inspector was called and Mrs Booth gave instructions for her husband to be removed from the house. While warning the inspector and servants that he would summons them if he was touched, Booth was seized and during a scuffle managed to knock one of the servants down before being finally ejected with the assistance of a groom, chauffeur, cowman, two gardeners and the police inspector.

Later Booth accused five of the servants and the inspector of assault and four of the servants were fined a nominal shilling. Booth himself was bound over for twelve months for using threatening behaviour towards his wife and was placed under court protection, which he considered unfair.

Now without a home, Booth entered Dorking Workhouse where he was allowed to stay for a week. During this time he had sought offers of employment in London and was given a week's work in a store dumping furniture. However, later offers of work did arrive as his difficulties became known.

According to a report in the *East Anglian Daily Times* (5 March 1926), Mrs Booth, who had changed her name to Pauling in January 1926, lost some of her jewellery which was being repaired by a London jeweller. The jeweller delivered it in October 1925 without permission to 34 Phillimore Gardens, which was one of her homes that Booth (later captain) was residing at while she was living at St George's Court, Hanover Square. She had taken this house in her husband's name in July 1922. Booth signed for the jewellery and it is not known what happened to it.

In November 1929 Booth attended the VC Dinner at the House of Lords, hosted by the Prince of Wales. Several years later and in preparation for the May 1937 Coronation of King George VI, he helped with the organising for the reception of Rhodesian troops visiting London.

Mrs Pauling, who had moved to France, died in July 1938, and it appears that when she and her husband separated she had agreed to pay an annuity of £500 'so long as he led a chaste life'. In 1941 Booth made a claim on his wife's estate and was awarded £6,547.

Between the two world wars the British South African Police used to hold regular reunions and Booth was a guest of honour at their annual dinner in 1938. After the Second World War broke out in September the following year, he volunteered for the Army and served with the Military Pioneer Corps in 1940 and was stationed in East Lancashire. He had been appointed second lieutenant in April and later left for France with the rank of captain.

After the end of the war, Booth attended the VE celebrations in London on 8 June 1946, followed by dinner at The Dorchester. In 1956 he attended the VC centenary commemorations in London and represented Rhodesia. At one point in the 1950s he was employed as a warehouseman in Bayswater.

Frederick Booth died in the Red Cross Convalescent Hospital for Officers, Percival Terrace, Brighton, on 14 September 1960, aged 70, and was buried five days later in the Red Cross Plot in Bear Road Cemetery, Brighton, reference ZKZ-36. His name is commemorated on a VC Roll of Honour Board at Cheltenham College. Other VCs remembered on the memorial include George Moor, Philip Neame and James Forbes-Robertson. His VC is not publicly held. In fact, his decorations, which also include the DCM, 1914–15 Star, BWM,

VM (1914–19) and MiD Oakleaf, King George VI Coronation Medal (1937) and Queen Elizabeth II Coronation Medal (1953) seem to have disappeared. It is probable that Booth returned them to his regiment in Salisbury, Rhodesia (now Zimbabwe), but they have not been seen in public since 1980.

INDIA

E. JOTHAM

Spina Khaisora (Tochi Valley), India, 7 January 1915

Stationed on the North-West Frontier prior to the First World War and acting as scouts, the 51st Sikhs' main duties were to guard against sporadic raiding parties by Pathan tribesmen. As part of this defence, a chain of outposts with telegraphic links was established along the frontier, which was 300 miles long and 100 miles deep. One of the provinces on the Punjab Frontier was Waziristan, which had been the scene of much fighting in the early part of the war.

The North-West Frontier had a history of conflict, although the responsibility for any fighting in the war years could hardly be laid at the British or even Turkish doors, but was still serious enough to need the involvement of at least twenty British or Indian regiments for the duration of the war. The main tribes involved in attacks against the British included the Tochi, Mohmand, Bunerwal, Swat and Mahsuds.

Despite Afghanistan having twice been at war with the British, the Amir of Afghanistan indicated in 1914 that the country would not make trouble for the British during the war. However, the subsequent entry of Turkey into the conflict on the side of Germany made the likelihood of disturbance on the frontier much greater. Although the 51st Sikhs had been initially ordered to guard the Suez Canal from November 1914, several officers had been left behind in charge of the remainder of the scout forces. Captain Eustace Jotham, who returned from leave in England in September 1913, was one of them and was ordered to join the North Waziristan Militia.

Each British officer in this militia was responsible for about 200 troops, drawn from the Pathan and Mahsud tribes, who were known for their fiery tempers and so required diplomatic handling. The North Waziristan Militia HQ was at Miranshah and was responsible for eighteen posts, each with between seventy and eighty men, in the upper and lower Tochi Valley on the 60-mile long Bannu–Datta road.

In November 1914 Jotham was involved in an operation which successfully dealt with a native attack against Miranshah.

Two months later, on 6 January 1915, Afghan tribesmen, supporters of Turkey, encircled one of the posts at Boya and then cut one of the telegraph lines to the HQ 15 miles away. To deal with this threat Capt. Jotham headed a column of thirty-seven mounted troopers early the following day, arriving in Boya at 9 a.m. They then moved on to Spina Khaisora, where hostile tribesmen were ready to attack. Reaching a post in a deep nullah (ravine), Jotham realised that his column was up against a much bigger force than was first thought. Quickly giving orders to turn around, the small group became encircled by approximately 1,500 tribesmen firing from both sides of the nullah. Desperate to escape from the trap, Jotham ordered the column to break into three sections, and two of these managed to get away while Jotham, in the last section, saw that one of his Indian troopers had been knocked off his horse; he was determined to save his colleague from being left behind in enemy hands.

Jotham allowed the rescued Indian sowar (cavalry equivalent of sepoy) to jump on his own pony, and the two men then struggled to escape. However, with the extra weight on the pony's back, a tragic end was inevitable and they were gunned down by rifle fire and finished off by knife and sword. Their bodies were severely mutilated.

Captain Jotham was to be awarded the VC for his extreme bravery, and his remains were buried in Miranshah Cemetery, North Waziristan, North-West Frontier, Plot 4, Grave 45.

After Capt. Jotham's death his father received letters from several of his son's fellow officers, including one dated 20 March 1915 from Maj. Walter St Hill of the Royal Fusiliers, who had become acquainted with Jotham when the latter was on leave. In this letter he described what happened during a train crash, when Jotham 'played a notable part' in rescuing trapped passengers in a railway coach following a crash of the Edinburgh and Glasgow expresses at Aisgill Junction. The rear coach of the Glasgow express was telescoped by the Edinburgh express and the coach caught fire; Jotham rescued four passengers. Sixteen people died in the crash. Hill was in the same coach and took part in the rescue where he:

> ... noticed a man working with ceaseless energy and pluck and always in the right directions. He was on the top of the compartment, already a mass of flames, handing out the poor people as we could extricate them. The while talking to them as if nothing was at stake and cheering them with kind words. He actually, to my certain knowledge, handed out four himself, his hair singed, his coat and cap on fire, working quite unconcernedly. . . . We travelled together to Leeds, and during this journey I took to him in a way that I think I have never done to any man before. We wrote to each other at Christmas, 1913, and on 12th Dec. [1914]. I received a regimental card from him, on which he wrote that 'it was hard to be shut up in a mud [?] sun-baked fort when he longed to be in France, where he hoped I now was.' I at once replied, and to my sincere regret the letter was returned to me marked, Deceased, killed in action.

Another of the many letters sent to Jotham's father was one dated 1 August 1915 from Lt Col G. Roos-Keppel, who was writing from the Chief Commissioner's camp, North-West Frontier Provinces.

> I hope you will excuse my writing to tell you how glad I am that your son's services have been recognised by the grant of the V.C. No V.C. can have been more nobly won. Your son having miraculously cut his way through hundreds of fanatical tribesmen, deliberately turned back and went in again to save one of his sowars who was down in the melee, although he knew that he was practically certainly sacrificing his life. He killed seven of the enemy before his death, and his gallantry has made a deep impression, not only on the men of the North Waziristan Militia, but even on the enemy. We were all proud of him, and grateful to him for setting such a magnificent example, which is specially valuable in a critical time like the present one.

For this gallant deed in the Tochi Valley, later to become part of Pakistan, Capt. Jotham was awarded a posthumous VC, which was gazetted on 24 July 1915 as follows:

> Eustace Jotham, Capt., 51st Sikhs, Frontier Force. For most conspicuous bravery on 7 Jan. 1915, at Spina Khaisora (Tochi Valley). During operations against the Khostwal tribesmen, Capt. Jotham, who was commanding a party of about a dozen of the North Waziristan Militia, was attacked in a nullah, and almost surrounded by an overwhelming force of some 1,500 tribesmen. He gave the order to retire, and could have himself escaped, but most gallantly sacrificed his own life by attempting to effect the rescue of one of his men who had lost his horse.

Jotham's name is included on Face 2 of the Delhi Memorial (India Gate), at the eastern end of the Rajpath or Kingsway. The memorial, designed by Sir Edwin Lutyens, commemorates 13,300 Commonwealth servicemen and 70,000 soldiers of 'undivided India' who served and died during the First World War. His posthumous VC was presented to his father at Buckingham Palace on 29 November 1916 and later passed to Margaret, Jotham's sister, whose son presented it to Bromsgrove School where it remains together with his BWM.

Eustace Jotham, second son of Frederick Charles and Mary C.A. Jotham (née Laxton), was born in Linden House, Chester Road, Kidderminster, on 28 November 1883. Having links with the wine trade and being a director of Charles Harvey & Co., Frederick Jotham had become a wealthy man. Linden House later became known as Stanmore House.

Jotham initially attended Lucton School, a boarding school near Leominster in Herefordshire, as a day-boy and was living in Kingsland nearby, possibly with relatives. He later went to Bromsgrove School in 1899–1901, where he became a member of the Cricket First XI and, more importantly, was groomed for entry into RMA Sandhurst, which he joined in 1902. He was commissioned into the 1st Battalion, the Prince of Wales's (North Staffordshire) Regiment on 22 April 1903. He then 'acclimatised' with the regiment before sailing with the 2nd Battalion to India in September 1903. On 23 June 1905 he was seconded to the Indian Army, whose officers were mainly British in command of Indian soldiers. He was promoted to lieutenant on 2 July 1905. He then became a member of the 102nd King Edward's Own Grenadiers. In 1908 he transferred to the 51st Sikhs (Frontier Force), who had been formed in the nineteenth century as the 1st Regiment of Infantry of the Frontier Brigade. In addition to guarding the 300-mile stretch of the North-West Frontier, they had fought in the Punjab Campaign (1848–49), the Afghan War (1878) and the Boxer Rebellion in China (1899–1901), and the role of his new regiment was to guard and patrol the Indian North-West Frontier on its border with Afghanistan. By 1911 Jotham had been attached to the North Waziristan Militia based at Miranshah, and on 22 April 1912 had become a captain. In 1913 he returned to England on leave.

Jotham is commemorated at Lichfield, Whittington Barracks, together with several other VCs. A memorial plaque was erected in the Sanctum Crypt at St Luke's Church, Chelsea, and he is also commemorated at Bromsgrove School. In 2015 he will have a commemorative paving stone laid in the Kidderminster area.

C. HULL

Hafiz Kor, North-West Frontier, 5 September 1915

Disturbances on the Peshawar border on the North-West Frontier began in the spring of 1915 when extremist mullahs (Islamic clergy) began to stir up hatred of the British in Mohmand territory. As a consequence, tribesmen began to gather and advance on a British fort at Shabkadr where the frontier constabulary had its HQ. One of the chief functions of the fort was to guard vital water supplies for the Peshawar region.

When the tribesmen made their attack, the fort held out for two days before assistance arrived in the form of the Peshawar Movable Column. An action took place near Hafiz Kor on 18 April when the Mohmands were pushed back and casualties were suffered on both sides.

Two months later, the safety of another fort, Chakdara, at Swat and the road to Chitral became threatened. However, owing to the presence of Allied troops at the fort, the threat of attack receded, but two months later it returned on 21 August when another tribal group moved down the River Swat to within a dozen miles of Chakdara. After a briefly fought action the Allied Malakand Movable Column returned to Chakdara, which it reached by 5 September.

By this time the Mohmands, under the leadership of Babra Mullah with 10,000 men, had decided to make another attempt to capture the fort at Shabkadr. However, the mullah's lashkars (militiamen) were attacked by three infantry brigades and cavalry from the 1st (Peshawar) Division, suffering over 1,000 casualties and were forced to retreat. The 21st Lancers (Empress of India's) had, according to R.V.E. Hodson, 'moved up from Adezai to the crossroads in sight of the fort at Shabkadr by 6 a.m. on the 5th. A long line of Mohmands on a sandy ridge to their front were visible and according to the regiment's war diary, numbered 5,000–6,000. More tribesmen could be seen in the hills and nullahs leading down to an open plain.'

At 8.30 a.m. the regiment left for Subhan Khwar Camp, moving north-westwards through Kodinak, and, as soon as their advance troops reached the ridge, they came under heavy rifle fire and B and C Squadrons came into action on the ridge. Their left flank was becoming vulnerable to attack and the two squadrons were ordered to fall back before B Squadron was instructed to attack tribesmen creeping along the Michni Canal bank. What remained of B Squadron, together with C Squadron, was then ordered to withdraw eastwards.

Later in the morning, B Squadron crossed the canal while C Squadron moved along the north bank, but, at a point opposite the village, the squadron came under heavy rifle fire. Col Scriven led the escape across the canal and through the village, but unfortunately two of his three officers became casualties. This left the adjutant, Capt. Learoyd, who crossed the canal after his colonel, but his horse was killed and he became trapped underneath it. It was at this point during the fighting in the foothills by Hafiz Kor that Pte Charles Hull, a shoesmith with the 21st Lancers (Empress of India's), gallantly rescued Learoyd from his predicament under very close-range fire. As with Capt. Jotham eight months before, Hull scooped up the captain and galloped with him to safety. This time the deed was successful and Hull was to receive a VC for his endeavours. Col Scriven had his horse shot from under him as well and was rescued by two lance corporals, but was later shot through the heart.

Later in the morning, after the Mohmands had retired to the hills, the dead and wounded were gathered in. Both sides had suffered heavy casualties, with the 21st Lancers losing three officers killed and three wounded, five NCOs and men killed and thirteen wounded. Casualties among the tribesmen were said to be much higher.

Charles Hull's VC citation was published in the *London Gazette* on 3 March 1916 as follows:

> Charles Hull, No. 1053, Private (Shoeing-Smith), 21st Lancers. For most conspicuous bravery. When under close fire of the enemy, who were within a few yards, he rescued Capt. G.E.D. Learoyd, whose horse had been shot, by taking him up behind him and galloping into safety. Shoeing-Smith Hull acted entirely on his own initiative, and saved his officer's life at the imminent risk of his own.

Further attempts to capture Shabkadr were made in October and November, but, despite harsh fighting, the Indian Army held firm.

Later in the war in France, the regiment provided a service squadron as part of XIV Corps Cavalry Regiment from June 1916 to August 1917. Charles Hull was with them and, according to the *White Lancer and the Vedette*, he was at one point captured by the Germans but managed to escape and rescued two French generals as well. This earned him the *Croix de Guerre*. When asked about this award, he used to tell the questioner that he got it for being 'first into the canteen and last out'.

Charles Hull, son of a Harrogate Corporation employee, was born at 3 Albert Terrace, Harrogate, Yorkshire, on 24 July 1890. He attended St Peter's School, the same school as Donald Bell VC had attended. Hull joined the 21st Lancers on 1 April 1908 at the age of 18, serving with them in Egypt in 1910, before leaving for India two years later, where he served on the North-West Frontier. When the war began he was with the 21st Lancers in Rawalpindi, and, in 1915, the regiment was ordered to form a 'flying column' to stand by for emergencies, the first of which arose at the end of August.

Hull arrived back in England in November 1919 and left his regiment on 1 December. He was decorated with his VC by the King at Buckingham Palace two days later. He also received the *Croix de Guerre* (6 November 1918), the Italian *Medaglia Al Valore Militare* (Bronze) for various deeds (2 November 1918) and was also Mentioned in Despatches. He was discharged in 1919 with the rank of private and joined the Leeds City Police Force in February 1920 where he remained until 1943, reaching the rank of sergeant. He then retired early owing to poor health. During his life he was keen on sport, playing cricket and football for his regiment and later for Leeds Police.

In 1920 he was sent a gold watch and chain as a thank you gift from Capt. Learoyd's father. On 26 June he attended the Buckingham Palace Garden Party for holders of the VC and in October he married Mrs Eliza Ann Brown at All Hallows' Church, Leeds. A few weeks later Hull attended the House of Lords' VC Dinner on 9 November 1929. On 21 March 1930 he attended a dinner for West Riding VCs in Leeds.

After the Second World War he took part in the Victory in Europe (VE) Parade in London on 8 June 1946, which was followed by dinner at The Dorchester. Apart from Hull, the other Leeds men who won the VC in the First World War were W.B. Butler, J.C. Raynes, W. Edwards and A. Poulter.

Charles Hull died at 74 Harold Grove, Leeds (or, according to Harvey, at his home at 11 Chapel Place, Headingley, Leeds) on 13 February 1953, and was buried at Woodhouse Cemetery, Section A, Grave 11,804. A detachment of the regiment from its Yeomanry HQ at Newark acted as the bearer party. His grave at Woodhouse Cemetery was one of those levelled in 1969 when the ground was absorbed by the University of Leeds.

On 5 September 1955, forty years to the day after his VC was won, Hull's decorations were presented during an Old Comrades' Reunion Dinner to the 17th/21st Lancers Regiment Museum, Belvoir Castle, by Mr F.W. Clarkson, who had accompanied Charles Hull on his famous charge. A plaque also commemorates him and Donald Bell VC at St Peter's Primary School, Harrogate, which was unveiled on 4 July 1956. Hull's name is also included on a VC Memorial in the Victoria Gardens in Leeds, which was unveiled in November 1992.

Fifteen years later, a VC plaque was unveiled at the Town Cenotaph in Harrogate on 4 July 2007. The names of Charles Hull and Donald Bell were both included.

Apart from his VC, *Croix de Guerre* and *Medaglia Al Valore Militare* (Bronze), Hull was also awarded the 1914–15 Star, BWM, VM (1914–19), King George VI Coronation Medal (1937) and Defence Medal (1939–45). At the present time the 17th/21st Lancers Regiment Museum is in Thoresby Park, near Ollerton, Nottinghamshire.

ITALY

C.E. HUDSON

Near Asiago, 15 June 1918

After the Austrian/German rout of the Italian Army at Caporetto at the end of October 1917, the Italian Army retreated to the River Piave. The Austrians were seemingly unconcerned with following up their success and any plan of a further advance was to be much influenced by events happening within the now collapsing Austro-Hungarian Empire. For example, there was a great shortage of food in Austria, which caused considerable unrest – a problem aggravated by the return of POWs from Russia, many of whom turned themselves into small groups of marauding bands. However, the Austrian Army, by now without German support, and having many Slavs among its ranks who were becoming increasingly rebellious, was still planning to make a great offensive, probably in June 1918. The aim was to push the Allies off the mountains and to penetrate the Italian Army's positions on the Piave. The Venetian Plain was also an objective and, as a consequence, Venice soon became deserted.

On 13 June the Austrian Army made its first move when it unsuccessfully attempted to penetrate the extreme left of the Italian forces at the Tonale Pass. But two days later they began a major offensive which was to concentrate on the Allied positions in the mountains at the Asiago and Monte Grappa sectors, as well as eastwards between Montello and the Adriatic.

The Allied positions on the Asiago Front consisted of Italian troops on the left, the British 48th Division in the centre and part of the British 23rd Division and French troops on the right. By chance many of the British guns were close up to the frontline as the British had been planning a limited attack of their own for the 18th.

On the right of the line in the 23rd Division area at San Sisto Ridge, its 70th Brigade was told that, in the event of an enemy attack, they were to hold the line while assaulting troops were to form up behind them. The frontline battalions north of San Sisto Ridge were the 11th (S) Sherwood Foresters and the 9th (S) York and Lancaster Regiment. Lt Col Charles Hudson, in command of the Sherwood Foresters, had his HQ in a quarry at the back of a ridge and below the top to:

> ... form the junction, on the right of the British, with the French. On the near side of the ridge the ground was steep, but on the enemy side the ground sloped more gently down through fir woods to the front line itself which ran just inside the edge of the woods. Two companies ... held the front trench; a third was disposed in platoon areas along the top of the ridge, and a fourth was held back in trenches behind the ridge.

These were the dispositions on 14 June and, from information received from patrols and prisoners, it was clear that the enemy, consisting of

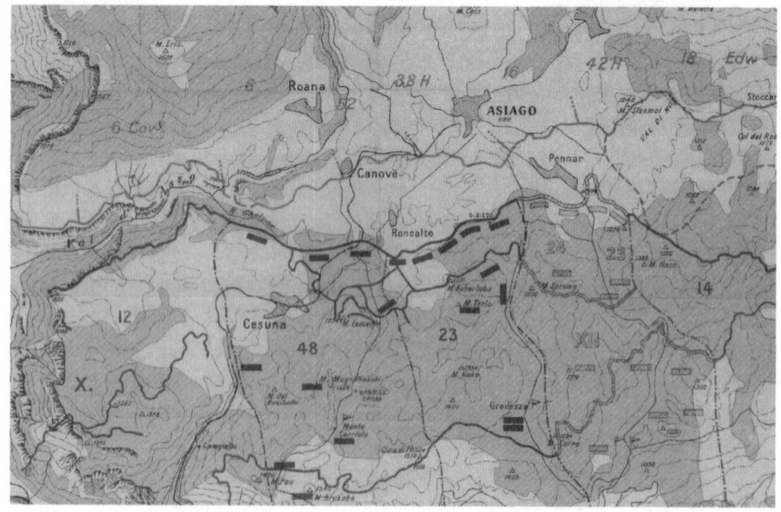

Asiago, 15 June 1918.

the Austrian Eleventh Army, was planning a heavy bombardment and attack on the following day. Given a four-hour warning of this event, Hudson ordered his frontline troops to be on the alert and for everyone to check on their gas masks.

At 3 a.m. on 15 June, Hudson was woken up by the sounds of a very heavy bombardment and the smell of gas; shells were bursting all around the quarry. The enemy had begun to bombard the Allied first and second lines, in addition to the back areas, and the British guns did not reply, either because they awaited the expected SOS call or because they were knocked out early in the bombardment. An observation platform had been erected in a high tree above the quarry and later 'it was possible to see over the ridge and on to the plateau'. The tree would be used by the battalion intelligence officer as the sky lightened. A heavy Italian mortar battery was close to Hudson's HQ in a tunnelled position and was only to be used as part of an offensive and not for defensive purposes. Telephone communication had broken and, at around 6.45 a.m., the first reports came in from the tree platform that the observer could see 'columns of infantry advancing across the plateau', including a leader 'mounted on a white horse'. The attackers, beginning to advance through the pinewoods, were spearheaded by assault troops together with bombers, machine-guns and *Flammenwerfer* (flamethrowers), while carrying parties brought up the rear. An extra hazard came as a result of artillery shells hitting rocks, bouncing off, often in splinters, and rebounding against people. Eyes were especially vulnerable and gas respirators had to be worn as protection. It was incredibly noisy; reverberations from the mountains increased the noise and many trees were brought down in the wooded areas and set on fire.

Hudson gave the artillery SOS signal, but their response was small and ineffective. However, the enemy advance was slowed by accurate rifle and machine-gun fire from the British frontline, apart from a section on the left of the front.

Hudson then sent orders back to his second-in-command, instructing him to bring his reserve company forward to a position behind the ridge and to be ready to make a counter-attack if necessary. Hudson had no wish to be caught in the quarry and, while waiting for the reserve company, he gave HQ details for orderlies, servants and runners to get ready, as they might be required to make a counter-attack on their own when the enemy arrived on the ridge. As soon as this happened, they were to provide 'ragged fire from the top of the ridge'. Hudson had already given the gas all clear and took his party of men from HQ details, together with some Allies, led them up the hill and drove the enemy off. However, in the confusion of the fighting Hudson lost contact with his men and was now with only two orderlies, and when there was machine-gun fire from the ridge he veered in its direction. By this time he had been joined by a mess sergeant and, just before 11 a.m., they came across a small group of about thirty Austrians some 30yd away. The sergeant offered to take the men prisoner and hurried off to try to do so, but was wounded in the rush. Not really knowing what to do, Hudson asked the party to raise their hands, which they reluctantly did, but almost immediately he was hit by a German stick bomb which landed at his feet. He was seriously wounded and thrown down on his back, but managed to roll himself into a trench where two bombs exploded just above him. Bits of the bomb had entered his body, and his right arm and right foot were badly damaged. However, he did manage to replace the rifle he had been carrying with his revolver, which he held in his left hand with difficulty. He fainted from the pain, only to be shaken awake by the slightly wounded mess sergeant. Somehow a stretcher was brought forward and Hudson was carried back up the rough hillside to the support company HQ on the ridge above. He had been expecting a British counter-attack, but was unaware of the situation with the rest of the line, where it was considered too dangerous as the flanks had been exposed. His second-in-command had remained in the rear trenches with his company, considering that it would be too dangerous to move forward. However, he had managed to arrange for another company, from the 8th (S) King's Own Yorkshire Light Infantry Regiment, to assist in holding the line, although they had yet to arrive.

Despite his serious wounds, on arriving by stretcher at battalion HQ Hudson was still keen for the counter-attack to proceed as originally planned; however, he fainted again. At this point the American-born battalion medical officer was able to bind up his wounds, but had little hope that he would live. His right leg, at the least, would have to be amputated. Ignoring this prognosis, Hudson challenged the American to a game of chess soon after, but was forced to abandon it.

Despite the initial Austrian Army's success on the 15th, they had severely underestimated the strength of the two British divisions and their assault was repulsed by an Allied counter-attack which left the British positions virtually intact. It is true that in a few places ground was given up, but their loss was not significant. The Austrians did take over 100 prisoners, but had to surrender a much higher number of their own men. The following day the battle had died down completely, although the artillery on both sides was again active. However, according to the war diary (WO95/4240) an extremely heavy enemy barrage was opened up at 9.44 p.m. on the same day. The British and French artillery replied and, by 11 p.m., the firing had died down again.

Hudson was taken by ambulance to a hospital in Genoa and there the doctors were keen to amputate his right leg, but he refused them permission despite having a gangrenous wound. From Genoa he went by ambulance train to Marseilles.

It was when he was recovering in hospital in Mount Street, London, that a staff officer he knew came to visit him and eagerly told him that he had won the VC for his work in Italy. Hudson was flabbergasted and clearly had no inkling that this would happen. His VC citation was published in the *London Gazette* less than four weeks later on 11 July 1918 as follows:

> Charles Edward Hudson, Capt., Temporary Lieut.-Colonel, D.S.O., M.C., Nottinghamshire and Derbyshire Regt. For most conspicuous bravery and devotion to duty when his battalion was holding the right front sector during an attack on the British front, at San Sisto Ridge near Asiago, Italy. The shelling had been very heavy on the right, the officers on the spot were killed or wounded. This enabled the enemy to penetrate our front line. The enemy pushed the advance as far as the support line which was the key to our right flank. The situation demanded immediate action. Lieut.-Colonel Hudson, recognising its gravity, at once collected various headquarters details, such as orderlies, servants, runners, etc., together with some Allies, personally led them up the hill. Driving the enemy down the hill towards our front line, he again led a party of about five up the trench, where there were about 200 enemy, in order to attack them from the flank. He then with two men got out of the trench, and rushed the position, shouting to the enemy to surrender, some of whom did. He was then severely wounded by a bomb which exploded on his

> foot. Although in great pain, he gave directions for the counter-attack to be continued, and this was done, successfully, about 100 prisoners and six machine guns being taken. Without doubt the high courage and determination displayed by Lieut.-Colonel Hudson saved a serious situation, and had it not been for his quick determination in organising the counter-attack a large number of the enemy would have dribbled through, and counter-attack on a large scale would have been necessary to restore the situation.

On the same day as Hudson won his VC, Capt. Edward Brittain, one of Hudson's company commanders, was killed. The two men had been the only surviving officers from the original battalion in 1914. By 8 a.m. the Austrians had penetrated the left flank of Brittain's company and consolidated.

Brittain led a counter-attack and his company regained the positions, with a little help from the French, but during the fighting he was reported to have been shot by a sniper. The following day he was buried in his blanket in the small Granezza British Cemetery, Plot 1, Row B, Grave 1. Four other officers from other units killed on 15 June were buried in the same cemetery. Three months later, Lt Col J.M. Knox of the Royal Warwickshire Regiment and brother of Maj. Cecil Knox VC was also buried there.

A week later, the War Office sent a telegram announcing Brittain's death to his father, Arthur Brittain, at Oakwood Court, Kensington. The cable announcing the dreadful news was opened by Edward's sister, Vera (later author of *Testament of Youth*), who was at home at the time with her father.

On learning that Hudson, her brother's commanding offcier, had been wounded in the same action, and extremely anxious to find out further details about Edward's last hours, Vera Brittain tracked him down from a newspaper casualty list and found that he was in hospital at Mount Street, near Park Lane, recovering from a leg wound. Vera was aware that her brother had respected his commanding officer without actually liking him. They were simply different sorts of personalities, with Hudson probably being more practical and Brittain more artistic. Vera was determined to cross-examine Hudson for further details of her brother's last hours.

At first Hudson was sympathetic and described the visit in his diary:

> I tried to give as much comfort as I could to the poor girl by telling her that since he was shot through the head he could have suffered little pain, but at this she flared up and said she was tired of hearing this story. Why was it that all her friends and acquaintances killed in the war had been shot through the head. Did I think that because she was a woman she was too weak minded to be told the truth, or so gullible that she could not recognise such nonsense?

Clearly Hudson was withholding information, but he considered that telling Vera the whole story would have been even more upsetting for her and difficult for the family to bear. So despite Vera's continuous attempts to extract more details about her brother, Hudson held firm.

On 13 September 1918, during Hudson's absence, the 11th Sherwood Foresters became part of 74th Brigade (25th Division) and left for France, arriving five days later. It was during this time of convalescence that he was decorated by the King at Buckingham Palace on 18 September, and Vera Brittain attended the same investiture. Hudson had also been awarded the *Croix de Guerre* and *Medaglia Al Valore Militare*. Having passed a medical board on the following day, he was allowed to return to France with the intention of being reunited with the battalion he had been with in Italy, but when calling in at the offices of the base commandant in Calais, he was informed that he was to take command of the 2nd Battalion with immediate effect. He caught up with his new battalion just after they had come back from an attack close to St Quentin, where they had suffered 400 casualties. He was to remain in command until January 1919.

On 4 October 1918 the battalion set out on a long march, which took them across the St Quentin Canal and through the recently captured Hindenburg Line. In effect, Hudson ended his active role in the war at the gas-filled village of Ors on 23 October.

Charles Edward Hudson was born on Oakapple Day, 29 May 1892, in Derby, a second son and third child of Lt Col H.E. Hudson, Sherwood Foresters, and of Mrs Hudson. Lt Col Hudson was the adjutant of the

1st Volunteer Battalion Sherwood Foresters and had joined the Army in 1873. He had gained his commission by examination as opposed to purchase.

Charles was educated at a preparatory school near East Grinstead, which he must have hated as he later described the joint head 'as an ogre of almost unbelievably sinister proportions'. He escaped to Sherborne School in Dorset where he studied between 1905 and 1910, before attending the RMA Sandhurst. He left before the end of the course and sailed to Ceylon where he became a rubber planter for two years. He returned to Britain on the outbreak of war and, through his father's links with the regiment, as well as his brother having a commission with them, he joined the Sherwood Foresters and was awarded a temporary commission on 17 November 1914, joining the 11th Battalion, which had been formed in Derby on 3 October. The volunteers were men mainly drawn from the Nottinghamshire and Derbyshire coalfield. Hudson was made a temporary lieutenant on 10 February 1915.

After ten months training, the battalion, part of 70th Brigade (23rd Division), arrived in France on 27 August 1915. Almost immediately Hudson suffered from a bout of malaria, but it was a medical problem which was not to reoccur during the rest of the war. He was due to be evacuated home, but instead he decided to discharge himself from hospital. The battalion's first tour of duty was in Belgium in the Armentières sector and, during this time, his company commander was killed by a sniper and Hudson took his place. The battalion was fortunate enough to only play a minor role in the Battle of Loos (September/October) and all told spent eight months in the Salient during 1915/16. They left for the Somme in March 1916. Hudson had been promoted to temporary captain on 11 October 1915 and remained with this rank until 1 March 1917.

During the preparations and opening of the Battle of the Somme, Hudson's battalion was part of a brigade which was temporarily attached to the 8th Division for 'blooding purposes' until 17 July. As the 11th Sherwood Foresters were then part of the reserve, they were not involved in the initial 7.30 a.m. attack on 1 July, but were active around the strongly held Mouquet Farm; nevertheless, they later suffered 500 casualties out of 700 available men on this disastrous day. When brought into action they had to move forward over the bodies of the 8th York and Lancaster Regiment. During the morning Edward Brittain, another officer in Hudson's battalion and who was later to feature in Hudson's life, was wounded in his left arm by shrapnel and by bullet wounds in his right thigh; he returned to 1st London General Hospital a few days later, where he was visited by his sister, Vera, on the 6th. He was to stay in Britain for several months before returning to light duties on 14 November, having joined the 3rd Battalion on 16 August. He had received news of his Military Cross (MC) gained in the attack against Mouquet Farm.

After having returned to their own division, the 11th Sherwood Foresters were left out of the battle for a month – time they spent on reorganising and training. Later they were briefly sent to Belgium, but were back on the Somme on 18 September 1916 when Hudson was still in charge of a company. Just over a week later, the 23rd Division was in the Martinpuich area and the objective was the village of Le Sars to the north. As a preliminary to an attack, Hudson was able to secure a trench known as 26th Avenue and it was for his good work here that he was awarded the MC (the official citation of 25 November 1916 wrongly says the date was 1 October). The citation was as follows:

> He led his company with great courage and initiative, capturing two enemy bombing posts. He has on many previous occasions done very fine work.

In November 1916 the 11th Sherwood Foresters returned to the Salient and, by now, Hudson was acting major and, later, battalion second-in-command. Eight months after he won the MC, he won his first DSO in the Battle of Messines Ridge on 7 June 1917 (*London Gazette*, 16 August 1917). The citation read:

> For conspicuous gallantry and devotion to duty. During an attack on the Wytschaete–Messines Ridge on 7. 6. 17. and before the objective was gained, he showed great promptitude and disregard for his own safety in reorganising his Battalion and leading it forward to the objective, which was secured and consolidated through his successful efforts. He has on many occasions showed capacity of the highest military value, notably in repulsing hostile counter-attacks upon his Battalion at a critical moment.

During the fight for the ridge, forty-three men from the battalion were killed and 175 wounded. A few weeks later, Hudson was once more rewarded for his gallantry and leadership when, in the first weeks of August during the Battle of Passchendaele, he won a Bar to his DSO (*London Gazette*, 26 November 1917). The citation read:

> For conspicuous gallantry and devotion to duty at Passchendaele between 31. 7. 17 and 6. 8. 1917. He was in command of a sector of the front line for several days during an action, and organised and carried out the defence of the position under continuous and violent enemy shelling. It was entirely due to his organisation and personal supervision of the work that the line was able to resist heavy enemy counter-attacks, he showed splendid leadership and great energy and courage [when in temporary command of his battalion].

After the Italian disaster at Caporetto, Hudson was given command of his battalion, which was ordered to leave for Italy as part of Allied reinforcements for the Italian Army against the Austrian Army and to travel to the Italian Front in the Alps above Vicenza. He was promoted to temporary lieutenant colonel of 11th Battalion (23 November 1917 to 28 September 1918) and then acting lieutenant colonel (29 September to 9 April 1919).

After a long and wearisome march the battalion took over from the 136th Italian Regiment on the River Piave on 3 December 1917. Two months later they relieved the 130th Italian Regiment in the line on the Asiago Plateau, near Granezza, in the mountains of northern Italy. Later they were to hold part of the frontline at the San Sisto Ridge, where there was a junction point with troops of the French Army.

Three days after the Armistice on 14 November 1918, the battalion began its journey to Cologne across the frontier, and on arrival Hudson, not yet part of the Control Commission, was struck down with a severe attack of flu. After he recovered, not yet wanting to leave the Army and with no better alternative, he made enquiries about serving in north Russia. The authorities were lukewarm to say the least and, as he was getting no help and had a spare month's leave due to him, in April 1919 he sailed to Murmansk on an American ship, having paid for his own fare. To his relief, when he got to Russia he found that Gen. Ironside, in command of the force, was short of officers and appointed him as brigade major to Gen. Turner on the railway front. His role was to be part of the Vlozda force in support of the White Russians against the Bolsheviks. By coincidence, while in north Russia he met up with another holder of the VC, Lt Col J. Kelly, in command of a Hampshire battalion, whom he found to be a very 'burnt out case'. Hudson was made a brevet major on 1 January 1919.

After serving in north Russia Hudson did consider leaving the Army at the end of hostilities, but instead continued to serve during what became the inter-war years. He became captain and adjutant in the 3rd Sherwood Foresters from 11 March 1920 to 9 March 1923.

Soon after his return from Russia, Hudson married Gladys Elizabeth Lee, who had first caught sight of her future husband when, serving in a hospital as a Volunteer Aid Detachment (VAD), she saw him carried in on his way back from Italy in June 1915. The couple were later to have two sons, John and Miles.

Hudson attended the 26 June 1920 VC Garden Party at Buckingham Palace, and the Cenotaph and Unknown Warrior ceremonies in November when he was part of the guard of honour.

He held the rank of major from 27 July 1928, brevet lieutenant colonel on 1 January 1932, was chief instructor at Sandhurst 31 January 1933 to 1937 and lieutenant colonel from 1 January 1935.

In 1933, Vera Brittain published her classic memoir of a generation, *Testament of Youth*, and in it she records having taken a violent dislike to Charles Hudson, the 26-year-old former battalion commander, and describes him as his regiment's 'professional survivor', almost as if daring him to remain alive. She is fairly dismissive, too, about the various medals that his service since 1914 had entitled him to. She wrote that he plainly had no wish to talk to her and that he stated that Edward had been sniped through the head by an Austrian officer. Vera was convinced that Hudson was concealing something from her, which indeed he was.

Long after Charles Hudson's death in 1959, his son Miles privately published a memoir in 1992 under the title *Two Lives 1892–1992* and the whole story of what happened to Edward Brittain on 14/15 June 1918 was revealed. In June 1934, after Hudson had been chief instructor at Sandhurst for eighteen months, he wrote to Vera and confessed that he had been deliberately withholding information about the circumstances surrounding her brother's death. The two arranged a meeting at her home in Glebe Place, Chelsea, for 9 July when they could talk in private when her children were in bed.

Hudson told Vera that on the eve of the Austrian attack on the San Sisto Ridge, he 'was called down to the track in the valley behind my headquarters to meet the Divisional General', who had an urgent and confidential matter to impart about a letter received from the Base Provost Marshal. 'A letter written by an officer in the battalion while on leave in England to another officer in the battalion, had been censored at base. From the context of the letter it was unmistakably plain that these two were involved in homosexuality with men in their company.'

Hudson was told to take no action while further enquiries were made, but nevertheless he did decide to tell Edward enough on the 14th to alert him to what was going on. He simply said '"I did not realise that letters written out here were censored at the Base." He had turned white, but made no comment and I knew that I had said enough to warn him. After that it was up to him.'

In her heart of hearts Vera could not really have been surprised by this information, and perhaps her mother was more worldly wise as she had previously destroyed an intimate diary which Edward had kept during his time at Uppingham when a close friend was expelled for 'acts of beastliness'. One hopes that by now Vera realised just how much she had vilified Hudson and understood why he had held back further information.

The name of the officer to whom Edward wrote a letter is not known as it was picked up by the censor. One suspects that Vera's biographers knew the answer, and it is certain that any surviving letters to the unnamed officer were destroyed by Vera to prevent them from being placed in the public domain.

There is a possible clue in Edward's service file, which states that he owed 15*s* to a Capt. Basil Bird MC and Bar, but the debt was not redeemed as Bird himself died of wounds in Rouen in September 1918 and was buried in St Sever Cemetery Extension S, V, 1, 3. However, Edward's chequebook survived and in it is a stub dated 14 June 1918 for 15*s* 6*d*. A bullet went through the rest of the chequebook, which was presumably kept in his breast pocket. This would also indicate that he was shot in the chest as well, not the head. The chequebook might have come into Vera's possession on the death of her mother in 1948.

In 1938, on the eve of the Second World War, Hudson was in command of 2nd Infantry Brigade at Aldershot, which left for France soon after the war began when the Germans were about to invade Belgium. He served with the 46th Division from December 1940. After many escapades when the British Army was in danger of being trapped in France, Hudson found himself in charge of his brigade's withdrawal to Dunkirk and its evacuation to England in May 1940. He was subsequently awarded a Companion of the Order of Bath (CB) medal for his services in France. Fourteen months later on 14 July 1941 he was appointed to command a division.

Hudson spent the rest of the war in 'a number of command appointments in the UK and Middle East where he commanded Iraqi Levies ... or in senior posts in Northern Ireland and the Middle East'. Tragically, he lost his eldest son, Lt John Hudson, who was killed on 24 April 1943 when serving with the 2nd Sherwood Foresters in Tunisia. During 1944–46 Charles Hudson was an aide-de-camp to the King and held the rank of brigadier.

Soon after the war, in his early 50s, Hudson retired to Devon. He lived at Kerswell House, Chudleigh, which was later burnt down after he had left a cigarette burning in his study. Most of the contents of the house were lost in the fire. The Hudsons then moved to Denbury Manor, Newton Abbot. From 1949 to 1954 Hudson was County Commissioner of the St John Ambulance Association, Devon, Deputy Lord Lieutenant of the County of Devon, and a JP. In June 1956 he attended the VC centenary anniversary in London and, on the following Armistice Day he opened the war memorial at Sherborne School to the memory of staff and old boys who had died in the war. The memorial took the form of an enlarged and revamped speech room.

While on holiday with his family at St Mary's, Isles of Scilly, on 4 April 1959, when he was 66 years old, he was suddenly taken ill and was rushed by launch to St Mary's Hospital, St Mary's, where he died. The cause of death was coronary thrombosis.

Hudson's funeral took place five days later when representatives of the many bodies and associations with which he had been involved attended. He was buried in St Mary's churchyard near his home at Denbury. Vera Brittain died twelve years later and after her cremation her ashes were taken to Italy and scattered on her brother's grave.

On 28 May 2003 Miles Hudson, Charles's surviving son, presented his late father's VC and other medals to the Sherwood Foresters Regimental Museum at a ceremony in Nottingham Castle. Miles, who was accompanied by his son Mark, had journeyed up from Hampshire. The medals had been under lock and key for years and the family considered that it was high time the VC was presented to the regiment. Miles stated:

> There is no particular reason why we have decided to hand over the VC now. . . . We just thought it was about time we gave it to the museum. I am sure my father would have been delighted, although he was a very modest man who did not like any fuss. [And again of his father he said:] He always reacted positively to any situation. I think that accounts for his bravery on so many occasions.

Hudson's decorations include the VC, CB, DSO and Bar, MC, Knight of Grace, The Order of St John, 1914–1915 Star with clasp (5 August–22 November 1914), BWM, VM (1914–19) and MiD Oakleaf, 1939–45 Star, France & Germany Star, Defence Medal (1939–45), War Medal (1939–45), King George VI Coronation Medal (1937), Queen Elizabethan II Coronation Medal (1953), *Croix de Guerre* with oak leaves (France), *Croce de Valore* (Italy), and *Medaglia Al Valore Militare* (Silver) (Italy). Hudson was also Mentioned in Despatches on six occasions: 15 June 1916, 21 December 1917, 30 May 1918, 6 January 1919, 9 July 1919 and 3 February 1920.

J.S. YOULL

South-west of Asiago, 15 June 1918

British forces first arrived on the Italian Front in November 1917, soon after Italian forces had been routed at the Battle of Caporetto. In March 1918 the 7th, 23rd and 48th Divisions took over the mountainous sector to the north of Vicenza in the Asiago region. In the small hours of 15 June the Austrian Eleventh Army opened what was to be named the Battle of Asiago with a heavy bombardment on the Allied 23rd and 48th Divisional positions. The weather was misty and visibility was poor.

At 3 a. m. the enemy began the bombardment against the Allied first and second lines, as well as the back areas. It used gas on the frontline and shrapnel on the second, and the 23rd Division HQ was forced to give orders for all outposts to be withdrawn. At 6.45 a.m. the Austrian infantry, headed by assault troops with bombers, machine-gunners and *Flammenwerfer*, followed by carrying parties, began advancing in large numbers along the whole front. The Austrian barrage was only responded to weakly as so many British guns were out of action.

Two patrols of the 11th (S) Northumberland Fusiliers, 68th Brigade (23rd Division) were in no-man's-land when the Austrian bombardment began. They managed to slow the attack on the area in front of the battalion as well as the 12th (S) Durham Light Infantry (Pioneers), and according to the brigade war diary:

> At 5.00 a.m. a message was received from one of these patrols saying they had dug in and were waiting for things to quieten down …

> 8.40am: The 11th N.F. (Left Front) reported that the 48th Division on their left had been driven back and the parties of the enemy were seen advancing through the woods. A Left Defensive Flank was formed and was heavily engaged. The situation here was not satisfactory owing to the retirement of the 1/4th T.F. Oxford & Buckingshire Light Infantry Rgt and it was principally about this time that the 11th N.F. under Major Gill, particularly distinguished themselves. Their numerous heroic efforts are too numerous to mention here but that of Lieut Youll who had brought in his patrol at 5.00 a.m. is an example. This officer behaved magnificently and by establishing a post on the Romcalto Road where it cut the 48th Divisional Front repeatedly restored the situation for short periods, and materially assisting in the capture of large parties of the enemy by cutting off their retreat, before this he had killed the team of an enemy machine gun, and used this gun (with another one captured) against the Austrians.
>
> The Assault Troops in this operation were the only dangerous element and these showed great gallantry and enterprise in such things as climbing trees and attempting to enfilade our trenches from the portion of the 48th Divisional front which they had captured.
>
> 12.30pm: ... the situation on the left was now reported restored, the British line being still intact and a defensive flank composed of the reinforcing Company of the 10th N.F. [10th (S) Northumberland Fusiliers] thrown back in touch with the 48th Division. In this operation the enemy had very nearly reached Battalion H.Q. the personnel of which turned out in defence.

The brigade's ammunition dumps were lost, but were regained later in the day:

> 7.10pm: The 11th N.F. on the left who had maintained their position against frontal and flank attacks all day had suffered heavily, and having already 2 Companies of the 10th N.F. under their orders I decided to relieve them by the H.Q. and remaining two companies of the 10th N.F. This relief was completed before midnight 15/16th June when the 11th N.F. returned to the Second Line behind the Right Battalion Front, one company being in Bde Reserve at Mt. Torle. Two companies of the 8th Yorks Regiment from the Reserve Brigade had been placed under my

> command were sent, one to the 2nd Line behind the Left Battalion, and one in Brigade Reserve at Mt. Torle.

By 9 a.m. on the following day the 10th Northumberland Fusiliers reported to Brigade HQ that the 48th Division had managed to retake their frontline and the situation was completely restored. The 11th Battalion had sustained 104 casualties. For his role in the operations, Lt John Youll was recommended for a VC, which was published in the *London Gazette* of 25 July 1918 as follows:

> John Scott Youll Second Lieut., 11th Battn. Northumberland Fusiliers. For most conspicuous bravery and devotion to duty during enemy attacks when in command of a patrol, which came under hostile barrage. Sending his men back to safety, he remained to observe the situation. Unable subsequently to rejoin his company, Second Lieut. Youll reported to a neighbouring unit, and when the enemy attacked he maintained his position with several men of different units until the troops on his left had given way and an enemy machine gun had opened fire from behind him. He rushed the gun, and, having killed most of the team, opened fire on the enemy with the captured gun, inflicting heavy casualties. Then, finding that the enemy had gained a footing in the portion of the front line, he organised and carried out with a few men three separate counter-attacks. On each occasion he drove back the enemy, but was unable to maintain his position by reason of reverse fire. Throughout the fighting his complete disregard of personal safety and very gallant leading set a magnificent example to all.

As well as the VC, Youll was awarded the *Medaglia Al Valore Militare* by the Italian Secretary of State for War, and the citation was as follows:

> During a whole day of fighting he was constantly displaying valour. As Patrol Commander, surprised by the enemy's barrage fire, he sent his men to safety and remained alone in observation. During the enemy attack he took command of men from various units, participating in the counter attacks, assaulted an enemy Machine Gun, killed the Machine Gun team and turned the Gun against the enemy's advancing waves. – Asiago 15th June 1918.

On 30 July 2/Lt J.S. Youll VC was presented with a VC medal ribbon by Maj. Gen. Sir J.M. Babington KCMG (Knight Commander, Order of St Michael and St George), CB, during a full-strength battalion parade which included two additional companies from the Durham Light Infantry. According to Norman Gladden's book, *Across the Piave*:

> This was a great honour for the battalion, and indeed to the regiment as a whole, as the Northumberland Fusiliers, despite its many battalions, had previously earned only two of these medals since the outbreak of war. Ardent Northumbrians sought to excuse this by alleging that the Fighting Fifth had on some occasions earned the displeasure of Queen Victoria and was thenceforth disqualified from receiving her most coveted award.

When Youll returned to Thornley after his VC had been announced, he was given a reception at the Thornley Hippodrome at an event organised by the local Soldiers' and Sailors' Memorial and Welcome Home Committee. He was presented with a gold watch with blue numerals and monogram initials JSY and chain, together with a large silver initialled cigarette case. He was 'received with rousing cheers and in reply to a speech of welcome he said: 'There were two kinds of honour – the seen and the unseen – and he hoped that the people of Thornley would give the boys the same reception on their return. Local children then sang "Blighty" and "The Village Blacksmith".'

Shortly after his return to Italy, a local newspaper published a further report: 'A few days ago a lad of the new V.C.'s Platoon came home on leave, bringing with him the Italian Silver Medal for Valour which had been presented to 2nd Lieutenant Youll by the King of Italy in person: "He is one of the lads," the soldier on leave told me. "And if anybody ever deserved the V.C. it is 2nd Lieutenant Youll."'

He was presented with his VC by the King at Buckingham Palace on 4 September 1918.

In October the 7th and 23rd Divisions left the Asiago Plateau in order to relieve the Italian XI Corps' front on the River Piave from Salletuol to Palazzon. The last Battle of Vittorio Veneto, which allowed the Allies to cross the River Piave, began on 23 October and the crossing was completed four days later with heavy officer casualties, including the commanding officer of the 11th Northumberland Fusiliers, Lt Col A.A. St Hill, and 2/Lt John Youll VC.

The battalion war diary of the 11th Sherwood Foresters (WO95/4240) recorded the incident:

> On 27 October the left of the divisional front the 68th IB with 12th DLI and 11th NF on right and left respectively met with stiff resistance and uncut wire. Considerable trouble was experienced from machine gun fire from the left flank and from certain forward machine guns which had escaped the barrage. At this point the 11th N.F. suffered severe casualties, their commanding officer, Lt.-Col. St. Hill, D.S.O. being killed. And all officers over the rank of Lieutenant becoming casualties. The command of the battalion fell to Lieut. J. Robertson. Both battalions, however, continued to advance with great gallantry, overcame all resistance and completed the capture of the first objective simultaneously with the 69th Infantry Brigade on their right.

A note in *Spinks' Prospectus*, which covered the sale of Youll's decorations on 17 December 1997, had the following details about the gallant officer's death:

> His Adjutant, Lieutenant Cowling, afterwards was ordered to attack, with three objectives to take. On the taking of the first objective all the Officers of Youll's Company, with the exception of Youll himself, became casualties. At the capture of the second objective, Youll was wounded in the arm, but the wound was only slight. About noon he was seen by Chaplain Wells in a captured trench and the pair had some lunch together. The Chaplain advised the young Officer to stay where he was, as the passage of the river was being heavily shelled. About 6 p.m. the Chaplain returned to the bridge and there was Youll's body laid out on a stretcher. He had been struck by a shell. His last words were, 'It's all right Cowling, we got them stone cold'.

A later note stated that, at 6.45 a.m. on 27 October 1918, the attack captured all objectives in spite of strong resistance and counter-attacks on Borgo Malanotte. During the day the division had captured 2,200 prisoners. A week later the Armistice came into effect and hostilities ceased.

After his death on 27 October 1918 crossing the Piave, Youll was first buried at Lonadina BC Spresiano and, later, in June 1919, reburied at Giavera BC, Plot 1, Row H, Grave 2. His family were notified of his death by telegram on 10 November 1918.

John Scott Youll was the younger son of Richard William and Margaret, and was born at his family home on 6 June 1897 at 'Thorncroft', Thornley, County Durham. John was educated at Thornley Council School and later became a student at the technical classes held by the Durham County Council at Wingate. When he was about 15 years old, John began work at Thornley Colliery as an apprentice electrician.

Nearly a year after the war began, Youll joined the Army as a sapper in the Royal Engineers (RE) (Durham Territorials, 1/1st Durham Field Company) when he enlisted on 24 July 1915. He trained for a year before leaving for France on 11 August 1916, and did such good service that he was recommended for a commission, returning home for officer training on 22 February 1917. In June he was gazetted to the Northumberland Fusiliers and returned to France at the end of July.

Two months later, Youll was Mentioned in Despatches for the part he took in the fierce fighting at Polygon Wood in September/October 1917. In October he was transferred with his battalion to the Italian Front.

John Youll was the first officer in his regiment to win the VC since the Siege of Lucknow (1857) and was decorated by the King in Buckingham Palace on 4 September 1918. He was also one of eight men from County Durham to be awarded the VC in the First World War. His watch and cigarette case are part of the Regimental collection, as are two ribbons – the purple one for the VC and a green one for the Italian Silver Star. Spinks sold the group on 17 December 1997 to a private buyer for £36,000. Including the BWM and VM, Youll's four decorations are on display in the Lord Ashcroft Gallery in the Imperial War Museum.

Eighty-seven years after Youll died, a new memorial to him was set up in his village of Thornley, close to the village war memorial, and unveiled in October 2005.

W. McNally

Piave, 27 October 1918

After the failed Austrian offensive in mid-June 1918, and owing to heavy rainfall and subsequent flooding, the Austrian Army found itself back across the River Piave, which in mid-June they had managed to cross in several places. The Italian Front was so quiet during the next three months that the War Office even planned to reduce the number of troops in order to strengthen the Army in France. Austria was also keen to reduce its commitment, partly owing to increasing domestic problems on the home front, and was keen to sue for peace.

In October Gen. Amando Diaz, who had been Italian commander-in-chief since November 1917 after the Italian Army's defeat at Caporetto, was planning what was to be the final Allied campaign of the war on the Italian Front. His scheme was for his troops to advance across the River Piave, with the Eighth Italian Army on the left, the Anglo-Italian Army in the centre and the Italian Third Army on the right stretching seawards. They were to be supported by British and French divisions and the objective was to drive a wedge between the Austrian Fifth and Sixth Armies. The two British divisions in the centre of the line were the 7th on the right and the 23rd on the left.

One particular battalion, the 8th (S) Alexandra, Princess of Wales's Own (Yorkshire Regiment), also known as the 8th Green Howards of the 69th Brigade (23rd Division), was to play a key role in the river crossing and began by moving towards the frontline on 21 October. Here they established themselves in farmhouse billets 2 miles behind the front. On the 22nd the battalion then moved up to support positions on the left of the British Front.

On 25 October 1918 A Company of the Green Howards left their billets to move up to Papadopoli Island, 2 miles wide and positioned in the Piave, and at 1 a.m. on the 26th the three companies of the 8th Green Howards also left their billets in order to embark for Papadopoli. Initially the Green Howards crossed a stream via a footbridge, while the second stage was carried out in small, six-man, flat-bottomed boats which were crewed by Italian boatmen, some of whom worked as gondoliers in Venice. As by now it was getting light, D Company was forced to return to their billets, leaving the already established A Company to be joined by B and C, together with Battalion HQ, and they dug-in at positions on the north side of the island where the Austrians had been garrisoned until they were 'surprised' by the 7th Division a short time before. The Green Howards were later rejoined by D Company at about midnight and the four companies in their assembly trenches were in touch with the 10th (S) Duke of Wellington's (West Riding Regiment), 69th Brigade, on their left, and the 7th Division on their right.

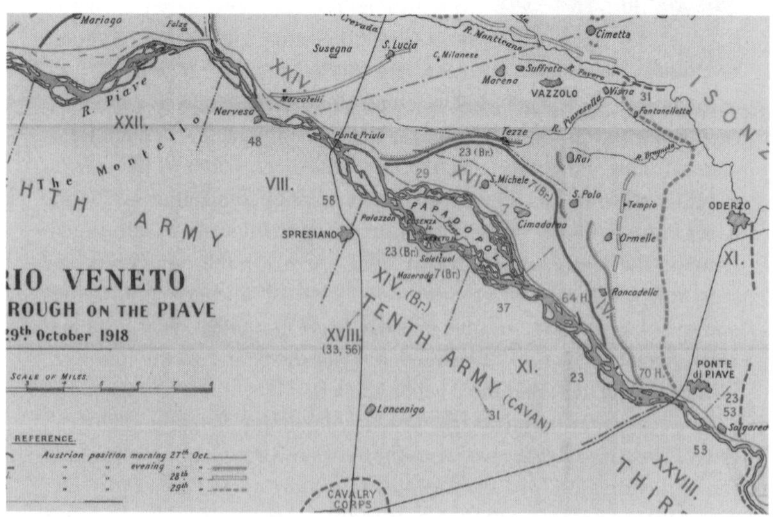

Vittorio Veneto – the breakthrough on the Piave, 27–29 October 1918.

Just prior to an advance, the British artillery began a preliminary bombardment against the enemy positions and the Austrians retaliated, especially against the north side of the island where they had previously been garrisoned, although the Green Howards suffered no casualties.

In the small hours of the 27th it was found that the Italian Eighth Army on the left flank were unable to reach their positions as they had failed to cope with the conditions of the flooded Piave. This was to lead to severe flanking problems over the next couple of days. At 5.20 a.m. the Green Howards' advance across the Piave began with A Company marching to Zandonadi. The actual crossing was very difficult as one of the further streams was deep and faster moving than anticipated, and several men were drowned. The battalion diary noted: 'The crossing of these streams was effected by the men forming long chains by linking arms.' When dawn broke, enemy shellfire and machine-gun fire became very strong and the Austrian infantry were in positions on the far bank of the river about 400yd away. In addition, the weather was cold and it rained heavily during the river crossings.

The Allied artillery continued to shell enemy positions and the battalion moved forward to within 60yd of the enemy. Some men were killed at this point. As B Company began to climb up a bank, Sgt W. McNally rushed an Austrian machine-gun post which had been set up in some deserted buildings on the right flank. He captured the position, killed the machine-gun team and took charge of the gun.

By 7 a.m. two of the Green Howard companies had reached the enemy first line at Zandonadi 'to a point about 400yds westwards'. The 7th Division right flank was not in touch, but on the left contact was maintained with a company of the 11th (S) The Prince of Wales's Own (West Yorkshire Regiment), also of the same brigade.

The remaining two companies of the Green Howards reached their final objectives at Tezze, 3 miles from the island, soon after midday when contact was re-established with the 7th Division on the right. In mid-afternoon the enemy attacked the 10th Duke of Wellingtons on the left, but the Austrians were quickly repulsed by the 11th West Yorks. During the day six guns and thirty-six machine-guns, together with 400 prisoners, were captured.

The advance continued the next day and met with very little opposition except for the occasional sniper. In the evening a patrol reached the town of Vazzola, which was devoid of enemy troops but full of cheering civilians. Here A Company moved forward to a bridgehead, capturing nine prisoners and two field guns in the process.

On the 29th the rest of the 8th Green Howards Battalion moved safely to Vazzola, where patrols were pushed forward to the River Monticano; the next objective was to capture a vital bridge and it was known that the enemy was in great strength on the north bank. It was at this stage of the battle that Sgt McNally of B Company, once again showing great initiative, earned the VC when he took charge of the situation as they:

> ... pushed forward to seize the bridgehead and after very severe fighting secured a footing on the North bank of the Monticano by 1000 hours. The enemy was well supplied with machine guns and artillery and McNally, realising that a frontal attack would prove disastrous, ordered his platoon to concentrate their fire on the enemy while he once more crept forward to a ruined building and took out the machine gun team and captured the position.

In winning his VC, Sgt McNally had the use of the regulatory four Mills Bombs, together with a revolver and sixteen rounds.

While on their way to the village of Cimetta, the Green Howards' final destination, McNally, directing the fire of his platoon with great skill, destroyed many of the attackers guarding the small village.

On the 30th the 23rd Division went into reserve and the remaining troops continued the move to Tagliamento while the Green Howards marched to billets near Orsago. At the beginning of November, news of the Armistice between Turkey and the Allies was announced and, three days later, an Armistice with Austria-Hungary was also completed. Hundreds of thousands of prisoners had been taken. Demobilisation began on the 23rd when troops began to leave for England, an operation completed by the end of January.

McNally was recommended for his VC by Maj. J.G. Smithson on 7 December, although the first McNally knew of it was when he was called out of an estaminet and told he was wanted at Battalion HQ. On arrival he was informed he had been recommended for the VC and ordered to visit Divisional HQ where he was told he had definitely been awarded it. When asked by Peter Liddle in an interview in December 1968 if he celebrated, he replied, 'Oh yes, I have celebrated ever since.'

His citation was published in the *London Gazette* of 14 December as follows:

> William McNally, No. 13820, Sergt., M.M., 8th Battn. Yorkshire Regt. (Murton Colliery, Co. Durham) For most conspicuous bravery and skilful leading during the operations on 27 Oct. 1918, [*sic*: and 29 October] across the Piave, when his company was most seriously hindered in its advance by heavy machine-gun fire from the vicinity of some buildings on a flank; utterly regardless of personal safety, he rushed the machine-gun post single-handed, killing the team and capturing the gun. Later, at Varzola, on 29 Oct 1918, when his company, having crossed the Monticano River came under heavy rifle and machine-gun fire, Sergt. McNally immediately directed the fire of his platoon against the danger point, while he himself crept to the rear of the enemy position. Realising that a frontal attack would mean heavy losses, he, unaided, rushed the position, killing or putting to flight the garrison, and capturing a machine gun. On the same day, when holding a newly captured ditch, he was strongly counter-attacked from both flanks. By his coolness and skill in controlling the fire of his party, he frustrated the attack, inflicting heavy casualties on the enemy. Throughout the whole operation his innumerable acts of gallantry set a high example to his men, and his leading was beyond all praise.

On 5 December a 69th Brigade parade was held when medal ribbons for awards won during the Battle of the Piave were distributed. However, they did not include Sgt McNally's VC, which was announced two days later by the corps commander when he informed the commanding officer: 'that No. 13820 Sergt. Wm. McNally had been awarded the Victoria Cross for his magnificent work in the Piave operations from 27th to 29th October. Sergt. McNally received hearty congratulations from all ranks.'

William McNally was born at 12 Bude Square, Murton, near Seaham, County Durham, on 16 December 1894, the son of a local miner. He was educated at Murton Colliery School from the ages of 4 to 14, when he began work in the Murton Colliery Pit. Initially he was employed as a pit pony driver, as his father had been before him, and worked six shifts a week. The colliery was owned by the Seaham Coal Co.

McNally enlisted from the colliery on 3 September 1914 and was attested at Havelock House, Sunderland. His height was 5ft 8in and after initial training he joined the 8th (S) Battalion Yorkshire Regiment in Halton Park Camp, Buckinghamshire. His colleagues were drawn mainly from Yorkshire, the Middlesbrough area and Richmond in North Yorkshire. However, he was not in Richmond long before continuing his training at Aylesbury and Halton Park, Buckinghamshire, and Berkhamstead, Hertfordshire. He spent a year in training before embarking for France just before the Battle of Loos. The Battalion, 69th Brigade (23rd Division), arrived in Boulogne on 26 August 1915 and moved by cattle trucks to their base town of St Eloi. McNally first saw action in the Battle of Loos, which began on 25 September. He was only in France for three weeks before returning to England on 1 October, remaining there until 11 December. During this time he had ten days' leave between 19 and 29 November, although he was home having received the first of three leg wounds which he suffered during the war. He returned to France and won his first medal, the MM (*London Gazette*, 23 August 1916), when taking part in an assault against Contalmaison on 10 July 1916 during the Battle of the Somme. He went to the assistance of a wounded officer shot through the thigh; he administered first aid and later arranged for the officer to be pulled in by fastening his legs with rope and dragging him back as far as the barbed wire. Sadly, despite these efforts, the officer later died. The recommendation for the MM was made ten days later by Lt Col H. Wilkinson of the 23rd Division. The 10 July was the same in that 2/Lt Donald Bell of the 9th Battalion died, having won the Victoria Cross five days earlier at Contalmaison. Presumably McNally was wounded in the legs a second time as he was back in England between 12 August 1916 and 9 January 1917. He returned to France on 10 January 1917 for six months before returning to England in mid-June 1917. He had possibly been wounded in the legs again. He remained at home for nearly eight weeks, during which time he had ten days' leave between 26 July and 4 August before returning to France and Belgium for the fourth time on 8 September where he remained before travelling to Italy, arriving there on 8 November 1917. He remained in Italy, apart from a spell of leave, until 19 February 1919.

McNally gained a second MM for actions near Passchendaele, which was recommended by Lt Col E.F. Faulkner on 13 November (*London Gazette*, 23 February 1918). The medal was sent to him by post and the citation read:

> The trench occupied by this NCO's Platoon was heavily shelled. One shell burst amongst him and his men killing one man and wounding three. With complete disregard for danger he got the remainder under cover and carried the wounded to safety. The following night at the same place his trench was heavily shelled and on three separate occasions he went to the rescue of men who had been buried and brought them to safety. The cool courage of this NCO is worthy of the highest praise and was a striking example to all ranks. Awarded bar to the Military Medal for the above.

Eleven months after McNally won his VC in Italy, he left for England. He was demobilised in February 1919 in Ripon, but was still suffering from one of three leg wounds and had a bullet lodged in his leg. He returned home to Durham (11 Shepperdson Street, Murton Colliery, was his address in the file). It is curious to note that on his demobilisation documents his date of birth is given as 1895 instead of 1894. When he got home he was met at Murton station by a Mr E.S. Wood and a welcoming crowd, and the local pit was closed for the day in his honour. Presentations were made to him on behalf of the villagers and he was accompanied by his pregnant wife whom he had recently married in July 1919, a short time before he was presented with his VC on the 17th. The couple were to have six children.

McNally returned to work at the pit and became a member of the Miners' Lodge Committee. He remained working there until about 1944 when he turned 50. He then had an office job for twelve years in a timber yard, supervising the making of pit props, before finally retiring in July 1958.

McNally attended the 26 June 1920 Garden Party at Buckingham Palace and the ceremony for the unveiling of the Cenotaph in November 1920; this included being a member of the VC Honour Guard who lined the processional route in Westminster Abbey at the ceremony of the Burial of the Unknown Warrior. He also attended the House of Lords' VC Dinner on 9 November 1929. In September 1933 he took part in a Drumhead Service, with Henry Tandy VC, and was occasionally a guest of honour at British Legion dinners. In 1937 he was presented with the 1937 Coronation Medal. After the Second World War he attended the VE Parade on 8 June 1946 and the dinner at The Dorchester in the evening, and the VC centenary celebrations on 26 June 1956.

After his retirement he spent sixteen years in his home village, taking an active part in the local community affairs, and was a regular attender of Green Howard Association reunions. He also attended the first two of the VC/GC (Victoria Cross/George Cross Association) dinners held at the Café Royal in 1958 and 1960, and one in July 1962; the day before he attended the VC/GC Garden Party at Buckingham Palace and a banquet given by the Lord Mayor of London.

In 1969 McNally was presented with a gold badge to celebrate fifty years of meritorious service with the Green Howards at the regimental reunion dinner near York. In 1975 a community hall for the elderly was named after him in his home village of Murton. In the following year Bill McNally died on 5 January at his home in 12 Bude Square, and was given a funeral with full military honours four days later at Holy Trinity Church. The procession was led by the Standard Bearers of the Royal British Legion, followed by two senior officers from the Green Howards and a bearer party of seven sergeants from the 1st Battalion. Two regimental buglers sounded the *Last Post* and *Reveille*, and many serving officers and old comrades attended the service. His body was cremated on 9 January at Tyne & Wear Crematorium, Hylton Road, Sunderland, and his ashes scattered in the Garden of Remembrance.

In McNally's obituary published in the *Green Howards' Gazette* of spring 1976, it was noted that:

> Billy came from Durham mining stock and lived at Murton Colliery, Co. Durham, where he was a much loved and respected member of the community. There will be many Green Howards who will remember him as a familiar figure at the Annual Reunions – accompanied by his sons, an event he hardly ever missed. A warm-hearted, kindly, modest man who was a friend to all. He took the greatest of interest in his old regiment and could always be relied upon to support any Regimental occasion. We shall miss him very much in future years.

Two years later on 28 October 1978, a memorial to McNally was unveiled in his home village by his widow. It had been planned shortly after his death in January 1976 by the people of Murton as a tribute to their most famous son and paid for from the proceeds of the William McNally Memorial Fund; the land in Murton Park on which it stands was given by East Murton Parish Council. Later the surrounding area adjacent to the war memorial garden was landscaped with nearly 300 rose bushes and the Parish Council agreed to pay the costs. The project cost £2,000 and was set in a small park in the shape of the letter E, and consists of a central plinth on which the following words are inscribed under the Green Howards' badge:

To the sacred memory of
William McNally VC, MM & Bar
1894–1976
who by his Courage and Unselfish
Devotion to Duty during the Great War 1914–18
Brought Honour and Glory to this
Village and his Regiment

Two wings extend from the plinth and in front of them are two benches on which people can sit. A small group from the Green Howards took part in the service and a parade was led by the Murton Silver Band. A short service of dedication was held before the unveiling by Mrs McNally, who was accompanied by two of her sons and a daughter, together with other members of the family.

In 1993 information about McNally's career appeared in the Gordons Catalogue of May 1993 and noted the existence of several official items, including his original invitation and travel pass to London for the November 1929 House of Lords' VC Dinner, together with a copy of the Legion Book which the Prince of Wales had signed and presented to each of his guests. He is also one of eight men born in County Durham who won a VC in the First World War. His decorations apart from the VC, MM & Bar inlude the 1914–15 Star, the BWM, the VM (1914–19), Defence Medal (1939–45), King George VI Coronation Medal (1937) and Queen Elizabeth II Coronation Medal (1953). These were in the keeping of the Green Howards' Museum in Richmond, Yorkshire, but in 2006 were sold to Lord Ashcroft for his collection in the Imperial War Museum.

W. Wood

Near Casa Vana, 28 October 1918

A day after Sgt William McNally won his VC in the Piave operations, a second man, Wilfred Wood, a private in the 10th (S) Northumberland Fusiliers of the 68th Brigade (23rd Division), gained the same honour when taking part in the divisional advance close to Casa Vana on 28 October.

Two days before, the 68th Brigade was in 23rd Divisional reserve in positions between Maserada and Lovadina, south of the River Piave, when A and B Companies were based on islands in the river, forming part of the left boundary of the division while the main attack moved forward on the 27th. After the barrage had lifted, the 11th (S) Northumberland Fusiliers, in the same brigade, advanced and were followed by the two companies from the 10th Battalion in support. Reading the 10th Battalion war diary it seems the 11th Northumberland Fusiliers were held up by wire in front of the first objective, which was then dealt with by A Company, thus allowing the advance to continue towards the Bund defences. At this point an enemy machine-gun held them up, which was dealt with at around 7 a.m., despite several officer casualties. Lt Wrighton shot the machine-gunner in the head and took command of A Company.

At 9.45 a.m. the 10th Northumberland Fusiliers, less two companies, moved up to the south bank of a river where they were instructed to remain while the commanding officer, adjutant and intelligence officer, who wished to reconnoitre the situation, began to cross the river in order to reach one of the islands. At this point the intelligence officer was killed by a shell and the adjutant wounded. The commanding officer found the attack was proceeding, but B Company, previously in support, was ordered to move up in order to strengthen the left flank.

After the commanding officer of the 10th Northumberland Fusiliers reached the HQ of the 11th Northumberland Fusiliers and 12th (S) Durham Light Infantry, the remaining companies of the 10th Northumberland Fusiliers, C and D, were brought over. Owing to the Italian Eighth Army having not shown up on the left as they were unable to cross the Piave, there were continuous problems and both A and B Companies were under great pressure as the plan had been to hand over these flanking defences to the Italians two hours after the advance began.

That night A and B Companies, using searchlights, sent out several patrols and brought in fifty to sixty prisoners. Between 4 and 6.30 a.m. on the 28th, six Italian battalions came up to begin a relief of the 10th Northumberland Fusiliers. Prisoners spoke of an imminent counter-attack and the relieving battalions took up positions in depth in order to defend the left flank. The 10th then took over from the 11th Northumberland Fusiliers, a relief completed by 9.30 a.m. At 12.30 p.m. the battalion made a successful attack and three machine-guns firing from ruins close to Casa Bravada were dealt with and sixty Austrians taken prisoner. The battalion war diary noted:

> Pte. Woods [*sic*] with a Lewis gun attacked a machine gun and while advancing fired from the hip, knocked out the gun and killed the crew. The Green Line was captured, many civilians being found in houses at this point.

Owing to the presence of several machine-guns, as well as sniper fire and despite attempts to capture the machine-guns, the battalion was forced to remain where it was through the night. It was impossible to advance to Ramera, where they planned to establish a bridgehead.

However, at 8.30 a.m. on the 29th, the battalion, without assistance from the left and with no contact with the right, was able to advance towards their last objective and reached the River Montecana. The advance then slowed down because of machine-gun and sniper fire from Ramera. In addition, the river bridge was destroyed by the enemy, although the man who lit the fuse was killed. The enemy held the position in strength and, with its machine-guns placed in buildings, forced the Fusiliers to dig in. A message was sent for either artillery support or assistance from the left flank. When dusk fell the battalion was withdrawn 200yd from the riverbank in advance of an expected bombardment. At 7 p.m. patrols, managing to cross the river, discovered that the 11th Northumberland Fusiliers had 'turned the position' and the 10th Battalion successfully advanced, taking fifty prisoners as they went. Contact with the right flank was still giving trouble, but by dawn, with more prisoners taken, the situation was totally cleared up.

The battalion war diary noted:

> During operations several hundred prisoners, many machine guns, 3 transport wagons and horses, many small dumps, and one large ammunition dump of 10 to 12,000 rounds, were captured by the battalion.

Clearly Pte Wilfred Wood of B Company of the 10th Northumberland Fusiliers was responsible for a considerable contribution, as indicated by the citation for his VC published in the *London Gazette* of 27 November as follows:

> Wilfred Wood, No. 59812, Private, 10th Battn. Northumberand Fusiliers (Stockport). For most conspicuous bravery and initiative on 28 Oct. 1918, near Casa Vana, Italy, when a unit on the right flank having been held up by hostile machine-guns and snipers, Private Wood, on his own initiative, worked forward with a Lewis gun, enfiladed the enemy machine-gun nest, and caused 140 enemy to surrender. The advance was continued till a hidden machine-gun opened fire at point-blank range. Without a moment's hesitation, Private Wood charged the machine-gun firing his Lewis gun from the hip at the same time. He killed the machine-gun crew, and without further orders pushed on and enfiladed a ditch from which three officers and 160 men subsequently surrendered. The conspicuous valour and initiative of this gallant soldier, in the face of intense rifle and machine-gun fire, was beyond all praise.

Nearly five weeks later, and after a Church of England service in the theatre at Montecchia di Crosara on 1 December, Maj. Gen.

H.F. Thuillier presented awards to several members of the 10th Northumberland Fusiliers at a parade which took place in a field opposite the theatre in the afternoon. These included a VC ribbon awarded to Pte W. Wood of B Company.

Wilfred Wood was born in Stockport, Cheshire, on 2 February 1897 at 25 Adcroft Street. After the death of his father, he moved to 52 Chester Road, Hazel Grove, near Stockport, where his mother married again, becoming Mrs Daniels. Wilfred was educated at Norbury Church of England School. He was a regular member of the Norbury Church congregation and a member of the local football club. After leaving school he got a job with the railways on his seventeenth birthday in February 1914 and was employed at the Edgeley sheds on the London and North Western Railway (LNWR) as a shed cleaner.

Nearly three years later, Wood enlisted in December 1916 as a stretcher-bearer, but soon transferred to the 10th Northumberland Fusiliers. He had joined the Army with two colleagues from the Edgeley sheds. He began his training at Oswestry and he became a stretcher-bearer with the Cheshire Regiment after he left for France, but later joined the 10th Northumberland Fusiliers who had left for France in August 1915. His new battalion was one of the first to be sent to Italy after the Battle of Caporetto and left France in November 1917; it was still part of 68th Brigade (23rd Division).

After Wood's VC was announced in November 1918, the residents of Hazel Grove and Bramhall Urban District agreed to club together and present their local hero with a testimonial. On 19 December, after being decorated by the King at Buckingham Palace and accompanied by his fiancée, Bessie, from Toronto Street, he arrived home at Edgeley station by train in the early evening, where he was escorted by a brass band to a public reception at Hazel Grove. The official welcome took place at the Worsley Street Chapel. The local newspapers stated that Wood was well known in Hazel Grove and his grandmother had been licensee of the White Hart Hotel for forty years. His mother displayed a flag of welcome in an upstairs window of her home.

Wood's brother, James Henry, was serving in the Army in Ireland and a third brother was 15 years old. Wood was demobilised in 1919 and returned to the LNWR, where he was soon promoted to fireman and later trained for a job as a driver in Newton Heath, Manchester. After he qualified as a driver, having worked his way up from shunting: 'He used to work in the northern region especially Blackpool to Birmingham, Leeds to Liverpool.'

In July 1919 Wood duly married Bessie in St George's Church, Stockport. The couple had first met when Bessie was a conductress on the Stockport trams and Wilfred used to wait for the tram she was working on. In 1920 Wood attended the Garden Party at Buckingham Palace on 26 June, the ceremony at the Cenotaph on 11 November 1920, the Burial of the Unknown Warrior in Westminster Abbey and the House of Lords' VC Dinner on 9 November 1929. In the following year he was presented to Lady Haig at Stockport on 11 April 1930.

On 12 May 1937, Coronation Day, he presented a glass bowl to the Matron at Stepping Hill Hospital on behalf of the local branch of the Ex-Servicemen's Association. On 8 June 1946 he attended the VE Parade, followed in the evening by the dinner at The Dorchester. Ten years later he took part in the VC centenary commemorations in London, which included a VC reception at the Guildhall in London. He later attended the first two VC/GC dinners.

The railways had been nationalised in 1948 and, at the age of 63, Wood retired on 27 August 1960 when supervisor at the Longsight railway shed. He had completed forty-six years' service with the LNWR, which later became the London Midland and Scottish Railway (LMS). He attended the Garden Party at Buckingham Palace on 17 July 1962, the banquet in the evening at the Mansion House and the third VC/GC dinner the following day. He also attended the Second Service of Remembrance at St Martin-in-the-Fields and, in September 1967, the funeral service for John Christie VC held at Stockport Crematorium.

Wilfred and Bessie Wood celebrated their golden wedding anniversary in July 1969 and the couple were paid an official visit by Councillor Kenneth Starkie, who presented them with a telegram of congratulation from the local council, together with a bouquet of flowers for Bessie.

In July 1974 a LNWR engine was named 'Private Wilfred Wood VC', and, although he had previously travelled in it, he never drove it. The nameplate, made in Crewe, was initially passed to the Regimental Museum, but was later presented to his old school, Norbury Church of England, on 28 October 1976. The locomotive was one of the 'Patriot Class' first introduced in 1930 and so named because the first one was numbered 1914. It was named 'Patriot' in memory of the employees of the LNWR who had died in the First World War. Two other engines were named after VCs: J.A. Christie and E. Sykes. The Patriots were in fact rebuilds of the 'Claughtons' and Wood's engine was No. 5536, later 45536. It was first built in 1933 and later rebuilt in 1946. It was used 'mainly on the express passenger services between London, Manchester and Carlisle and covered more than 1.5 million miles before being withdrawn and scrapped in 1962'. Of the forty-one engines in this class, none survive.

When interviewed by the *Stockport Express* in November 1975, Wood said of his VC: 'That medal means a lot to me ... I wouldn't part with it for anything, but I'm in a fortunate position, so I don't need to sell it.'

Bessie died in 1976. Apart from a great interest in railways, Wood was also a Freemason and his son, a clerical officer with Freight Management in Rail House, Manchester, would occasionally take him to Lodge Meetings. In the late 1970s Wood's health began to fail and he suffered from a slight stroke as well as cataracts in both eyes. At the age of 84, Wilfred Wood died in Stepping Hill Hospital, Stockport, on 3 January 1982. His home since 1929 had been 23 Butley Street, Hazel Grove. He left one son, Harry, and two grandchildren. In his will he left £42,205 gross.

Wood was cremated at Stockport Crematorium on 8 January and his ashes were scattered in the crematorium's First Garden of Remembrance. His name is included in the Book of Remembrance. His engine nameplate is now with the Northumberland Fusiliers Museum, Alnwick Castle. His decorations are not publicly held and, apart from the VC, they should include the BWM, VM (1914–19), King George VI Coronation Medal (1937), Queen Elizabeth II Coronation Medal (1953) and Queen Elizabeth II Silver Jublilee Medal (1977). A model of Wood's engine has been made by Messrs Hornby, which uses the engine number 45536.

On 10 September 2010 a Wetherspoons pub was opened in 204 London Road, Hazel Grove, Cheshire, and was named 'The Wilfred Wood'. It includes a plaque and a hanging sign which incorporates Wilfred's image. After his son, Harry, died in May 2013, the family decided to hold a wake in the pub on the 30th in his memory. However, as one of the family group was under 16 years of age the Wood family was asked to leave the establishment. At the time of writing there are active plans to build a replica of a Patriot class engine and it is hoped to use LMS parts as much as possible and have it ready by 2018. It will be named the 'Unknown Warrior'.

MESOPOTAMIA:

A LAND BETWEEN TWO RIVERS

G.G.M. WHEELER

Shaiba, 12 April 1915

In 1908 large oil reserves were discovered at the head of the Persian Gulf, which were then worked by a consortium named the Anglo-Persian Oil Co. Fortuitously, this new source of cheap fuel came at a time when the Royal Navy was busy converting its ships from coal to oil. Hence large quantities of oil would be needed by the Royal Navy when its ships were moving in the Middle and Far East. During the First World War these oil deposits were a prize which Germany and Turkey were desperately keen to own, and, in addition, Germany was involved in building a vital railway which would run from Berlin to Baghdad, the capital of Mesopotamia. By 1914 this line was only 400 miles short of completion. Most of all, the Kaiser wanted to expand his territories and be able to cut Great Britain off from her Indian possessions. Prior to the war he had approached Turkey with a view to combining their two armies in the region. The agreement was that Turkey would supply most of the manpower while Germany would provide the finance, the brainpower and the military leadership.

Even before the declaration of war against the Allies, the British, realising what was obviously to happen in Mesopotamia, despatched an Indian force, including some British battalions, which would protect this vital source of oil in the Persian Gulf. The threat of capture came from troops of the Turkish Army, who could also count on Arab support. The British landed a force of 600 troops at Fao in the Persian Gulf on 7 November 1914, and two days later they landed 4,500 troops at Sanniyeh, close to Abadan. Thus the British were in time to establish defensive positions from which they could prevent the oilfields from Turkish capture. It was during this period that the Allied force suffered its first casualties of the campaign in the subsequent fighting.

After few difficulties, the Anglo-Indian 6th (Poona) Division entered Basra on 21 November, where there was little opposition as the Turks had already withdrawn. The town, on the west bank of the Shatt-al-Arab, 55 miles from its mouth in the Persian Gulf, was to become the base for the Mesopotamian Expeditionary Force for the duration of the war.

After leaving Basra, the Turkish Army was holding on to the town of Qurna close by. Owing to the difficulties in crossing the River Tigris, initial attempts on the Turkish-held town failed, but it later surrendered on 9 December after being surrounded. By the end of the year the British force had moved towards the confluence of the Tigris and Euphrates rivers and then proceeded to make full use of both rivers.

In early February 1915 the Central Powers struck back by targeting Britain's main defence artery, the Suez Canal, with the aim of raising

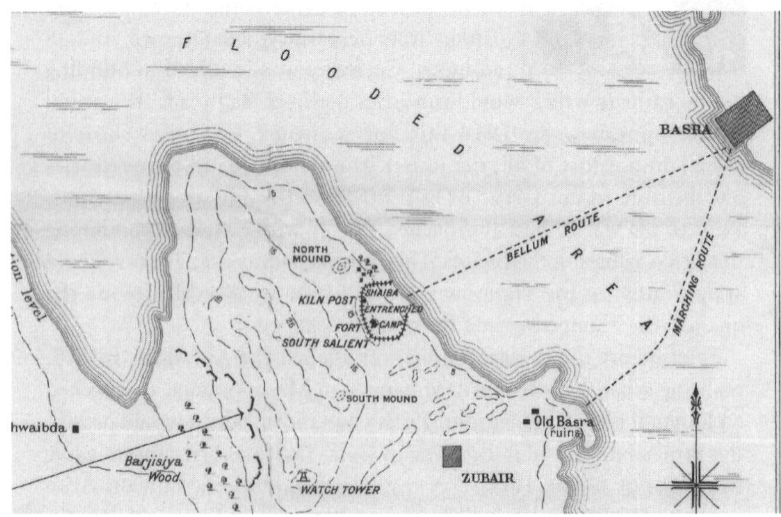

Basra and the North Mound, 12 April 1915.

an Islamic revolt in Egypt, but the attack failed with heavy losses. However, four months later it became known that the Turks were planning to retake Basra and the small British force was expanded to cope with the threat. After a series of actions during the period 12–14 April at Shaiba, 14 miles to the south-west of the town, in which three Indian cavalry regiments, the Bombay Engineers, three British and ten Indian infantry regiments took part, the immediate threat of the capture of Basra receded. The British force of 6,156 men, of whom 1,265 became casualties, routed a 12,000-strong Turkish force whose casualties totalled 3,177.

The first intimation of an enemy attack had been the presence of the enemy cavalry at Barjisiya Wood, combined with reports of a large body of infantrymen moving into Shwaibda. The divisional commander, Maj. Gen. C.I. Fry, considered these troops to be the advance guard of a much greater force and, as a consequence, the Anglo-Indian force was about to have a fight on its hands.

According to the 6th Indian Cavalry Brigade diary entry for 7.50 a.m. on 11 April, reconnaissance reported there were about 800 horsemen advancing towards Barjisiya Wood from the direction of Shwaibda and about 1,500–2,000 beyond Shwaibda. The wood itself was already held by an unknown number of horsemen. Later in the morning a force of Arabs, estimated to be about 1,000, were seen near Shwaibda.

In the evening the Cavalry Brigade received orders to leave Shaiba camp at 5.30 a.m. the next morning and march towards Old Basra and Zubair. As the advanced guard began to move off, counter orders were received from Shaiba HQ as apparently the enemy was beginning a strong attack towards Basra. The brigade was ordered to remain where it was.

The hours went by until, at 4 p.m. on the 12th, Maj. G.G.M. Wheeler of the 7th Lancers:

> ... volunteered to take his squadron by a covered route to attempt to surprise a trench from which snipers were firing at the Artillery observation point. The squadron, which made the whole manoeuvre at a gallop, was unable to attack the trench owing to coming under numerous infantry in a hidden position. These were ridden over and many were lanced. Artillery and Machine Guns acting in support repulsed an attempt of the enemy to make a mounted attack. The squadron returned with

> 1 man slightly wounded & 3 horses wounded. The whole manoeuvre inflicted considerable loss on the enemy & the squadron was admirably led with great dash by Major Wheeler.

The Lancers' own war diary gives the time as being an hour earlier and notes:

> 'A' Squadron led by Major Wheeler galloped to a point 1500yds S.E. of No. 8 Picquet: as the squadron emerged from camp the R.H.A. who were in position at No. 8 Picquet & the M. Gun section opened fire on the enemy, who left their trenches when they saw 'A' Squadron galloping for them. 'A' Squadron got home with the lance, and at the same time great execution was done by the guns on the enemy footmen and also on the enemy's cavalry, who suddenly emerged at a distance of about 2500yds from the high ground N.E. of Old Basra. 'A' Squadron, having delivered their charge, rallied and cantered back to camp. In this action 'A' Squadron had one man and one horse wounded.

A note in the war diary also states: 'The idea of this manoeuvre, which was a brilliant piece of work, was conceived by Major Wheeler who asked to be allowed to carry it out with his own Sqdn.'

Shaiba camp was now under shell and rifle fire, and some men and horses were wounded.

During the evening the commanding officer, Maj. Gen. Fry, issued orders for a move towards North Mound and beyond, to take place at 5.30 a.m. the following morning. The move was slightly delayed in order to allow for artillery and extra infantry support. At 7 a.m. the 7th Lancers, under Lt Col C. Cook, were ordered to rush the 'Groves' along with House 'B' and North Mound, leaving the rest of the brigade in support. Though their advance was heavily repelled, they captured the North Mound but were unable to hold on to it owing to heavy fire. Even so, the Lancers had been busy with the enemy, 'getting well among 50 to 100 of them with the lance'.

Seeing the forced retirement of the 7th Lancers, it was decided to retire the brigade as casualties were mounting severely. At 11.50 a.m. orders were given for the cavalry and infantry to recover some abandoned hostile guns. During this operation many of the enemy began to retire and, in doing so, were severely cut down. The chance of inflicting further damage on the enemy was missed owing to the recovery of the guns.

It was for the charge on the 12th that Maj. George Wheeler of the 7th Hariana Lancers gained the first VC of the Mesopotamian Campaign, but sadly he was killed the following day in the attack across unreconnoitred ground and trenches against the North Mound when trying to capture the enemy's standard. Seven Indian NCOs and men were killed at the same time and, apart from the eighteen wounded, no fewer than thirty-six horses were killed as well as seventy-nine horses of the 7th Lancers. It appears to have been a suicide mission. Wheeler was later buried in Basra War Cemetery, Plot III, Row C, Grave 22. Sadly, the cemetery has been virtually destroyed during recent conflicts, first during the Iran–Iraq war and later during the Allied invasion of 2003–04.

Summing up the two-day operation, the adjutant of the 7th Lancers wrote:

> Although the operations, as a whole, were not successful, the 7th Hariana Lancers under the leadership of Lt. Colonel C.C. Cook acted with splendid push and resolution. The Division Commander Major General C.J. Melliss, V.C., expressed his admiration of the way in which they attacked North Mound.

It may be significant to remember that Melliss was awarded his VC for a similar act to Wheeler's, but this time during the Ashanti Wars fifteen years before.

The citation for Wheeler's posthumous VC was published in the *London Gazette* of 1 September 1915 as follows:

> George Godfrey Massy Wheeler, Major, late 7th Hariana Lancers, Dates of Acts of Bravery: 12 and 13 April, 1915. For most conspicuous bravery at Shaiba, Mesopotamia. On the 12th April 1915, Major Wheeler asked permission to take out his squadron and attempt to capture a flag, which was the centre-point of a group of the enemy who were firing on one of our picquets. He advanced and attacked the enemy's infantry with the lance, doing considerable execution among them. He then retired, while the enemy swarmed out of the hidden ground and formed an excellent target to our Royal Horse Artillery guns. On the 13th April 1915, Major

> Massy Wheeler led his squadron to the attack on the 'North Mound'. He was seen far ahead of his men, riding single-handed straight for the enemy's standards. This gallant officer was killed on the Mound.

George Wheeler was born 31 January 1873 at Chakrata, United Provinces, India, a son of Gen. Hugh Wheeler (who died in 1910) and grandson of Gen. Sir Hugh Massy Wheeler KCB, of Indian Mutiny fame (1858) when he and his wife were massacred at the Cawnpore Entrenchment. George Wheeler was educated at Bedford Modern School (1886–91). Later he went to RMA Sandhurst and joined the Army on 20 May 1893, serving in the 1st Wiltshire Regiment. On 13 October 1897 he transferred to the Indian Army, 7th Hariana Lancers, and was promoted to captain in May 1902. Between 1908 and 1912 he was made commandant of 50th Camel Corps and served in operations in the North-West Frontier in 1908, for which he received a medal with clasp. In 1911 he was promoted to major. He was married to Nellie Purcell, a daughter of a prominent surgeon, Ferdinand Wheeler.

George Wheeler was a keen sportsman in every sense of the word: a good polo player, a most devoted regimental officer, and a great favourite in the regiment. In the latter part of his life he was known as Massy Wheeler and his English address was at 5 Gwydyr Mansions, Hove, Sussex. His VC was presented to his next of kin, after it had been sent to the India Office, on 4 September 1916. His VC and medals are kept in the National Army Museum. Apart from his VC they include the BWM, VM (1914–19) and MiD Oakleaf, India General Service Medal with two clasps ('Waziristan 1919–21' and 'Waziristan 1921–24').

Another distinguished soldier and sportsman who attended Bedford Modern School was Lt Col Edgar Mobbs DSO (1882–1917). He arrived at the school a year after Wheeler left and was killed on 31 July 1917 on the first day of the Third Battle of Ypres. He is commemorated on the Northampton War Memorial and by the annual Mobbs Memorial Rugby Match in Northampton. His name, together with that of Wheeler, is remembered on Bedford Modern School's First World War Memorial, which was dedicated in 1923. It was transferred to the new building at Manton Lane in 1974. In addition, two portraits of Wheeler and Mobbs were commissioned in the 1920s and painted by Barbara Chamier. The one of Wheeler was the gift of a school contemporary, Mr G.M. Aclom, and is a life-size, three-quarter-length portrait which shows him in the uniform of the 7th Hariana Lancers and wearing a military turban.

In addition to these school commemorations, Wheeler was also remembered by being listed on the family stone in Deans Grange Cemetery, Dublin. His name is also included on the Hindhead War Memorial, next to St Andrew's Church, although it is not clear what his links with the town were. We do know, however, that a Reverend (Revd) George Massy Wheeler was in the Guildford area between 1901–11 and was Vicar of Hindhead from 1912–18. The memorial was unveiled by the Bishop of Winchester on 14 December 1919 and it is not known whether the Revd Wheeler attended the service. The name of a second holder of the VC, Lt Col Philip Bent, is also included on the memorial.

In 1974 in the *Victor* comic of 3 August, Wheeler's adventures in capturing the Turkish flag were told in graphic detail.

C. SINGH

The Battle of Wadi, 13 January 1916

Between the Turkish attempts to recapture the major town of Basra in April 1915 and their subsequent retreat from Shaiba to the south-west two days later, the first phase of the Mesopotamian Campaign ended – a campaign which was to be fought up and down the River Tigris, across a featureless landscape, and which continued towards the goal of Baghdad via Amara, Kut, Aziziya, Ctesiphon and back to Kut again. A major factor in the campaign was that the Tigris was liable to flood between March and May and occasionally even overflow as early as January. On 14 May 1915, Turkish troops had withdrawn to Amara and were defeated on the 31st at Kurna on the River Tigris where they were pursued by a Royal Naval flotilla of launches. Three days later, and despite having a force of 2,000 men, they surrendered the town to the British.

The 6th (Indian) Division was under the command of Gen. Sir Charles Townsend, who had arrived in Basra from India on 22 April. Townsend had been in India at the outbreak of war and had been made a major general and given an Indian division to command. This was a decision which was to have far-reaching consequences for the campaign in Mesopotamia.

In early May Gen. Nixon, the commander-in-chief of the Anglo-Indian force, made the decision to conduct a Tigris offensive with the aim of reaching the capital city of Baghdad, headquarters of the Turkish Army in Mesopotamia, and sought permission from London

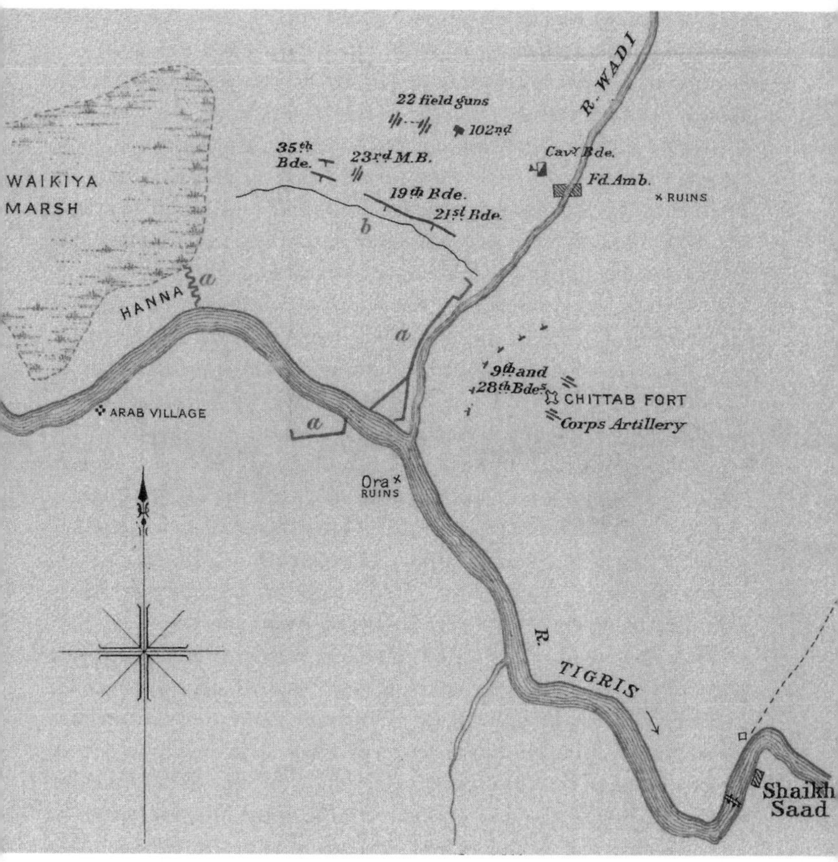

Battle of Wadi, 13 January 1916.

to carry it out. The force set out and made rapid progress to the town of Amara, which was then captured.

Seemingly unaware of the dangers, Nixon ordered Townsend to continue the advance, but by now conditions were becoming extremely trying, mainly owing to the men suffering from disease; dysentery, malaria and the heat taking a huge toll. Soon casualties from sickness alone had reached over 1,000 men and the climate was particularly hard to cope with as temperatures in the day were reaching 125°F. In addition, all water to be used had to be purified first and there was no supporting line of communication. Even Gen. Townsend himself became ill and returned to Bombay in July on sick leave.

Despite the extremely trying conditions the Anglo-Indian force moved steadily north-westwards and after returning to Amara on 27 August Townsend was instructed to advance on Kut, a task which began on 12 September with a force of 11,080 men and thirty guns. The advance was made over land and water, using the River Tigris as a main source of transport. It was still very hot during the day and the nights were correspondingly cold. It followed that much of the marching was carried out at night and, on reaching the outskirts of Kut on 28 September, Townsend's force stormed the Turkish defences outside the town and managed to overwhelm them. In the battle for possession of the town of Kut-el-Amara, the two sides endured heavy fighting in extremely hot weather; the enemy suffered 1,850 casualties and Townsend's force 1,233. The Allied force successfully occupied the town the next day. Although strategically important and situated in a loop of the River Tigris, to say that Kut was an extremely drab and unhealthy place would be a considerable understatement.

While Townsend's force rested and recuperated in Kut, and awaited essential supplies, the enemy had retreated towards Baghdad, 120 miles to the north-west. In early October Townsend continued the advance towards the capital, but with two weakened divisions. In addition, the next stage of the advance was delayed by the War Office for three weeks until Gen. Nixon was given permission for it to continue. On 11 November Townsend renewed his advance with a force which was clearly far too small and which had already travelled 300 miles from Basra. By the next day they reached to within 7 miles of Ctesiphon, 25 miles south of Baghdad. The attack on this town on the 22nd was successful, but of the 8,500 British and Indian troops who took part in the fighting almost half became casualties. The Turks also lost heavily.

Holding on despite several Turkish counter-attacks, and on receiving news gathered by aerial reconnaissance of a Turkish return, the British force wearily retired from Ctesiphon on the 25th to the River Tigris a few miles away via Azizia, which they reached on the 28th, and returned to garrison Kut, where they arrived on 3 December having journeyed 90 miles. Townsend sent eleven boats away and the cavalry was also sent back downstream. Then with a small and very weary force he was quoted as saying: 'I mean to defend Kut as I did Chitral.' This was a reference to his actions in India twenty years before when he was in his early 30s.

However, the enemy, bolstered by 30,000 reinforcements, had other ideas and the Turkish forces quickly surrounded the town. Two days later the Siege of Kut-el-Amara began. Townsend rejected an offer of surrender on 9 December and Gen. Aylmer sent a message to Townsend the next day to give him news of a planned early relief. Over the next few weeks the Turks continued to lay siege to the town, whose garrison had to survive in dreadful conditions and was faced with being starved to death as well as having a lack of medical supplies, let alone arms, with which to defend itself. Several attempts were made to relieve the beleaguered troops with Gen. Aylmer making the first move on 6 January. Leaving from Ali Gherbi, with a force 19,000 strong, the Tigris Corps, made up of the 7th Division (35th, 21st and 19th Infantry Brigades), the 28th Brigade, a cavalry brigade and a brigade of the Royal Field Artillery, moved astride the Tigris on the 4th and, despite a strong attack on 7–8 January, the Turkish defences remained intact, as they were much stronger than previously thought.

On the 9th the Turks retreated to Wadi and the British force occupied Shaikh Saad to the north-west. On the 13th Gen. Aylmer's force captured Turkish positions in the Battle of Wadi, together with 2,000 casualties as opposed to 1,613 of his own. During the day heavy rains caused the British bridge across the Tigris to collapse.

In the Battle of Wadi the enemy's main position faced south-east, and, according to the 21st Brigade war diary:

> The task of the 21st Bde was to hold the enemy on his left without committing itself too closely, while the 19th Bde on the immediate right of the 21st Bde and the 35th Bde and Cavalry Bde still further to the right manoeuvred him out of his position by action against his rear.

It was during this fighting that a supreme act of heroism was carried out by an Indian sepoy, one Chatta Singh of the 1st Battalion of the 9th Bhopal Infantry, 21st Infantry Brigade, 7th Division, when he saved the life of his commanding officer. The 9th Bhopals became part of 21st Brigade when they arrived at Ali Gerbi to take part in the relief of Kut by the Tigris Corps. On 13 January the brigade was in the line with the 9th Gurkhas on the left and the 41st Dogras and 6th Jats to the right. Leading companies crossed the River Wadi with little opposition, although the artillery was unable to use the steep banks. The companies came under heavy fire from well-concealed enemy positions and Lt Col T.W. Thomas, commanding officer of the 9th Bhopals, was hit by a burst of bullets when he went forward towards B Company in order to give them instructions. Thomas was lying on flat and open ground and became an easy target for the enemy 200yd away. At this point Sepoy Chatta Singh rushed over to assist the colonel and to bandage his wounds. Being in a totally exposed position the sepoy attempted to shield Thomas with his own body and then, using his entrenching tool, began to dig a bullet-proof cover for the two men. The 21st Brigade advance was now at a standstill.

According to the regimental history:

> Colonel Thomas's left leg was shattered half-way between the knee and ankle, and he suffered such agony that at times the pain drew from him groans that could be heard by his men during lulls in the fighting. Chatta Singh's efforts to comfort and reassure his commanding officer could also be heard. Further aid was impossible before nightfall, for any attempt to carry Colonel Thomas to safety during daylight would have meant the destruction of the whole party. When eventually Colonel Thomas was rescued, he was nearly delirious through pain and loss of blood, but in spite of this, he did not forget to impress on his rescuers the great and unselfish gallantry of Chatta Singh.

Captain B.W. Browning, 9th Bhopal Infantry, wrote a slightly different account:

> I was not actually with the regiment in Mesopotamia when Chatta Singh did his deed for which he was awarded the V.C. He was awarded his V.C. for the Battle of the Wadi 13 Jan. 1916. As far as my memory serves me, the story is this: The regiment attacked the Turkish position and was driven back, leaving among the wounded in No Man's Land the Colonel (Colonel T.W. Thomas), wounded in the thigh. The Colonel of the regiment on our left was also left wounded in No Man's Land. Chatta Singh remained with these two officers for over 24 hours – I'm not sure

> of the length of time – dug a small parapet round each to protect them as much as possible, and fed them, all the time under very heavy fire. They were subsequently brought in, and Colonel Thomas died later at Amara from shock and exposure.

Colonel Thomas was buried in Amara War Cemetery, Plot I, Row C, Grave 29.

Although there was sporadic sniping during the night, it petered out before dawn and patrols discovered the enemy had withdrawn. The rest of the day was quiet and the 21st Brigade bivouacked close to the Tigris. As a consequence of this action, seventy-two men were killed, including sixty-three Indians, and 368 men wounded, 316 of them Indians.

While the relief advance was making very slow progress, Townsend's rations were rapidly dwindling; on the 16th he wired Aylmer to say that he had from seventeen to twenty-one days left. Aylmer considered that now was the time for Townsend to attempt to break out from the besieged garrison, but Gen. Nixon refused permission; however, three infantry brigades were added to the relief force.

Owing to much of the ground being marshy, combined with a break in the weather, the landscape was reduced to a quagmire. So there could be no advance against the enemy-held trenches at what was known as the 'Hanna Position' between the Suwaikiya Marsh and the Tigris until the 21st when a second VC was gained by another Indian member of the 7th Division, this time with the 35th Brigade to whom the 41st Dogras had been lent.

Sepoy Chatta Singh's well-earned VC was published in the *London Gazette* of 21 June 1916 as follows:

> Chatta Singh, No. 3398, Sepoy, 9th Bhopal Infantry, Indian Army. For most conspicuous bravery and devotion to duty in leaving cover to assist his commanding officer, who was lying wounded and helpless in the open. Sepoy Chatta Singh bound up the officer's wound, and then dug cover for him with his entrenching tool, being exposed all the time to very heavy rifle fire. For five hours until nightfall he remained beside the wounded officer, shielding him with his own body on the exposed side. He then, under cover of darkness, went back for assistance, and brought the officer into safety.

Chatta Singh was born at Tilsara, Cawnpore, India, in 1887 (or 1886), son of Ishu Singh, who was a cultivator. He was educated at Tilsara Village School, and joined the Indian Army on 5 July 1911 as a sepoy in the 9th Bhopal Infantry. His VC was sent from the War Office to the India Office on 26 June 1916, a few days after the citation had been published, and was possibly presented to him by Capt. Ralston, India Army, OC Depot, 9th Bhopal at Fyzabad, India, in July.

In 1934 he was still a member of the Indian Army, serving with the 16th Punjab Regiment. He died in his early 70s on 28 March 1961 at Tilsara, Kanpur, India and was cremated at Tilsara Village. Apart from the VC his medal entitlement included the 1914–15 Star, BWM, VM (1914–19), King George VI Coronation Medal (1937) and Queen Elizabeth II Coronantion Medal (1953). They are not publicly held.

LALA

El Orah, 21 January 1916

The actions at El Orah in Mesopotamia on 21 January 1916 were part of an attempt to capture Turkish positions at Hanna, ¾ mile north of the River Tigris, near the Suwaikiya Marsh. Of the 7th (Indian) Division under the command of Maj. Gen. Sir George Younghusband, the 2nd Black Watch, 6th Jats and 41st Dogras battalions were attached to the 35th Brigade and the 9th Bhopals to the 19th Brigade. The attack against strongly held Turkish positions was planned to take place on 21 January.

The prospect of a successful attack must have seemed pretty slim; the morning of the assault turned out misty and at 7.45 a.m. the day began badly with an inadequate bombardment against the enemy positions. With the marshy ground in such a poor state, together with a very well-organised foe established in sunken loop-holed trenches, and with the cavalry nowhere to be seen, the actions were a total failure with the initial advancing battalions suffering many casualties when attempting to go forward over a flat landscape. After an initial pause, the assault continued, the artillery having lifted its guns at 7.55 a.m. To add to the British problems, a broken bridge across the Tigris had prevented guns from being taken to the right bank from 'which a flanking fire might have been effective'.

As to the battalions themselves, the 2nd Black Watch had its left flank on the Tigris, entrenched 200yd from the enemy frontline, and the 41st Dogras continued this line further to the right. This two-battalion front extended for about 450yd and was covered by about 570 men.

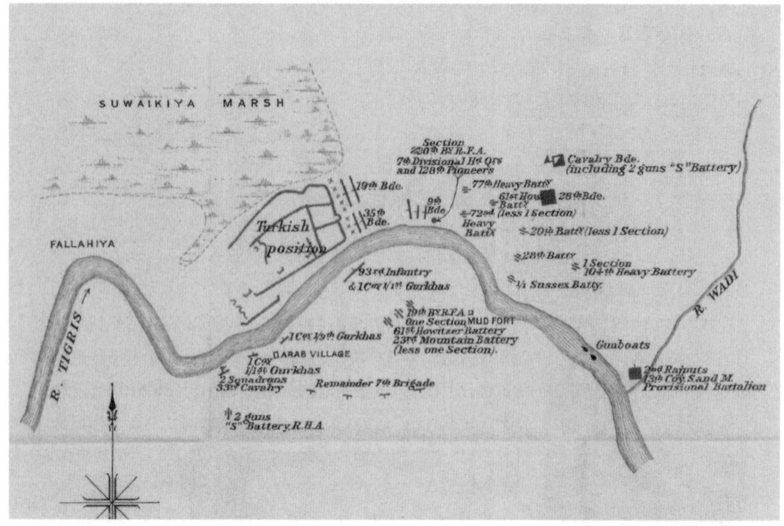

Near Suwaikiya Marsh, 21 January 1916.

Later in the morning the enemy made a counter-attack, and a further attempt at an advance was made by the Indian Division after a second bombardment, but again without success. By 11 a.m. it had begun to rain heavily. By nightfall the attacking troops, from battalions which had become extremely weakened in the dreadful conditions, were back at their starting point and, just to make matters worse, the rain became torrential, turning the landscape into a sea of mud. Casualties for the five battalions directly involved in the day's action came to 541.

This failed action was a severe reverse for the Kut relief force, but with Townsend's garrison trapped inside Kut and now reduced to half-rations with ever-diminishing supplies, Gen. Aylmer had little choice but to take on the Turkish defences.

During the fighting Capt. Nicholson, the adjutant of the 37th Dogras, a supporting battalion, was badly wounded in no-man's-land in pouring rain and was saved by Lance-Naik (Lance-Corporal) Lala who, on 'seeing him in a shallow nullah and much exposed, got out to him and dug a trench which gave him good cover, while later on he came out to him again and got both him and the wounded Adjutant of the 41st, Captain Lindop, back to our trenches, neither of them being equal to crawling through the mud, for which acts of devotion and gallantry he was awarded the V.C.' (9th Bhophal Battalion history)

In his book entitled *A Soldier's Memories*, Maj. Gen. Younghusband wrote extensively about Lance-Naik Lala's bravery after the initial advance had failed:

> At this point Sepoy (now Lance-Naik) Lala came across a Major in his regiment, 150yds from the enemy, lying completely exposed in the open, and trying to bandage a grievous wound. Lala dragged him a few yards to a very slight depression only a few inches deep and there bound up the Major's wounds. Whilst doing so he heard other cries for help, and sallying forth dragged four more of his comrades into the meagre shelter, and bound up their wounds.
>
> Meanwhile it had come on to rain hard, and a pitiless icy wind sprang up. Then Lala heard another voice calling for help about fifty yards to the front, and only one hundred yards from the Turkish trenches. He recognised the voice and said to the Major:
>
> 'That is my Adjutant, Sahib, calling. I must go out to help him.'
>
> 'No, Lala, it is quite useless,' said the Major. 'You will certainly be shot dead and therefore be of no use.'
>
> Then seeing that Lala was still preparing to go, he added: 'I order you not to go. Lie down.'
>
> Lala lay still for a bit, and then the voice from the front again called for help.
>
> Up jumped Lala, and calling out 'I'll be back in a minute,' dashed out to his Adjutant to save him.
>
> Later the Adjutant, just before he was taken into the operating room in hospital, where he died, dictated his evidence to a brother officer. He said:
>
> 'I was shot down in the open about a hundred yards from the enemy, and lay in great agony. An Officer of the Black Watch, who was lying a few yards off, tried to crawl to my assistance, but he was instantly shot dead. Every time I made the slightest movement bullets whistled past me, or through me. Then came a Sepoy to my assistance, and he was instantly shot dead. Then it came on to rain, and a bitter wind sprang up. Then as I lay in great pain suddenly appeared Lala and lay down beside me with cheering words. First he bound up my wounds, and then taking off his own coat spread it over me. Then he lay down lengthways so as to protect

me from the enemy's bullets. For five hours he lay like this in the wet and cold, and all the time kept talking cheerfully and encouragingly to keep my spirits up. At length when it grew dusk he crept off and said he was going back to get assistance and would soon return. I slept or dozed for sometime and then heard Lala return.

'It is good, Sahib, very good. I have brought some stretcher-bearers up not far from this. I will lie flat whilst you get on my back, and then I will crawl away with you on hands and knees.'

With great difficulty the Adjutant obeyed these instructions and was borne painfully many hundred yards by Lala to the stretcher-bearers.

Then Lala said:

'I must return and fetch the Major, Sahib, and these four Sepoys.'

And this he did though he was not touched by bullet, or shell, all day or night. Next morning he was hale and hearty and cheerful as ever, and grinned with great joyousness when he heard he was a brave man.

The Victoria Cross has only recently been acceded to Indian soldiers, and perhaps there is no worthier wearer of that badge of honour and bravery than Lance-Naik Lala of the Dogras.

Another account of Lala's deeds was published in E. Candler's book, *The Sepoy*, in which he wrote:

There was a freeezing wind and the wounded lay out in pools of rain and flooded marsh all night; some were drowned; others died of exposure. It was a Dogra-like act of Lala to strip himself, and to make a shield of his body for his Adjutant, an act of devotion repeated by the sepoy in Mesopotamia; and the Adjutant was only one of five officers and comrades whom Lala saved that day.

In a special issue of orders the Divisional General spoke of the splendid gallantry of the 41st Dogra in aiding the Black Watch to storm and occupy the enemy's trenches. The 6th Jats and the 97th Infantry were mentioned with the Dogras.

Of the collective achievement of the four regiments on that day, the general wrote:

They showed the highest qualities of endurance and courage under circumstances so adverse as to be almost phenomenal.

Lala was duly awarded the VC and the citation was published in the *London Gazette* of 13 May 1916 as follows:

> War Office, 13 May, 1916. His Majesty the King has been graciously pleased to confer the Victoria Cross on No. 501 Lance-Naik Lala, 41st Dogras, Indian Army, for most conspicuous bravery. Finding a British officer of another regiment lying close to the enemy, he dragged him into a temporary shelter, which he himself had made, and in which he had already bandaged four wounded men. After bandaging his wounds he heard calls from the Adjutant of his own regiment, who was lying in the open severely wounded. The enemy was not more than a hundred yards distant, and it seemed certain death to go out in that direction, but Lance-Naik Lala insisted on going out to his Adjutant, and offered to crawl back with him on his back at once. When this was not permitted, he stripped off his own clothing to keep the wounded officer warmer, and stayed with him till just before dark, when he returned to the shelter. After dark he carried the first wounded officer back to the main trenches, and then, returning with a stretcher, carried back his Adjutant. He set a magnificent example of courage and devotion to his officers.

Two days later he was also awarded the 1st Class Order of St George.

Lala was born on 20 April 1876 in the village of Parol in the district of Hamipur, near Jullundar, Kangra District, Punjab, India (or Himachal Pradesh Province, North-West India).

He was a son of Dinga, belonging to the Maila caste, and also a landowner, or Zeminder. He received no schooling but could read and write Hindi. He joined the Indian Army on 21 February 1901 and served in the First World War from 1914. He later said:

> I was in the first batch of Indians that came to France, and returned in 1915; guarded the Suez Canal for three months, and then moved to Mesopotamia, and there got my V.C., beyond Shaikh Saad, and then returned to India with the regiment in 1917. Kept fit all through, except got trench feet in France, and came to England to the Brighton Hospital, but soon rejoined my regiment. I am in the first eleven regimental football

> team. I have no newspapers here. I won my V.C. on 21 January 1916. Indian papers would contain certain accounts.

Lala was probably decorated in India in 1917 on his return home with his regiment, and later his medals were split up. He died at the age of 50 on 23 March 1927 at Parol and his body was cremated the same day in the village. His ashes were scattered locally and no plaque was erected.

In 1993 Gurdai Lala, Lala's second wife who was then aged 95, won her case for a pension, although she had previously been ruled ineligible as she was his second wife and only the first would be entitled to a widow's pension. The case had been dragging on since 1932 and the pension was backdated, giving her more than thirty years' payments. Lala's medal entitlement apart from the VC would have included the 1914–15 Star, BWM and VM. They are not publicly held.

J.A. Sinton

Orah Ruins, 21 January 1916

On 21 January 1916, during the Battle of El Hanna, Capt. John Sinton was medical officer to the 37th Dogras of the Indian Division. They were in action at Shaikh Saad in the area of the Orah ruins during one of the several attempts to relieve Kut-el-Amara, 23 miles away, where Gen. Townsend was besieged together with troops of his 6th (Indian) Division.

During the fighting, Sinton went forward to attend the wounded and in so doing was shot several times, both through his arms and his side. Despite his wounds, though, he would not be moved and remained at the front attending the wounded under heavy fire from the Turkish positions.

The corps war diary gave full details of how the casualties sustained on 21 January 1916 in the Battle of El Hanna were dealt with after only a few men from the attacking force had reached the Turkish trenches. After it began to rain at 11 a.m., a steady downpour continued into the night and turned the already marshy ground into a landscape of knee-deep mud.

The war diary of the 3 (Indian) Corps Deputy Director of Medical Services (December 1915–March 1917) on the following day noted:

> 22 Jan 1916 – Al Orah – Rain continued through the night. Country is a quagmire and nearly impassable for wheeled transport. Got over 1500 casualties yesterday evening and during the night. The 'Salimi' left here 6 p.m. yesterday and evacuated 6 British Officers and 450 British and Indian rank and file from a Dressing Station on the bank of the river. Another group of 120 who were 100yds nearer the front were brought

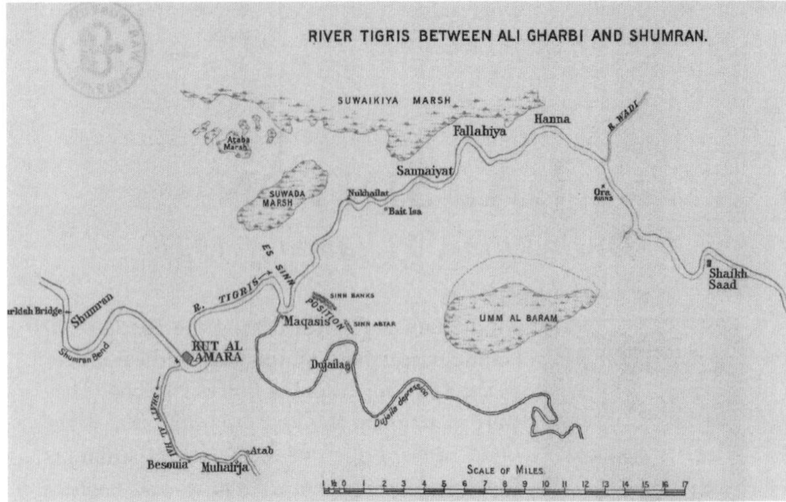

Orah ruins, 21 January 1916.

in this morning by small river craft as the 'Salimi' would have been under the fire of the enemy's guns if she had gone to them. Had interview with Corps Commander 1 p.m. I told him I estimated our casualties at 3000, also that he must expect a great deal of sickness.

'Salimi' left for base at 11a.m. with 6 B.Os [British officers] and about 450 British and Indian ranks referred to above. P.1 left 2p.m. for base with following wounded: BOs 6; British R & F [rank and file] 186, IO's [Indian officers] 12; Indian R & F 726. Total 930.

Number evacuated on 'Salimi' and P.1 approximate as owing to deficiency of Staff and urgency of getting them away they could not be properly checked.

Camp of 20 CFA [?] pitched close here is a morass and am putting as many wounded as possible on ships as they come in.

Gen Douglas DA [deputy assistant] & QMG [quartermaster general] went out about noon with flag of truce and arranged for 6 hours armistice to allow us to collect our wounded and bury the dead. Enemy would not allow us to collect our wounded close to his trenches but took them to his ambulances.

> We sent out all available A F carts – about 200 – accompanied by 3 Combatant Officers and one parson who volunteered to assist, also one troop British and one troop Indian cavalry to search the battlefield. They found all had already been collected and were in the advanced dressing station. All wounded were in by 6 p.m. with exception of 2 British Soldiers who arrived at 8.30 p.m.
>
> A F carts bringing in the wounded had great difficulty in reaching the ships, as the country was knee deep in mud and many of them were stuck for hours. Some of them were lying out all night on the battlefield and were very much exhausted.

The citation for Sinton's well-deserved VC was published in the *London Gazette* of 21 June 1916 as follows:

> John Alexander Sinton, M.B., Capt., Indian Medical Service. For most conspicuous bravery and devotion to duty. Although shot through both arms and through the side, he refused to go to hospital, and remained as long as daylight lasted, attending to his duties under very heavy fire. In three previous actions Capt. Sinton displayed the utmost bravery.

Sinton was presented with his decoration on 31 January 1918 by the Viceroy of India, Lord Chelmsford, at a special ceremony in Delhi.

John Alexander Sinton was born in Victoria, British Columbia, Canada, on 2 December 1884, the third of seven children of Ulster parents, Walter Sinton and Isabella Mary (née Pringle). The family returned from Canada to Ulster in 1890 and from 1893 to 1899 John was a pupil at Nicholson Memorial School, Lisburn, before moving to the Royal Belfast Academic Institution between 1899–1902. He then matriculated at the Royal College of Ireland and entered the Arts School of Queen's College, Belfast. A year later he passed the First Arts Examination of the Royal University of Ireland and entered the Medical School at Queen's College. He appears to have had no difficulty in winning prizes and honours in most of the subjects he studied.

In 1908 Sinton graduated with first-class honours in Medicine, Surgery and Obstetrics and became the Riddell Demonstrator in the pathology department. He also held an appointment in pathology at the Liverpool School of Tropical Medicine. On graduation he was appointed house surgeon and house physician at the Royal Victoria Hospital, Belfast. He was later a pathologist at the Ulster Eye, Throat and Ear Hospital, and clinical pathologist at the Mater Infirmorum Hospital, Belfast. Other qualifications included MB, DPH (Cantab and Belfast), DTM (Liverpool), and B.Ch., BAO, RUI (Indian Medical Service).

In August 1911 this very highly qualified doctor entered the Indian Medical Service having gained first place in the entrance examination. Prior to this he had been medical officer to the 31st Bengal Lancers (31st Duke of Connaught's Own Lancers), stationed at Kohat in the North-West Frontier Province.

On the outbreak of war, Sinton was on active service in India as regimental medical officer with the Movable Column, Kurram Valley, North-West Frontier, and later joined the Mesopotamia Expeditionary Force. He was made a captain on 21 June 1915 and posted to the Indian Expeditionary Force D (Mesopotamia) as regimental medical officer to the 37th Dogras, together with several other units. In January 1916 he was serving with the Dogras against the Turkish forces in Mesopotamia. It was when taking part in an action brought about by the attempt to relieve Kut-el-Amara that he won his VC on the same day as Lance-Naik Lala.

The following is from *Biographical Memoirs of Fellows of the Royal Society*:

> On return to duty (from India) after being wounded he remained on active service in various theatres of war until 1920, and for a time he was Sanitary Officer with the rank of A/Major in the Mahsud Operations on the NW Frontier, later in East African Field Force (Tanganika) and then with the East Persian Cordon Field Force commanding a Cavalry Field Ambulance and Agency Surgeon, Khorassan. From August 1918 to April 1919 he was in the Turkestan Military Mission as S.M.O [Senior Medical Officer]. and commanding a Cavalry Field Ambulance with the rank of Lt.-Col. In 1919 for a year he was D.A.D.M.S [Deputy Assistant Director of Medical Services] (San.) successively in the Afghanistan Campaign

> 1919, the Mahsud Campaign 1919–20 and the Waziristan Campaign 1920. Many times Sinton was Mentioned in Despatches and received many awards and medals.

In 1919 Sinton was promoted to brevet major and the Queen's University conferred the honorary degree of Doctor of Medicine on him, in recognition of his treatment of the wounded in the field during the war.

He continued to serve on the North-West Frontier in Afghanistan and Waziristan, and was Mentioned in Despatches on two occasions.

Sinton was made temporary major on 26 October 1920 and received the OBE (Mil.) in 1921. After a period at home he returned to India, having retired from the Army and taken up a career in research; he joined the Medical Research Department of the Indian Medical Service, taking charge of an enquiry into how malaria was treated, and he was one of the men involved in the setting up of a malaria treatment centre at Kasauli in the Punjab. As part of a team of experts he became known as a foremost authority on malarial and parasitical diseases, and in 1923 was made a full major.

On 19 September 1923 Sinton married Eadith Steuart Martin, only daughter of Edward Steuart Martin, a former indigo planter; the couple had a daughter, Eleanor, born on 9 December 1924 at Kasauli, where Sinton was serving with the Indian Medical Services in a civilian appointment.

On 24 March 1927 Sinton was awarded the Degree of Doctor of Science and in the same year was made the first Director of the Malarial Survey of India. He founded a scientific journal in order to be able to publish new information on the control of the breeding of the mosquito. He wrote over 200 papers on entomology. In 1928 he was presented with the Chalmers Memorial Medal of the Royal Society of Tropical Medicine and Hygiene, and continued with his researches for a further ten years before finally retiring from the Indian Medical Service in August 1938. (He had been promoted to lieutenant colonel on 29 January 1931.) He was then made Manson Fellow of the London School of Hygiene and Tropical Medicine, and adviser to the Ministry of Health. When war broke out again in 1939 he was recalled to India and posted as quartermaster to a military hospital where he proved a great success. In the following April, having reached the retirement age of 55, he was placed on the retired list and sent home, where he joined the Home Guard. However, between June and November 1940 he was recalled to be consultant malariologist to the East African forces; a position which was later expanded to cover the whole Middle East force. He travelled throughout the Middle East in this role and in 1942 took part in an extensive tour in order to be able to report on health conditions on projected air routes for troops across Africa. Between March and July 1945 he took part in an inspecting and advisory tour for the Army to inspect malaria conditions further afield in Assam, Burma, Ceylon, Australia, New Zealand and other countries. He was responsible for directing the advanced planning to ensure that specialised medical supplies were available to combat the dangers of malaria to the masses of troops newly arriving from the United Kingdom. Largely through his efforts, incidences of malaria in the Middle East force were minimal.

In 1944 Sinton was retired a second time, but was recalled once more as consultant to the War Office as there had been many outbreaks of the disease among the troops moving into Sicily and Italy. He retired for a third time at the end of the war and was awarded the Blisset-Hawkins Medal at the Royal College of Physicians in London. In 1946 he became the Robert Campbell Memorial Orator and Medallist of the Ulster Medical Society. In the same year he was made a Fellow of the Royal Society for his research into the problems of malaria. On his very last retirement he returned to his home at Slaghtfreedan Lodge, Cookstown, County Tyrone, where he planned 'to play the role of a country gentleman' and study ornithology, fish and gardening. In 1949 he was awarded the Mary Kingsley Medal by the Liverpool School of Tropical Medicine. Having planned a quiet retirement, it did not stop him from taking part in local affairs and he became a JP, a Deputy Lieutenant and, in 1953, High Sheriff for Tyrone.

According to the *Biographical Memoirs of Fellows of the Royal Society*:

> He was Pro-Chancellor in 1952 at Queen's and President of Queen's University Association 1953–4. Governor of the Royal Academical Institute, Belfast, 1946–50, President of the Co. Tyrone Branch of the Forces Help Society 1946–52 and Vice-President of the North Ireland Branch of this Society from 1952. He was President of the Cookstown

> Branch of the British Legion 1946–53, member of the Council of the North Ireland Branch 1949–52, and represented North Ireland at the 11th Conference of the British Empire Service League at London in 1951. In 1946 he was made Hon. Member of the Royal Society of St George. He was President of the Queen's University Service Club from 1946; Vice-President 1946–52 and President 1952–3 of the Old Instonians Association. He was Magistrate (JP) for Co. Tyrone from 1947; High Sheriff for that county in 1953; and Deputy Lieutenant in 1954.

Sinton was also a member of the National Arbitration Tribunal of Northern Ireland. John Sinton died on 25 March 1956 at his home at Slaghtfreedan Lodge, near Lough Fea, Cookstown, County Tyrone, having been ill for eight years. Described as a tall, spare man and full of energy, he was surely one of the most talented men to win a Victoria Cross and during his career achieved a very great deal in the service of others.

Sinton's funeral took place on 28 March at his home, and his coffin, on which rested his dress sword, cap, medals and the Union Jack, was carried into the Creggan Presbyterian churchyard by the vice-presidents of the Cookstown British Legion, together with the Branch's Standard. The procession was led by two pipers from the Royal Inniskilling Fusiliers Depot at Omagh, who played the *Lament*. At the graveside the 'Final Salute' was fired by two NCOs and twelve Fusiliers, and the *Last Post* and *Reveille* were sounded by a bugler from the same depot. As a final tribute, members of the British Legion filed past the grave and each one dropped a poppy into it. The ceremony was also attended by the medical profession, representatives from Queen's University and many other figures representing Sinton's considerable interests in the community at large.

Each year a ceremony takes place at Sinton's grave where a poppy wreath is laid by the local Legion branch on the Saturday afternoon before Remembrance Sunday.

Sinton's widow, Edith, died on 1 October 1978 and is buried in the same grave as her husband. In 1987 their daughter, now Eleanor Watson, opened a small housing complex organised for the use of Legion members, named Sinton Court in honour of her father's memory. The Musgrave Park Military Hospital, Belfast, also had a ward named after him. In addition, he is also remembered by the naming of Sinton Hall, a hall of residence for students at Queen's University, Belfast. In 2009 a new medical centre named after him was opened by his grandson.

Edith donated her late husband's decorations to the RAMC (Royal Army Medical Corps) Museum (later Army Medical Services) in Aldershot. They were considerable in number and, apart from his VC and OBE, include the 1914–15 Star, BWM, VM (1914–19) and MiD Oakleaf, India General Service Medal (1908–36) with three clasps ('Afghanistan NWF 1919', 'Mahsud 1919–20', 'Waziristand 1919–1921'), 1939–45 Star, Africa Star, Burma Star, Defence Medal (1939–45), War Medal (1939–45) and MiD Oakleaf, King George V Silver Jubilee Medal (1935), King George VI Coronation Medal (1937), Queen Elizabeth II Coronation Medal (1953), Order of St George (4th Class, Russia) and Egypt Gambia Medal.

G. STRINGER

Es Sinn, 8 March 1916

Since 21 January 1916 when two VCs had been gained during an attempted relief to extract Gen. Townsend's force at Kut-el-Amara, there had been painfully slow progress in covering the last 20 miles to relieve the besieged troops. By the 28th the Kut garrison was reduced to 8,356 fit personnel, 2,157 sick and 2,908 followers. Also on the same day, Lt Gen. Sir Percy Lake, now commander-in-chief Mesopotamia, having taken over from Gen. Nixon on the 19th, visited Gen. Aylmer's HQ and Gen. Gorringe was made chief of staff. On 7 February the Chief of the Imperial General Staff (CIGS) gave orders for the 13th Division from Gallipoli and the 7th Mountain Artillery Brigade to join the Mesopotamia Force. Six days later, the enemy bombed Kut from the air for the first time, but on the 22nd the garrison personnel must have much cheered when they heard the sound of Allied guns.

On the 26th Gen. Aylmer informed Gens Lake and Townsend that he was hoping to launch a further relief attempt on 7 March. Meanwhile, on 1 March Turkish guns continued shelling the Kut garrison, causing thirty-seven casualties.

Aylmer duly made his second relief attempt on the 7th with a force of 23,335 men and sixty-eight guns. The advance began with a night march with the idea of turning the Turkish southern wing. The subsequent battle was known as the Battle of Dujaila and, although the Turks were initially caught off guard, Aylmer's force made an attack which was too belated and thus the element of surprise was lost. It probably came as no surprise to Gen. Aylmer on the 11th when he learnt that he was to be replaced by Gorringe as General Officer Commanding (GOC) Tigris Corps. Few senior officers survived very long in this theatre of war before being replaced. Indeed, despite the closeness of the relief force, Kut was not to fall for another seven weeks.

On the 8th the third VC gained during the Kut relief campaign was won at Es Sinn by George Stringer, a private in the 1st Manchesters, 8th Infantry Brigade, 3rd (Lahore) Division during the attack against the Dujaila Redoubt. The attack began at 4.40 p.m. and companies of the 1st Manchesters and 59th Rifles advanced against heavy enfilade fire from Turkish positions. The trenches had not been targeted by Allied artillery, which concentrated on the redoubt itself. At 5.20 p.m. a footing was made on the redoubt and two lines of enemy trenches were quickly occupied. The attack swept over the crest of the redoubt, but then became immersed in the dust and smoke.

Under the weight of a very heavy counter-attack, the advanced positions became untenable and the Manchesters were forced to retire. It was during this period that Pte George Stringer won his VC for guarding his part of the line against enemy counter-attacks. The VC was published in the *London Gazette* of 5 August 1916 as follows:

> George Stringer. No. 15818, Private, 1st Battn. Manchester Regt. For most conspicuous bravery and determination. After the capture of an enemy position he was posted on the extreme right of his battalion to guard against any hostile attack. His battalion was subsequently forced back by an enemy counter-attack, but Private Stringer held his ground single-handed and kept back the enemy till all his grenades were expended. His very gallant stand saved the flank of his battalion and rendered a steady withdrawal possible.

On 11 March 1916 Stringer also saved the lives of two officers and this bravery was rewarded with the Serbian Gold Medal.

In the following July, Stringer wrote home to his wife from India, where he was now in hospital suffering from enteric fever and jaundice. On 12 June he returned home to a great welcome by a large crowd in Albert Square. During his leave he visited his old school and former

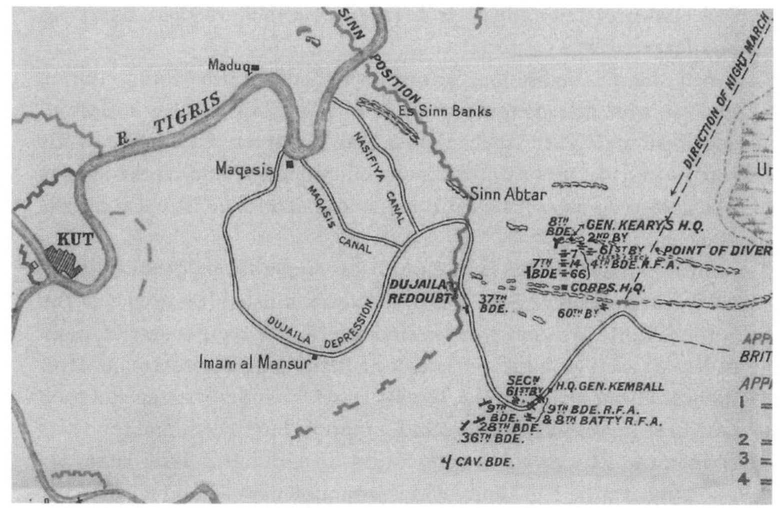

Dujaila Redoubt, 8 March 1916.

place of work. He was decorated with the VC by the King in an investiture at Buckingham Palace on 21 July 1917.

George Stringer, the son of a chemical worker after whom he was named, was born at Newton Heath, Manchester, on 24 July 1889. Young George went to school at the Albert Memorial School, Queen's Road, Miles Platting. After he left school he worked for a firm of dyers and bleachers, Messrs Kerr & Hoegger, in Grimshaw Lane.

In 1905 at the age of 16 George became a member of the Lancashire Fusiliers Volunteers at Cross Lane Barracks, Salford. He later married Florence Marie and the couple set up home at 1 Bath Street, Newton Heath. Prior to the war he joined the 8th (Ardwick) Territorials, Manchester Regiment and on the outbreak of war he transferred to the 1st Manchesters, who fought in France between 26 September 1914 and 10 December 1915. During this time Stringer took part in the disastrous Battle of Loos. The Manchesters, part of the

3rd (Lahore) Division, left Marseilles and landed at Basra on 8 January 1916.

After his demobilisation, Stringer, who had lost two brothers during the war, was offered employment at William Hall & Sons of Monsall and lived in Higher Openshaw in Stanley Street. As a result of his war wounds he was awarded a disability pension and worked at the Manchester Assistance Board as a doorkeeper until he retired at the age of 62.

Stringer attended the House of Lords' dinner for holders of the VC on 9 November 1929. In 1939 he offered himself for service in the Second World War but was rejected as unfit for regular service, so in order to assist with the war effort he made munitions instead. After the war ended he joined the Territorial Army at Stalybridge and took part in the peace celebrations in London in June 1946, and ten years later in the VC centenary celebrations in London in June 1956. He also attended the 1937 and 1953 Coronation parades and received the appropriate medals. They were later put on display at Queen's Park Art Gallery, Harpurhey.

Stringer presented his decorations to the Manchester Regiment at Ashton Barracks on 28 October 1954 but retained a set of their of miniatures. At the present time they are kept in the Regimental Museum in the Town Hall of Ashton-Under-Lyne.

From 1956 Stringer's home was at 203 Oldham Road, Failsworth, and he had become a well-known personality in the district, attending many functions. Two months before he died he was guest of honour at a meeting of the Delph (near Saddleworth) British Legion. He died from bronchitis at Oldham General Hospital on 10 November 1957 and his funeral took place at Holy Trinity Church, Failsworth. He was buried with full military honours in Philips Park Cemetery and the arrangements were made by the Manchester Regiment. His wife survived him until 4 July 1959 and his mother, Esther Hewitt, who died on 24 January 1939, also shares the family grave. In the mid-1960s the Manchester Regiment Old Comrades Association erected a headstone over Stringer's grave (Section M, Grave 1826) and a sister of George, now Mrs Wrenshall, was one of those who visited the new memorial, which she did in April 1965.

Stringer's name was also commemorated by a plaque on the wall of a chapel in the same cemetery which was set up in 1985. A Rorke's Drift

VC winner, Pte William Jones, is also buried in Philips Park Cemetery and both men had wall plaques to their memory. However, the chapel wall was later knocked down and the plaques put into storage. In addition the cemetery was becoming vandalised and neglected. As is so often the case a group of volunteers got together – 'Friends of Philips Parke Cemetery' – and have come to the rescue, putting the cemetery in good order. As part of these improvements the two plaques to Stringer and Jones were brought out of storage and set in granite blocks and repositioned at the cemetery entrance. Their new site was unveiled on 24 July 2011 together with commemorations at the graves of four other soldiers buried in the cemetery.

Stringer's decorations apart from the VC included the 1914–15 Star, British War Medal,Victory Medal, MiD Oakleaf, King George VI Coronation Medal (1937), Queen Elizabeth II Coronation Medal (1953) and Obilitch Medal of Bravery (Serbia). His VC was stolen in 1975 but was later recovered.

A. BUCHANAN

Fallaniyah Lines, 5 April 1916

Since 8 March 1916, when Pte George Stringer had won his VC at Es Sinn, the Tigris Corps had made slow progress towards Kut-el-Amara in order to try and relieve Gen. Sir Charles Townsend's force trapped there.

Townsend was given a chance to surrender by Khalil Pasha on 10 March, but he rejected the offer. On the following day the chief of staff, Gen. Gorringe, replaced Gen. Aylmer as GOC Tigris Corps. Five days later the Tigris, often liable to flooding, rose 3ft and damaged a British boat bridge as well as flooding the Dujaila Redoubt. On the 18th Townsend sent a message stating that his food rations would only last until 15 April and that the British element of his force had their rations already cut by 2oz a day.

The relief force was still suffering from a severe shortage of boats and, in a region where rivers were the main system of transportation, the relief was extremely hampered by the conditions. However, the 13th (Western) Division, fresh from Gallipoli, was now close to the front and would be able to take part in the campaign.

General Gorringe planned to make an assault on the Hanna Positions in early April, but he postponed it by three days in order to acquire aircraft support.

The state of his force at the outset of the third attempt to relieve Kut in the battles of Hanna and Fallaniyah was 30,357 men, 127 guns,

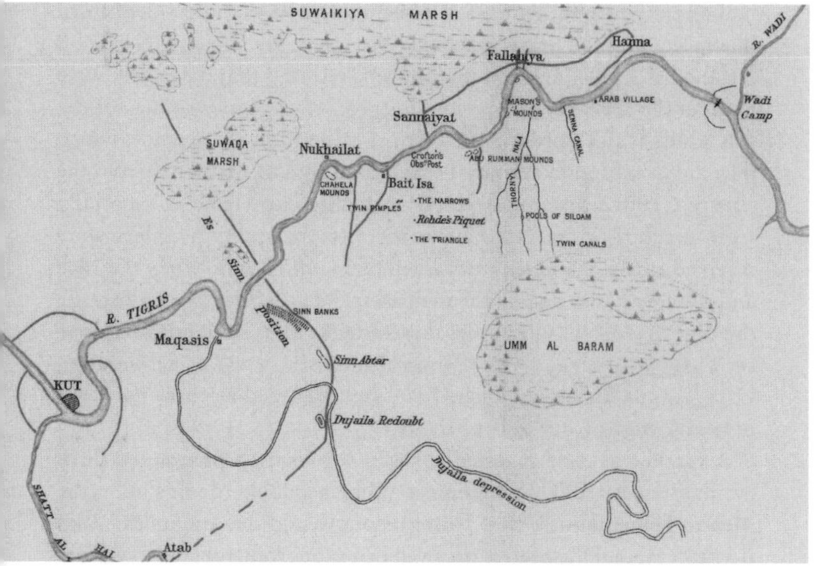

Fallaniyah lines, 5 April 1916.

11 aircraft and 4 gunboats. There was, however, a shortage of officers. On the other hand, their Turkish opponents fielded 20,000 men and 88 guns.

On 5 April 1916 the 4th South Wales Borderers, being part of the 40th Brigade of the 13th Division, were going into the line at the Hanna trenches to assist the 7th (Meerut) Division, whose numbers had been greatly depleted in the previous weeks. The three divisional brigades, from right to left, were the 38th, 39th and 40th, who were to attack simultaneously, and the 4th South Wales Borderers, who were in positions close to the river and were to be part of the third wave.

The Borderers climbed out of their trenches at 4.50 a.m. in support to the 5th (S) Wiltshires and Royal Welsh Fusiliers, and the assault began five minutes later. With the help of artillery and machine-gun fire from both sides of the river, the first and second lines were carried within a quarter of an hour. The guns lifted at 5.15 a.m., by which time it became obvious that, apart from a small rearguard, the Turks had already retired. At 5.45 a.m. an attack on the unmanned third line began and the line was quickly occupied. The advance covered a distance of 3 miles and information was received that the enemy were holding the 'Fallaniyah Position' in force. It was now the turn of the 4th South Wales Borderers and 8th (S) Cheshires to advance, which they did over ground devoid of cover, soon coming under fire from the enemy 1,200yd distant; fire grew gradually more intense, especially from machine-guns. After covering a further 500yd, orders were received to dig in and they remained there until 7 p.m. when the 38th and 39th Brigades passed through their lines on their way to capture the objective. It was in one of these attacks that Lt Hemingway was seriously wounded, as were several men who tried to rescue him. Capt. Angus Buchanan dashed out and managed to carry back not only Hemingway but also a private.

A further assault planned for 12.30 p.m. was postponed until evening when artillery support would be available. At this point the Meerut Division took over frontline duties and the 4th South Wales Borderers found themselves involved in a supporting role, and a further attack was called off.

That same evening Capt. Buchanan was wounded and later left for India to recuperate. Seven other officers from the battalion had also been wounded on the same day. All told, the 13th (Western) Division had 1,868 casualties in the battle; however, the prize was an advance of 6 miles from the Hanna Positions as far as Sannai-I-Yat.

Buchanan was awarded the VC for his selfless acts of bravery on 5 April and the citation for his VC was published in the *London Gazette* of 26 September 1916 as follows:

> Angus Buchanan, Lieut. (Temporary Capt.). 4th Battn. South Wales Borderers. Date of Act of Bravery: 5 April, 1916. During an attack an officer was lying out in the open severely wounded about 150yds from cover. Two men went to his assistance and one of the men was hit at once. Capt. Buchanan, on seeing this, immediately went out and, with the help of the other man, carried the wounded officer to cover under heavy machine-gun fire. He then returned and brought in the wounded man, again under heavy fire.

For some months Buchanan was in India recovering from his second wound. Meanwhile, his commanding officer wrote a letter to Dr Buchanan, Angus' father, dated 8 April 1916:

> I regret to say that your son was wounded in the arm on the evening of 5 April, when we were attacking and driving back the Turks, but I am very glad to tell you that the wound was only a slight one. The real reason for my letter is a far more pleasant one. During our advance in the morning we came under very heavy machine-gun fire, and suffered rather heavily. One of our officers, Lieut. Hemingway, was badly wounded, and lying in the open about 150yds from cover. Your son, seeing his condition, and that the effort on the part of two men to carry him in had ended in one of them being shot, himself left his trench, and with the help of the unwounded man, brought Hemingway into the trench under a heavy fire. During the journey the man with him was wounded in the foot, but got into the trench. Angus then went back and fetched in the other man who had been wounded. I have forwarded a recommendation in his case for the Victoria Cross, and the Brigadier has sent in one and supported it. We sincerely hope he may be awarded it, but there is always a chance that he may only be awarded an honour of lesser degree. I should like to tell you that I have previously brought his name to the notice of the General for gallant conduct at Helles on 7 January.

Buchanan was wounded a third time on 24 September 1916, but returned to B Company three days later.

Probably soon after 26 September 1916, the date of the official announcement of Buchanan's VC in the *London Gazette*, there was great rejoicing in Coleford, Gloucestershire, his hometown, and the bell in the church tower rang out in tribute to the 'local hero'. The news was particularly well received by his former school colleagues. The news was even flashed up on the screen of the local cinema on an evening when the film of *The Battle of the Somme* was being shown. On 7 November Buchanan was one of four VC winners presented with a ribbon of the Victoria Cross by Lt Gen. Sir Frederick Maude, GOC Mesopotamia Force at Amara.

On 13 February 1917 Buchanan was wounded again, but this time very seriously as his injuries led to the loss of his sight and, as a consequence, he relinquished his commission on account of his wounds on 2 September 1917, but retained the rank of captain. He was Mentioned in Despatches (*London Gazette*, 17 October 1916), and he was also awarded the Order of St Vladimir with Swords (4th Class). Buchanan was presented with his VC and MC by King George VI when the monarch was on a visit to Durdham Down, Bristol, on 8 November 1917:

> For the investiture a large square had been barricaded off near the Reservoir, on the Westbury side of the Stoke Road. At the King's special wish, the troops on parade were marshalled in such a way as to give the largest possible number of civilians a clear view of the ceremony. The Royal dais was draped in Imperial purple bearing in relief gilded lions' heads. A battalion of the Inland Waterways and Docks Transports, R.E., 800 strong, was drawn up inside that part of the square nearest to the city. On the opposite side of the square was the Bristol Volunteer Regt., while at the side of the square which faced the dais were Bristol University O.T.C., Clifton College O.T.C. and the Bristol Grammar School contingent of the O.T.C. Also facing the dais, but very much nearer to it, was a smart Guard of Honour of the 3rd Officer Cadet Battn.

Seats for 127 recipients were provided for those who were to receive decorations and medals, and provision was also made for family members and wounded soldiers. Other VCs who were present included Sgt Harry Cator and Sgt Thomas Rendle:

> The investiture was that of a hero who had been sorely stricken in performing deeds of the utmost gallantry. This was Capt. Angus Buchanan of the South Wales Borderers, whom the King decorated with the Victoria Cross and the Military Cross. Unhappily, Capt. Buchanan is now blind, and had to be led on to the dais. After decorating him, His Majesty kept him for some time in sympathetic conversation. The huge assembly also showed their sympathy with the gallant officer by according him a special ovation.

Another VC winner to be decorated was L/Cpl F.G. Room from Bristol and the parents of 2/Lt Hardy Parsons also received their son's posthumous award.

The following day, Coleford took its turn in welcoming their local hero home when the whole town was bedecked with flags and bunting. After the official speech of welcome, Buchanan was presented with a solid gold watch with the braille inscription 'A Tribute to Captain Buchanan, V.C., M.C., by Dean Foresters, 9th November 1917'.

Angus Buchanan was a son of Dr Peter Buchanan, medical practitioner in Coleford and deputy coroner for the Forest of Dean, and Hanna Allen Buchanan (née Williams). Hanna was a widow and already had five children. Angus was born at the Old Bank House, Coleford, Gloucestershire, on 11 August 1894. The town was the capital of the Forest of Dean. Buchanan was educated at St John's Boys' School, Coleford, and from 1905 at Monmouth Grammar School where he became one of the school's most accomplished athletes. He was a good all-round sportsman, being captain of the school and captain of rugby. He was also a member of the cricket and rowing teams. In addition, he joined the School Cadet Corps and became a colour-sergeant. He also won the school essay prize three years running before leaving the school in 1913. Having won a classical scholarship to Jesus College, Oxford, he took part in the University Rugby Trials and played for the Oxford University 'A' Team 1913–14. He was also a member of the Officer Training Corps (OTC).

Soon after the outbreak of war when he had just turned 20, Buchanan was commissioned as a temporary second lieutenant in the 4th Battalion, South Wales Borderers on 27 November 1914 and left for Gallipoli on 28 June 1915; he was promoted to lieutenant on the same day. He was wounded at Suvla Bay on 7 August soon after B Company landed and was sent to hospital in Cairo, returning to his battalion on the Peninsula in early December, together with seventy-two recovered sick or wounded men. He was awarded the MC on 7 January 1916 for bravery at Helles when in command of B Company in trenches east of Gully Ravine, and he was made a temporary captain on 21 December 1915. He took part in the evacuation from the Peninsula and during his time there had been Mentioned in Despatches on two occasions. After a few weeks' rest he left for Mesopotamia, arriving there on 4 March 1916.

After Buchanan returned from the war he spent a year at St Dunstans learning braille and then returned to Oxford University in order to study law. While there he became a member of the College rowing eight. On 26 June 1920 he attended the Garden Party for VCs at Buckingham Palace. He later qualified as a solicitor and took up a practice in his hometown, going into partnership with Mr G. Brocklehurst Taylor. From 1933 he ran the practice on his own until his death. He was a regular figure in the local area and was assisted by one of his clerks, Clifford Wintle or Joan Hart. His original office was at the then Number 1 Gloucester Road and later he moved the practice to larger premises in Coleford High Street. As he was blind he did not accept court cases and instead worked on conveyancing and estate work.

After the war in 1919 a 'spacious parkland' to the west of the town was purchased by public subscription as a tribute to their local VC and subsequently laid out as a recreation ground. In 1935, the year of the King's Silver Jubilee, two gates were added and one of them commemorated Buchanan's deed and read:

> In 1919 this Recreation Ground was purchased by public subscription to commemorate the Award of the Victoria Cross to Captain Angus Buchanan in the year 1916.

In 1921 Buchanan had taken part in the dedication and unveiling ceremony of his school war memorial.

The original parish church was built in the centre of the town in 1820, but owing to a gradual increase in the town's population it became too small and was taken down in 1882. However, the church tower was retained, and after the Great War it was dedicated to Angus Buchanan. The British Legion began holding remembrance services there. A replacement church, St John the Evangelist, was built in Bowen's Hill and the church bells were rung out after it was announced that Buchanan had been awarded the Victoria Cross.

Buchanan's lack of sight never prevented him from enjoying a full and active life; he was said to be the best salmon fisherman in the district and had an excellent knowledge of the River Wye. He was vice-chairman of the Coleford branch of the British Legion and always attended the clock tower two-minute silence on Remembrance Day. In November 1929 he attended the Prince of Wales's VC Dinner in the

Royal Gallery of the House of Lords. In the years between the wars he was a very prominent member of the community in Coleford, making many friends. He continued his interest in local sporting clubs and despite his blindness was fond of bridge. He was vice-chairman of the Forest of Dean Golf Club. His disability did not prevent him from going on accompanied walking holidays in North Devon, the Norfolk Broads and more locally in Monmouthshire.

He was also fond of light opera and was very familiar with the words and music of Gilbert and Sullivan, often playing records of the shows.

Angus Buchanan died at the early age of 49 from the effects of his war wounds on 1 March 1944 in Gloucester Royal Infirmary, having been taken ill in his office in Coleford High Street. Five days later he was given a funeral with full military honours. The words on his civilian headstone in Coleford Cemetery state quite clearly that he died from the effects of his old wounds. Two days after his death, the following 'obituary letter' was published in *The Times*:

> Few men have faced adversity with greater cheerfulness and patience than Angus Buchanan, 'the blind V.C.' At school everything fell into his lap – he had the makings of a fine classical scholar and a great athlete; in war, distinctions such as many a professional soldier would have given his life to win came easily to him. Then, soon after winning the Victoria Cross in Mesopotamia in April 1916, a grievous wound in the temples condemned him to blindness. His friends thought that life was over for him. But we had under-estimated his fortitude. Reading to him at Oxford (for his text-books were not yet in Braille) I found that, though his sight had gone, he had lost none of the keen perception of the scholar; in walks in the pleasant countryside around Oxford or in Monmouthshire, I came to understand how cheerfulness can overcome difficulties. Never a murmur about his affliction, but always a determination to live a normal life, and in it to share with his friends their pleasures and pains. To accompany him to Gilbert and Sullivan was to probe into the depth of his sense of humour; to watch his interest in his godchild was to know how highly he rated moral duty. To have set up in practice as a country solicitor, after taking his degree in Law at Oxford, was the sort of thing one would expect Angus Buchanan to do; for him there was no such thing as an obstacle in his path.

A former clerk in his office and 'minder' said this of his former employer:

> He is a shining example to the people of Coleford as to what can be done in triumphing over affliction, and making a positive contribution to life and the district and his country.

In the late 1960s Buchanan's home, Old Bank House, close to the King's Head Hotel, was demolished to make way for a new road. The town hall was also demolished at this time owing to severe traffic congestion in the town centre.

Angus Buchanan was later commemorated in a number of ways, in addition to the playing fields in Coleford named after him and the plaque to his name on the gate. On 10 October 1987 his life was celebrated in his hometown when wreaths were laid on his grave in Coleford Cemetery and a tablet unveiled in St John's Church, above the triptych on which the names of those who died in the First World War had been recorded. St John's had a full congregation for the service, which included relatives and friends of the blind hero. In addition, the Royal British Legion sent representatives, as did various military and school contingents. The address was given by Maj. Gen. L.A.H. Napier, colonel of the Royal Regiment of Wales, who gave the details of Buchanan's life and career. At one point he held up the late captain's medals, drawing attention to the VC and MC. Later the new memorial was unveiled by Ian Buchanan, a nephew of Angus. After the sounding of the *Last Post* and Binyon's famous exhortation, 'They shall grow not old...', Maj. Gen. Napier read out the VC citation. Later the congregation was invited to Coleford Community Centre for refreshments.

In Monmouth there is a Buchanan Close and he is also remembered in the Havard Chapel, the South Wales Borderers regimental chapel in Brecon Cathedral.

Until December 2013 his decorations were on loan as part of the collection belonging to the South Wales Borderers Museum in Brecon. However, they have been acquired by Lord Ashcroft for the VC collection held at the Imperial War Museum. In addition to the VC, which Buchanan used to keep in a drawer in his bedroom, they include the MC, 1914–15 Star, BWM, VM (1914–19) and MiD Oakleaf, King George VI

Coronation Medal (1937) and Order of St Vladimir (4th Class) (Russia). In total he was Mentioned in Despatches on four occasions: 6 March 1916, 24 August 1916, 17 October 1916 and 15 May 1917.

In recent years Buchanan has also had a plaque set up to his memory in the 'Angus Buchanan VC Recreation Ground' next to Coleford Cemetery. In addition, a trophy in his name is now presented to a senior army cadet at Monmouth School.

S.W. WARE

Sannai-I-Yat, 6 April 1916

The beginning of the third attempt to relieve Kut was made by the 13th (Western) Division on 5 April 1916, and during the operations T/Capt. Angus Buchanan of the 4th South Wales Borderers, 40th Infantry Brigade (13th Division), won a VC when rescuing two wounded men lying out in the open.

On the following day the 7th (Meerut) Division took part in the First Battle of Sannai-I-Yat, and although they made three charges, they suffered considerable losses and only gained 500yd. There was still 16 miles to go before the Tigris Corps could reach the gates of the besieged town. During the day 24-year-old Cpl Sidney William Ware of the 1st Seaforth Highlanders, 19th (Indian) Brigade, gained a posthumous VC for also rescuing wounded men from the battlefield.

The citation of the VC was published in the *London Gazette* on 26 September 1916 as follows:

> Sidney William Ware, No. 920, Corpl., 1st Battn. Seaforth Highlanders. For most conspicuous bravery. An order was given to withdraw to the cover of a communication trench. Corpl Ware, whose cool gallantry had been very marked during the advance, was one of a few men remaining unwounded. He picked up a wounded man and carried him some 200 yds to cover, and then returned for others, moving to and fro under very heavy fire for more than two hours until he had brought in all the wounded and was completely exhausted.

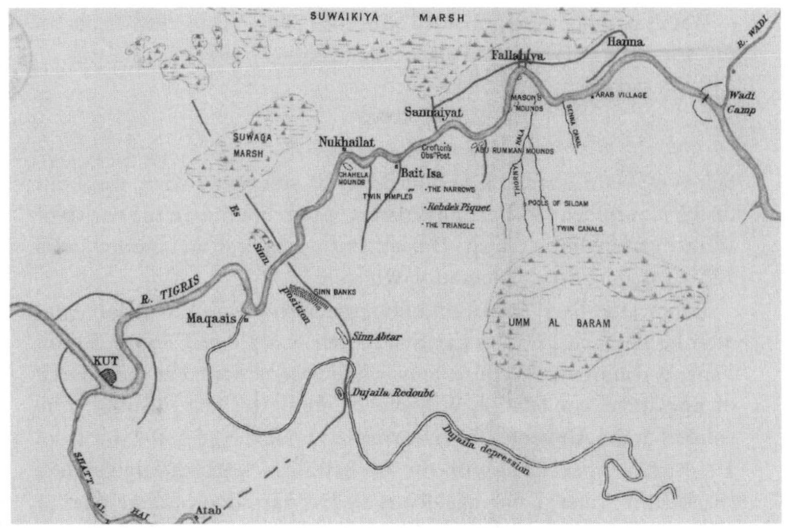

Fallaniyah lines, 5 April 1916.

Four days after the advance, Sidney Ware was severely wounded and was taken back to hospital in the Persian Gulf where he died on 16 April in Rawal Pindi Hospital, near Basra. He was originally buried in the Amara War Cemetery on the left bank of the Tigris. In 1933 all the headstones were removed when it was found that the salt in the soil was 'causing them to deteriorate'. Later a screen wall was put up which listed the names of those men who were known to have been buried in the cemetery. Ware's reference is Plot VI, Row H, Grave 1.

Sidney Ware was described as 'a very steady and trustworthy man, very fond of football and reading'. Two of his brothers were also killed in the war and neither of their bodies was recovered: Sgt Albert Ware of the 1st Dorset Regiment was killed on 1 July 1916 and commemorated on the panels of the Thiepval Memorial, and 21-year-old Pte Archibald Ware of the Wiltshire Regiment died on 11 March 1915 and was commemorated at Le Touret, panels 133–4. Two remaining brothers returned home safely.

Also buried at Amara War Cemetery were two other holders of the VC: Lt Cdr E.C. Cookson and Lt Col Edward Henderson.

Ware's parents were presented with their son's VC by the King at an investiture at Buckingham Palace on 28 February 1917.

Sidney William Ware, son of William Uriah and Maud Ware, was born on 11 November 1892 at Whitcombe, Winterbourne, in the parish of Whitchurch, Milton Abbas, Dorset. During the war their address was 127 Earlscourt Road, Amesbury, Wiltshire.

Sidney later lived at Milton Lilbourne, near Pewsey, Wiltshire, and after his death in 1916 his parents' address was 1 Pine Cottage, Sutton Veny, Warminster, Wiltshire. Sidney had been educated at the Church of England Boys' School, Whitchurch, and after just turning 19 he enlisted in the Army on 29 November 1911. He served in the war from 1914 to 16 April 1916 with the 1st Battalion Seaforth Highlanders (Ross-shire Buffs, Duke of Albany's). His battalion became part of Debra Dun Brigade of the 7th (Meerut) Division, and on the outbreak of war was stationed at Agra. It left for France in mid-September as part of the Indian Expeditionary Force.

Having reached Marseilles on about 12 October, Sidney Ware was wounded a month later on 11 November. After ten days' leave in hospital he returned to France. The 7th (Meerut) Division left for Mesopotamia in December 1915 and Ware was wounded on 7 January 1916. On 4 February his brigade was renamed the 19th Highland Brigade. Owing to heavy casualties the Seaforths had amalgamated with the 2nd Black Watch.

On recovering from his wounds, Ware rejoined his regiment and won his VC on 6 April 1916. His decorations are with the Regimental Museum of the Queen's Own Highlanders (Cameroons and Seaforths) at Fort George, Inverness-shire. It is part of the Highlanders' Museum. Apart from his VC they include the 1914–15 Star, BWM and VM (1914–19).

W.R.F. ADDISON

Sannai-I-Yat, 9 April 1916

The Tigris Corps, using troops from the 13th (Western) Division and 7th (Meerut) Division, began the third attempt to relieve Kut on 5 April 1916 when the 13th Division bore the brunt, suffering nearly 2,000 casualties in exchange for very little ground captured. On 6 April the first attempt against the Sannai-I-Yat positions in the Battle of Sannai-I-Yat began with the 7th (Indian) Division charging three times against the enemy with the reward of 500yd of ground captured. This battle continued unsuccessfully for three days, before it was decided to bring the 13th Division forward again in order to renew the attack.

Of the three brigades, the 38th Brigade took up positions on the right, with the 40th on their left and the 39th in support. According to an account in Gen. Maude's diary:

> At 4.30 a.m. line moved forward to assault, orders being to rush the first three lines.... Line advanced steadily and noiselessly till 4.28, when leading line was within 100yds of position. The Turks then sent up a flare from their left which made our left lose direction slightly. About half a minute later another flare went up from the enemy's right, followed by heavy outburst of machine-gun and rifle fire. Second line lay down while first line pushed on. Consequently first line, which did splendidly, got into the Turks' trenches in a good many places – North Lancs, King's Own, Welsh Fusiliers and Wilts especially. But being unsupported by second line had to give way.... We held on tenaciously where we were all day, the

> troops scratching holes in the ground and digging themselves in as best they could, and at night we withdrew into the trenches we started from in the morning.

At 7 p.m. the 38th and 39th Brigades moved back to bivouacs to the east of Fallaniyah, leaving the 40th Infantry Brigade to remain with the 7th (Indian) Division to hold the Sannai-I-Yat position. In this attack the 13th Division suffered a total of 1,807 casualties.

Of the 6th Loyal North Lancs referred to above, seven men were killed, eighty-five wounded and 169 missing. The adjutant, Capt. Pennefather, wrote the following account:

> It was after the attack had failed and while troops were trying to dig in under intense machine-gun fire, that the Rev. W.R.F. Addison, the C. of E. Chaplain attached to the Battalion, gained the Victoria Cross for his unceasing attention to the wounded throughout the whole morning under incessant fire on perfectly flat ground within 400yds of the Turks. I saw him myself, having been wounded early in the morning.

A summary in the war diary of the 13th Division noted on the 9th:

> During the fight and in addition to the officers the Chaplains and Medical detachments, including the stretcher bearers particularly distinguished themselves by their splendid work.

Addison's VC was published in the *London Gazette* of 26 September 1916 as follows:

> The Reverend William Robert Fountaine Addison, Chaplain. For most conspicuous bravery at Sannaiyat, Mesopotamia. He carried a wounded man to the cover of a trench, and assisted several others to the same cover, after binding up their wounds under heavy rifle fire and machine-gun fire. In addition to these unaided efforts, by his splendid example and utter disregard of personal danger, he encouraged the stretcher-bearers to go forward under heavy fire and collect the wounded.

Addison was also awarded Russian Order of St George (4th Class) on 15 May 1917.

After Addison's VC was announced while he was serving in India, the rector of St Edmund's, Salisbury, had this to say of him:

> His experience in a lumber camp and of Colonial life caused him to mix with men of all kinds; and it was this experience that made him seek ordination that he might give himself more fully to the work of keeping men and boys from ruin and winning them to better things.

One incident reported at the time spoke of Addison having a near miss when conducting a burial service:

> He was reading the service by means of an electric torch, when a bullet from a sniper's rifle knocked his hat off. Several other shots followed, but Mr. Addison went on with the service in the dark.

On 7 November 1916 Gen. Sir Frederick Maude held a parade of the 13th (Western) Division, his former division, at Amara. It was for the purpose of presenting the VC ribbon to four members of the division who had earned the award during the fighting in April. Apart from Addison, the other three men were Lt (T/Capt.) Angus Buchanan, Lt E.K. Myles and Pte James Finn.

A few months later, on 19 July 1917, he got married at Christ Church, Brighton, to Miss Marjorie Wallis, who came from Caterham, Surrey. The couple were later to have two sons. Addison was Mentioned in Despatches on three occasions and was presented with his VC medal at Buckingham Palace on 3 August 1917. Some time in the summer of 1917, he received a presentation in Cranbrook on his return from active service and his honeymoon. The presentation took place in Queen Elizabeth's School and the Cranbrook Platoon of Kent Volunteer Regiment with a troop of local Boy Scouts formed a guard of honour, the troops with fixed bayonets. Addison later addressed the large audience:

> Officers, N.C.O.s and men of the Cranbrook Platoon, I compliment you on your smart appearance. I trust you will not be called on to do active defence duty and trust the war may soon be over, when you will feel that you have done your best to make men patriotic at home.

After letters from various people who were unable to attend the ceremony were read out, Addison was presented with a handsome Illuminated Address and a cheque by the Revd Canon Bell.

Another ceremony in his honour was held in the same year in the rectory gardens of St Edmund's, Salisbury, instead of in the usual Market Place. There were many guests, including the Mayor and the St Edmund's Company of Church Lads' Brigade, together with their bugle band. An Australian band was also in attendance. When Addison and his wife arrived there were loud cheers; the chaplain was wearing his uniform with his two medals together with two gold stripes denoting the number of times he had been wounded. Several congratulatory speeches were made and Addison was then presented with a cheque from the congregation of St Edmund's.

In his reply of thanks, Addison briefly outlined his links with Salisbury and gave an account of his two years in the Army working as a chaplain at Suvla Bay and the subsequent evacuation, the operations in Mesopotamia, the capture of Baghdad and the winning of his VC. He said that later, after the troops had been fighting, he held a service and nearly every man attended from all denominations. After more applause the chaplain presented stripes to several members of the Church Lads' Brigade.

William Robert Fountaine Addison was born in Cranbrook, Kent, on 18 September 1883. He was the son of an artist, William Grylis Addison of Goudhurst, and Alice Addison of Cranbrook. On the death of his father in 1904 he left home for Canada and firstly worked as a farmer, then in a lumber camp in British Columbia for two or three years, before taking holy orders. Two of his brothers made new lives in Australia. Lancelot was killed in action in Gallipoli in August 1915 and Philip F. in Mesopotamia in February 1917. William worked very hard in Canada, before returning to England in 1909 and studying farming in Devon. However, he had made up his mind to enter the Church and, once he had enough money, he attended Salisbury (Sarum) Theological College as a student in 1911. He was ordained in Salisbury Cathedral in May 1913 and became curate of St Edmund's, Salisbury, in the same year, a position which he held for about a year before war broke out. During this time he was an assistant chaplain to the Church Lads' Brigade. Having worked with a cross-section of men in a lumber camp, he was probably a very sociable person, which would have also helped when he joined the Army as a chaplain. According to the rector of St Edmund's: 'He was most regular at their parades, was zealous in gaining recruits, and most assiduous in his efforts to interest the lads.' A friend also wrote: 'He spent most of his time with the boys. He was a prodigious worker, and would often sit up until two and three in the morning writing – and always to help somebody or something, or other.' He was also keen on bird-nesting and took up boxing while in the Army.

In September 1915 Addison became chaplain 4th class to the forces and was accepted on the 22nd with the rank of captain. He later went to Suvla Bay and Mesopotamia. Addison wrote home to Mrs Butt, his landlady, saying: 'I often wish I was back at St Edmund's, but really I like the life out here. By the way, I can eat anything now, and not a bit faddy. It is fearfully hot here – 120 degrees in the shade, and the shade is only a tent.'

After the war and after deciding to remain in the Army, Addison was made a senior chaplain to the forces and served at Bulford Camp between 1920–23, Aldershot 1923–24, Khartoum 1924–25 and Malta 1924–27. He later served with the Shanghai Defence Force from 1927–29 and back in England at the Shorncliffe garrison from 1929–30. By then he was 3rd class with the rank of major. He later served at Shoeburyness from 1930–31 and at Tidworth from 1931–32. In May 1932 he was promoted to be chaplain to the forces, 2nd class lieutenant colonel, and appointed to Bulford Camp. From November he served as senior chaplain to the forces (Church of England) at Bulford, Wiltshire from 1933–34. He was subsequently posted to Bordon, Hampshire. Also in 1934 he answered charges at Salisbury City Petty Sessions that he had left a car 'in such a position as to be likely to cause danger to other persons using the road...'. He pleaded not guilty but was fined £1 and ordered to pay 5*s* in costs.

As for VC functions, he attended the June 1920 Garden Party at Buckingham Palace, the Cenotaph and Unknown Warrior services on 11 November 1920 and the House of Lords' VC Dinner in 1929. He also used to attend the annual dinner of the Royal Army Chaplains' Department and was said to be a 'fluent preacher ... who preached the Gospel all over the world' and was a popular chaplain with the troops.

In August 1938 Addison retired from Army service as a chaplain after serving for more than twenty years and having lived in twenty-one different houses. When he was in his mid-50s he became rector of Coltishall with Great Haubois in Norfolk for twenty years before retiring a second time. In July 1939 he assisted a Miss E. Flowerdew (a sister of Gordon Flowerdew VC) to open a fête at Harleston on the Norfolk–Suffolk border.

During the Second World War he was reappointed chaplain to the forces in 1939 and deputy assistant chaplain-general in South Wales. One parishioner, Ivan Williamson, stated in a local newspaper article:

> He was a real man's man, far more at ease in men's company than with women.... Unlike some parsons he was very down to earth. He used to swear sometimes, but that didn't make him any the worse.... He was very strict about church laws.

After the war he attended the centenary of the VC in June 1956, the Westminster Abbey service and the Hyde Park parade.

Addison made it a rule to visit every house in his parish at least once a year and, apart from taking his pastoral duties very seriously, he was also passionate about the game of cricket. After the war he rebuilt the Horstead and District Cricket Club, which had lapsed, and often acted 'as a most fair and strict impartial umpire'. He rarely missed a match and he only had a short walk to make from the tree-ringed rectory to the ground at Coltishall when the local team played at home. He became rural dean of Ingworth in 1948 and was also chaplain to the district branch of the British Legion, treasurer of the football club, chairman of the bowls team of the old people's society, 'The Good Companions'. His other interests included collecting butterflies, and he discovered a large tortoiseshell not previously seen in the Belaugh meadows. He was a keen birdwatcher and fisherman, particularly on Blickling Reach.

After Addison retired from being rector of Coltishall, his parishioners presented him with a cheque for £111 and a book inscribed with the names of nearly 300 donors. The church organist, Mr W.J. Allen, who made the presentation, stated: 'He thought he had heard some 1,500 sermons by the Rector and had been struck by his intense sincerity, by his sense of humour and by the vividness of the pictures he drew from his widely travelled life.' A road on the outskirts of Coltishall was later named Addison Close after him.

His wife predeceased him after the couple left Norfolk for Bexhill and he died in St Leonards-on-Sea, Sussex, on 7 January 1962. He had suffered from Parkinson's disease and underwent several unsuccessful operations. On 11 January his funeral took place at St Barnabas Church, Bexhill-on-Sea, and he was buried at Brookwood Cemetery, 220346, Plot 22. Five other men who gained the VC in the First World War are also commemorated or buried at Brookwood Cemetery. A memorial service was later held at Coltishall Parish Church, led by the Ven. Robert Meiklejohn, and during his address he stated that the late rector's life fell into two parts:

> First there was his distinguished service as an Army chaplain up to 1938 and then secondly when he became Rector of Coltishall and gave simple, unostentatious, unassuming and devoted service to that church and people.

In 1983 his eldest son, who gained the MC when serving with the Desert Rats in North Africa in 1943, lent his father's decorations to the National Army Museum. Apart from the VC they include the 1914–15 Star, BWM, VM (1914–19) and MiD Oaklaf, War Medal (1939–45), King George VI Coronation Medal (1937), Queen Elizabeth II Coronation Medal (1953) and Order of St George (4th Class) (Russia). Addison had been the second of three padres of the Anglican Church to win the Victoria Cross during the Great War; Revd Noel Mellish was the first in France/Belgium at the end of March 1916. Addison's decorations were returned to the lender in 1997.

The author visited St John the Baptist Church at Coltishall on 7 November 2003 just after a funeral had taken place. One of the churchwardens said she had been prepared for confirmation by Addison in the early 1950s. She added he was popular in the village and many of the men in the recent funeral would have known him from his cricketing days. The church lists Addison's name on the board under the patronage of the Norwich Diocese, 'Vicar 1938–58', and a prayer desk with brass plate is all that commemorates him apart from two pictures of him in the vestry. The two pictures are one of him in the Army as a chaplain and another taken at the vestry door of St John's. Opposite the church is Rectory Road, where the rectory used to be; the site is now occupied by houses. However, the tree-lined cricket ground still existed close to the village hall. The Imperial War Museum also holds a portrait of him in their collection.

At the turn of the century, Addison's grave in Brookwood Cemetery was in danger of collapsing and generally in a poor state, but it was restored in 2007.

J.H. Fynn

Sannai-I-Yat, 9 April 1916

The Second Battle of Sannai-I-Yat began on 9 April 1916 and three VCs were won during the action; the one gained by Pte James Fynn was the second such honour for a member of the 4th South Wales Borderers within four days. All three VC winners ignored their own safety in their attempts to save the lives of their wounded comrades.

The war diary of the 13th (Western) Division mentions that a general staff officer, brigade major and signal officer reconnoitred the Sannai-I-Yat positions and decided that the division would make the attack on its own and without the 7th (Meerut) Division. After operation orders were given, the troops moved up to their lines after dark. The 38th Brigade was to the right front, the 40th to the left, where there was a marsh which made conditions very difficult, and the 39th was in support. The 4th South Wales Borderers were the second battalion from the left of the 40th Brigade. The troops lay out all through a bitterly cold night without blankets or greatcoats, clad only in khaki drill uniform. When roused for the attack, many men were unsurprisingly tired and confused. Before dawn 'there was a good deal of lightning in the east, which may have helped to show up our advance in the early morning'.

The general attack began at 4.20 a.m. and, after the advance had proceeded about 300–400yd, the enemy sent up flares on the right flank and gave the advancing troops the wrong idea of where the main enemy positions actually were. Hence the advance made a major shift towards what was a false position. As a consequence, the eight battalions within the two brigades became hopelessly muddled up and this confusion was impossible to reorganise. When dawn broke, many of the troops were forced to dig in and, although the division made some progress by briefly entering the first Turkish lines despite heavy machine-gun and rifle fire, they were unsupported and subsequently bombed out from these positions. Later in the day, they were forced to withdraw to their original lines. The 38th and 39th Infantry Brigades returned to bivouac, while the 40th Infantry Brigade remained to contain the Sannai-I-Yat position together with the 7th (Meerut) Division. The day had not been a success for the 13th (Western) Division and the basic reason was that the advance troops had had to lie out all night in the cold. Whether the enemy deliberately set up flares on his left is not known, but it made the attacking troops even more confused than they already were. The division suffered 1,807 casualties in this abortive advance.

The battalion history of the South Wales Borderers notes:

> The stretcher-bearers did splendid work, bringing in many wounded; but the outstanding incident was the gallantry of Private Fynn of C Company, who crept out in broad daylight to two men who were lying within 300yds of the Turkish line, bandaged their wounds and brought one of them in.

For this gallant deed he was awarded the VC, which was published in the *London Gazette* on 26 September 1916 as follows:

> James Henry Fynn, No. 1/11220, Private, 4th Battn., South Wales Borderers. After a night attack he was one of a small party which dug in in front of our advanced line and about 300yds from the enemy's trenches. Seeing several wounded men lying out in front, he went out and bandaged them all under heavy fire, making several journeys in order to do so. He then went back to our advanced trench for a stretcher, and, being unable to get one, he himself carried on his back a badly wounded man into safety. He then returned, and, aided by another man, who was wounded during the act, carried in another badly wounded man. He was under continuous fire while performing this gallant work.

James Fynn kept a diary during the war, but his entry for 9 April is not very detailed: 'by 9 a.m. they had dug in and had then stopped in the open all day'.

On 10 April the 4th South Wales Borderers relieved the 5th (S) Wiltshires during the night and, at 8 p.m. on the 11th, they were in turn relieved by the amalgamated Black Watch and Seaforth Highlanders. The battalion history gives a grim picture of the conditions of the return to bivouac:

> The march from the trenches to the place of bivouac five miles distant was carried out under the most trying conditions, very heavy rain soaking the men and making the ground almost impassable. Three wounded men and all the Machine Guns had to be carried the whole way.

Fynn mentions that, after they had cleaned their rifles and kit, a service was held for their fallen comrades. On the 17th the battalion was once more in action and this time they took 180 prisoners: 'In getting to the firing line we have to go through a bog and river – up to our necks in water and waist deep in mud.'

In early June the weather was 'almost unbearably hot' and the diary speaks of 'a temperature of well over 100 degrees in the shade.... On June 10 Fynn was taken ill and placed in a regimental hospital. By early July he had recovered, and on the 5th of that month he mentions going Arab hunting at night for bounty money.'

On 4 October, eight days after his VC was announced in the *London Gazette*, he notes that he has become 'a V.C. wallah'.

Fynn was ill for three days in the first week of November, but was well enough to attend a parade in which he and three other VC winners in the 13th (Western) Division were presented with their VC ribbons at Amara by Gen. Sir Frederick Maude.

Sadly, nearly six months later Fynn died in Mesopotamia on 30 March 1917 and his body was not recovered. He was wounded in a battle north of Baghdad and died soon afterwards. His name is commemorated on panels 16 and 32 of the Basra Memorial in Iraq. Four other winners of the VC are commemorated at Basra. It is not clear from the records just exactly how Pte Fynn died, but it is known the 4th South Wales Borderers were involved with a Wiltshire battalion against Turkish positions at Marl Plain. Fynn might have been one of thirty-six other ranks wounded and he died the following day. David Harvey notes that Fynn had been wounded in the leg at Noel Plain, then shot when being taken to a field hospital.The Basra Memorial was moved in 1997 by presidential decree to a new site, which was once part of the Gulf War battlefield.

Fynn's VC was presented to his father at an investiture held in Hyde Park on 2 June 1917. He was also awarded the Serbian Medal. On 17 June Lt Col C.E. Kitchin, commander of the 4th South Wales Borderers, wrote to Fynn's father:

> Dear Mr. Fynn,
> I cannot tell you how sorry I am that you have not before received particulars from the Regiment of the death of your very gallant son Private J.H. Fynn, V.C. I should have written to you myself had I been here, but at that time I was in Hospital in India, having been wounded earlier in the operations, and I did not hear of your son's death until my return a short time ago. He was wounded in the leg during a fight on March 29th, on the Moel [*sic*] Plain, about 50 miles north of Baghdad, his Company Commander got a stretcher party to take him back to the field Ambulance, but on the way he was again struck by a bullet in the side, it was this wound that proved fatal.
>
> Gen Lavin told me that he went to the Ambulance and saw your son, who was at that time not suffering much, but seemed to know his end was near. He died that evening and was buried near the Ambulance. I am very sorry not to be able to give you a sketch of the grave, but the position has been marked and later on it may be possible to do this, at present the grave is outside our Outpost Line and some miles from our present position.
>
> It was a great blow to hear of your son's death as I was very proud of him, he having been my servant for a good many months last year, his devotion to the wounded was remarkable and I know that he has saved many lives by rendering first aid to his wounded comrades. He has shown me absolute contempt of danger when under fire and was always ready and anxious to do anything to help anyone, and we shall badly miss him in the Regiment. I expect he told you that he was awarded a Serbian Decoration of the Gold Medal, before he was killed. He added lustre to the record of the Regiment and we are all proud of him and shall reverence his memory. May I express to you and his family our very deepest sympathy with you in your sorrow.

James Henry Fynn was born in Union Workhouse in the St Clements Parish of Truro on 24 November 1893, one of four sons and three daughters of Mr and Mrs Frederick John Fynn. Mr Fynn was a cutler (a grinder of scissors and tools) who served with the Duke of Cornwall's Light Infantry during the Boer War and in the Special Reserve in the First World War. Mrs Fynn's maiden name was Mary Baxter and she came from Camborne. The family later moved as lodgers to Bodmin and lived in 19 Downing Street and later moved to 87 Higher Bore Street. Fynn attended the Board School at the top of Robartes Road.

Fynn worked in London for a short time and became a member of the Salvation Army. He left London for Wales, where he was employed as a miner in a colliery at Cwmtillery, near Abertillery, Monmouthshire. His home was then as a lodger in a mining colleague's home in Frederick Street.

In 1914 Fynn, known as Jimmy, enlisted in Abertillery and joined the TF battalion, the 4th Battalion South Wales Borderers. Initially he served in France and was wounded there. He later took part in the Gallipoli Campaign in 1915 and in January 1916 transferred to Port Said where, according to a diary quoted in L.E. Long's *An Old Cornish Town*, he worked in the Officers' Mess. On 14 February his company sailed for the Persian Gulf on board the *Oriana*.

Arriving in Basra, Mesopotamia, they waited for transport to take them up river. Moving up the Tigris they were fired upon by a Turkish cavalry patrol soon after they passed Amara. In November 1916 Fynn was one of four members of the 13th (Western) Division to be presented with the VC ribbon by Gen. Sir Frederick Maude, GOC Mesopotamian Force, at Amara. During 1916–17 he was servant to Lt Col C.E. Kitchin of the 4th South Wales Borderers and he was wounded and invalided home with a wounded knee and chest at some point. He later rejoined his battalion in Mesopotamia.

On the night of 31 March/1 April his company moved up to the frontline in torrential rain and he wrote in his diary: 'The most miserable night I have ever spent.' On 4 April final arrangements were made for an attack to begin at 4 a.m. the next morning. The battalion succeeded in driving Turkish troops from their trenches and, advancing 4 miles, dug themselves in. The next day they gained another 2 miles. Fynn and some of his colleagues then helped to clear the battlefield of the wounded and the many dead.

After the Second World War Fynn's medals were presented by his mother to Bodmin Borough Council on 16 February 1954 and, twelve years later, other items associated with him were handed over to the town by members of his family. Fynn is commemorated on a VC memorial in the Havard Chapel in Brecon Cathedral, and a housing estate was named after him in his hometown of Bodmin on Remembrance Sunday, 13 November 1966. His citation published in the *London Gazette* was read out by another VC holder, Lt Col Harold Marcus Ervine-Andrews. The Fynn VC Estate plaque read:

> The home of the late Pte James Henry Fynn, who was awarded the Victoria Cross at Sannaiyat Mesopotamia on the 9th April, 1916, was in Downing Street (19) the site of which forms part of this estate. Pte Fynn died of wounds in Mesopotamia on 30th March, 1917.

Apart from the VC, his decorations included the 1914–15 Star, BWM, VM (1914–19), and Order of Kara-George (1st Class) (Serbia). His VC is kept in a bank and there is a replica on display in Bodmin Town Museum. In their collection of Fynn memorabilia, they also have the following: a diary for 1916, a locket containing his portrait and a lock of hair, his bronze death plaque, a watch, various photographs, including one of King George VI speaking to his parents in 1937, and the letter from the commanding officer of the 4th South Wales Borderers, Lt Col C.E. Kitchin, to Fynn's father. A portrait of Fynn appeared in *The Sphere* on 16 December 1916, drawn by Ugo Matania. The Wellcome Library holds a copy. Fynn's name is also on a plaque held in the local library, on Bodmin's war memorial, on the family grave in Bodmin Town Cemetery and on the Abertillery War Memorial.

There has always been confusion as to whether the family name was Fynn or Finn and it appears that the family used both spellings.

From the short account above, it becomes clear that Fynn was a man who grew from humble beginnings and proceeded to live the rest of his life according to the strongest of Christian principles.

E.K. MYLES

Sannai-I-Yat, 9 April 1916

During the continuing attempts to relieve Kut, the capture of the Fallaniyah position in early April 1916 led to an advance on the northern bank of the Tigris. This allowed the 7th (Meerut) Division to push forward behind the retreating enemy as far as the Sannai-I-Yat positions. The enemy had withdrawn from its positions on the southern bank of the river.

The 7th (Meerut) Division's role in the First Battle of Sannai-I-Yat on 6 April 1916 was not a success and Gen. Gorringe, commanding the Tigris Corps, decided that, in spite of the northern bank being drier, an advance would be more successful if it was renewed against the enemy positions at Sannai-I-Yat. However, it was an ideal position to defend and was strongly held by Turkish forces. The 13th (Western) Division was chosen to make the renewed advance on the morning of 9 April.

The 9th Worcestershire Regiment, 39th Brigade, 13th (Western) Division, was spending 8 April in bivouac and providing working parties to repair gaps along the banks of what was becoming the increasingly flooded Tigris. At 8 p.m. they were ordered to march forward across the Fallaniyah trenches, which was over 4 miles of rough ground and trenches, the latter having been made by the 7th (Meerut) Division. The 38th and 40th Brigades were in advanced positions, with the 39th Brigade in support, and the deployment was completed by 2 a.m. The advance troops then lay down to await the hour of attack.

The waiting troops suffered severely from the lack of protection from the extreme cold and soon after 4 a.m., cold and exhausted, they moved off across 400yd of land before being challenged by frontal fire. The attackers, obviously very confused, veered to the right towards the Turkish front and the battalions became mixed; all the time the enemy was dropping shrapnel bombs and spraying the front with heavy machine-gun and rifle fire. A few men from the 38th and 40th Brigades did manage to enter the Turkish front trenches, but they were so few in number that they were unable to hold on to the positions. In the total confusion, the wounded who had been caught between the two firing lines were either trying to drag themselves to cover or crying out for assistance. Lt E.K. Myles, attached to the 9th Worcestershires from the 8th Welsh Regiment, rushed out again and again to assist in the carrying in of some of the wounded and was later awarded the VC for his bravery. The 9th Battalion lost nine officers and over 100 other ranks; the men left in the battalion spent the next six days in bivouac and were depressed by the results of the battle. However, the commanding officer, Gen. Maude, who shared the cold and misery of the attack, did his very best to keep up the men's spirits.

Instead of attacking the Sannai-I-Yat position a third time, Gen. Gorringe decided to use the partially flooded south bank of the Tigris to try to push through to Kut. Movement close to the river would obviously be particularly difficult and the 3rd (Indian) Division was chosen to attack and capture the Turkish position at Bait Isa. The attack took place on 17 April and the 9th Worcestershires were involved again after the initial advance.

Five months later, the citation for Myles' VC was published in the *London Gazette* of 26 September 1916 as follows:

> Edgar Kinghorn Myles, Lieut., Welsh Regt. For most conspicuous bravery. He went out alone on several occasions in front of our advanced trenches and under heavy rifle fire, and at great personal risk assisted wounded men lying in the open. On one occasion he carried a wounded officer to a place of safety under circumstances of great danger.

He was himself wounded during the action.

A day after his VC was published in the London Gazette, the principal of East Ham Secondary School, which Myles used to attend, announced the award of the VC to hearty applause from the school assembly on 27 September 1916. Later in the day, the students were given a half-day holiday. The staff sent Myles a congratulatory telegram to India where he was recovering from wounds received in Mesopotamia. Plans were also made for the school to make a presentation to the young lieutenant and to establish a permanent commemoration to him at the school.

On 21 October 1916 Myles was appointed acting captain in the Welsh Regiment on an evening when the film of *The Battle of the Somme* was being shown. In early November 1916, during a ceremonial parade, Myles (who had returned to the battalion on 20 October) was presented with a VC ribbon by Gen. Sir Frederick Maude, together with three other VC winners from the 13th (Western) Division.

Two months later on 12 January 1917, Myles was transferred to the Worcestershire Regiment with the rank of second lieutenant with seniority from 28 August 1915, and on the same day promoted to lieutenant with seniority from 19 October 1916. A week later he was made a captain in the Worcestershire Regiment, a rank he held until 30 September 1919.

The final Battle of Kut began on 25 January 1917 and the town was back in British hands by 23 February, remaining so for the rest of the war. During the fighting in January, the 9th Worcestershires, and in particular Capt. Myles, were heavily involved in the action. By 10 a.m. the enemy frontline had been captured, but officer casualties had been very high, leaving only four in the frontline positions, who then proceeded to organise a defence against the inevitable counter-attack, which duly occurred at noon. Myles was in charge of a party of signallers who laid telephone wire to keep in direct contact with battalion headquarters. Later, after the enemy counter-attacks subsided and two of the four officers had been killed, Capt. Myles, though wounded, continued to direct the defence and his colleague Lt Ainsworth manned a Lewis gun on top of the parapet.

For his gallantry on this occasion, Myles was awarded the DSO and Ainsworth the MC. Myles' DSO was published in the *London Gazette* of 25 January and he was presented with his award in Mesopotamia on 17 March 1917 by Gen. Maude:

> For conspicuous gallantry and devotion to duty. When all the officers except two had become casualties, he, for five hours, inspired confidence in the defence against two counter-attacks and sent back most accurate and valuable reports of the situation. His courage and fine example were largely responsible for the steadiness of all ranks under him.

Myles was wounded during this action and he returned to the battalion on 29 September after he recovered from his injuries. A few weeks later his battalion returned to Mesopotamia where Myles remained until April 1918. He was wounded twice and on at least one occasion was sent to India to recuperate; at one time he was at a hill station in the neighbourhood of Simla. At some point he was offered a staff appointment, but declined the offer as he wished to return to active service. He was Mentioned in Despatches twice: 19 October 1916 and 15 August 1917.

In July 1918 the 39th Brigade became a part of North Persia Force.

Myles was decorated by the King at an investiture held in Buckingham Palace on 4 September 1918. In an article in *The Echo and Mail* on 29 September 1918, after he had been presented with his VC, it was noted:

> His old school fellows and masters speak of him as a manly, clean living youngster, never behindhand when the quality of dare-devilry was needed, but never other than perfectly 'straight' and true.

Edgar Kinghorn Myles was born in Black Hall Crescent, Wanstead, Essex, on 23 July 1894. He was the fourth child and only son of Andrew Kinghorn Myles, a schoolteacher, and Agnes Jane Myles, daughter of John Bain, who he had married in 1890.

From 1899 Myles attended the Shaftesbury Road Council School, East Ham, close to his Milton Avenue home, where he gained a junior scholarship to the East Ham Secondary School in September 1906 (later the Technical College Secondary School). In January 1907 he joined the Boys' Brigade as a member of the 17th South Essex (East Ham) Company, and in 1910 he became a staff sergeant. According to the 1911 census the family home was at 'Brooklyn' (later 147) Milton Avenue, East Ham. In 1913 the family moved to 2 Lake House Road, Wanstead.

After taking second-class honours in the Oxford Local Examination, Myles left the secondary school in 1910 and retired from his position in the Boys' Brigade in 1912, soon after moving to Wanstead. The family house was a new semi-detached house at 2 Lake House Road and had a view over Wanstead Flats. On the outbreak of the war he was employed as a clerk with the Port of London Authority and soon gave this job up, enlisting in the Army on 20 August 1914 as a private in the 9th Worcestershire Regiment. His number was 9311.

On the recommendation of his colonel, he was soon offered a commission and on 27 November he was discharged as a lance corporal on his appointment to a temporary commission as a second lieutenant from 28 November 1914. His battalion, the 9th Worcesters, sailed from Avonmouth on 24 June 1915, reaching the Gallipoli Peninsula on 13 July 1915. He was promoted to lieutenant on the 22nd and made a bombing officer. In early December, when taking over some trenches, the battalion set to work to 'put things right'. Several trench mortars were brought into action by Lt Myles and 'rapid bursts of musketry were opened whenever a target offered'.

Later he was given a commission in the Welsh Regiment on 7 January 1916 as a second lieutenant with seniority dating back to 4 December 1915.

At the beginning of January the 9th and 4th Battalions occupied front trenches, while behind them the planned evacuation of the Peninsula was beginning to unfold. Myles took an active part in the withdrawal from the Peninsula, acting as a rearguard officer on 'W' Beach, where his company was one of the last to leave. His duties would have been to make sure fire was kept up against the Turks while troops were in the process of being evacuated. The final evacuation took place during the night of 8/9 January and, after carrying out their duties successfully, his party then escaped in a small lighter which, owing to a storm, was swept around for about eight hours. As a consequence, all their equipment was lost overboard, but fortunately the men were later picked up by a steamer. Not surprisingly, at around this time Myles was reported as missing, but arrived back in Egypt on 24 January. He was promoted to temporary captain in August 1916 and acting captain on 21 October. He returned to the Worcestershire Regiment with the rank of second lieutenant and was promoted to lieutenant on 12 January 1917, seniority dating back to 28 August 1915.

After the war, Myles was employed on staff duties at the War Office from 4 December 1918, and was a GSO 3 (General Staff Officer 3rd Grade) with temporary rank of captain from 1 October 1919 to 31 March 1920. He attended the Buckingham Palace Garden Party on 26 June 1920. He joined the 4th Worcestershire Regiment in 1920 and served with them in Cologne. In Glasgow in 1921 he was stationed at the depot of the Highland Light Infantry during the 1921 coal strike and later served in Belfast and Galway when the battalion took part in a march across Ireland from Dublin to Galway.

Myles was later seconded to the Royal Tank Corps on 5 December 1921, before being transferred to the King's Liverpool Regiment on 9 May 1923, being promoted to captain on 22 February 1925. He served with the Worcestershire Regiment in the Rhine Occupation, Aldershot, Malta and Khartoum. His chief recreations were polo and golf. On 10 March 1928 Myles retired from the Army with a gratuity, having latterly worked in the intelligence department of the government, and was placed on the Regular Army Reserve of Officers (the King's Regiment) with the rank of captain with seniority from 14 September 1921.

He then entered the film business and assisted in making news films. He joined Gaumont British Newsreel Productions and worked on a series of short films under the name of *The Cockney Spirit of War*. In November 1929 he attended the Prince of Wales' VC Dinner at the House of Lords and from 1930 he took a prominent role in the Wanstead British Legion. At the end of November 1934 Myles took over management of a cinema in Bristol known as the News Theatre, and in 1936 took part in a film about the Irish Rebellion being made at Elstree Studios. The film was called *Ourselves Alone*, an English translation of the Sinn Fein motto.

Myles must have left Bristol after a fairly short time, for he next crops up back in East London during the late 1930s, where in 1938 he becomes involved in 'preparing a scheme to protect Leyton in time of war emergency and is anticipating the co-operation of services such as the fire brigade, police and British Legion, as well as the ordinary civilian community'. Initially, he ran his office in Wanstead Town Hall before moving to the Electricity Department's showrooms at 280 High Road. He was later appointed Air Raid Precautions (ARP) officer for Islington as well as Leyton. During the early part of the Second World War he served briefly in the Army from 9 April 1939 to 22 January 1940 as a Staff Captain HQ Northern Command. On 23 July 1945 he ceased to be a member of the Regular Army Reserve of Officers, as he was now too old for recall.

In 1947 he married Ellen M. Illingworth in Hatfield. He attended the VE Parade on 8 June 1946 and later the first two VC/GC Association dinners. At some point he sold his medals to a collector, who later offered them for sale to Messrs Spinks in November 1960. The Worcestershire Regiment hoped to secure the set, and in correspondence with the regimental secretary Spinks mentioned that Gen. Maude had actually considered awarding a Bar to Myles' VC but later changed his mind, as he thought that at that time no second VCs had been awarded and he had no wish to create a precedent. With the aid of a grant from the Army Museum Ogilvy Trust, the Worcestershire Regiment managed to purchase the medals in April 1961 and a copy of the VC is on display in the City Museum, Worcester.

In the early 1960s it seems that Myles' regiment thought that he was dead; he wasn't, but he had fallen on hard times and had ended up living in a converted railway cattle truck together with two dogs. Though he was virtually destitute he would not agree to leave and live in an old people's home, because he did not want to be separated from his dogs. In February 1964 and only after one of his dogs had died, he was persuaded by the Welsh Regiment and Worcestershire Regiment to take a place in Huntley Royal British Legion Home, Officers' Association Country Home in Bishopsteignton, Devon, where he died on 31 January 1977 at the age of 82. His funeral took place in Torbay and he was cremated on 4 February at Torquay Crematorium, after which his ashes were scattered on the lawn in the Garden of Remembrance.

Myles' medals are held at the Worcestershire Regimental Museum in the Worcester City Art Gallery and Museum, and include the VC, DSO, 1914–15 Star, BWM, VM (1914–19) (replacement),

King George VI Coronation Medal (1937) and Queen Elizabeth II Coronation Medal (1953).

In Newnham there had been strong local support for a plaque to commemorate the connection between Myles and East Ham. Finally in 2010 a plaque to both Myles and Jack Cornwell VC was unveiled in Miller's Well Public House in Barker Road, close to the town hall.

T/Lt Wilbur Dartnell sacrifices his life by staying with his wounded men. (Deeds that Thrill the Empire)

Capt. Jotham is shot dead while attempting to rescue one of his men. (Deeds that Thrill the Empire)

Pte C. Hull saving the life of Capt. G.E.D. Learoyd under fire. (Deeds that Thrill the Empire)

Maj. Wheeler leading a charge of Indian Lancers. (Deeds that Thrill the Empire)

Sepoy Chatta Singh digging for cover for his wounded officer while under fire, after binding up his wounds. (Deeds That Thrill the Empire)

Lance-Naik Lala drags a wounded officer, whom he found lying close to the enemy, to a shelter and bandages his wounds. (Deeds that Thrill the Empire)

Capt. A. Buchanan (left), 8 November 1917. (IWM)

Amara War Cemetery. (David Harvey)

The Revd Addison carries a wounded man to the cover of a trench under heavy rifle and machine-gun fire. (Deeds that Thrill the Empire)

HOW WILL WOMEN VOTE? BY MR. H. BOTTOMLEY

SUNDAY·PICTORIAL

LATEST CERTIFIED CIRCULATION MORE THAN TWO MILLION COPIES WEEKLY

No. 117. SUNDAY, JUNE 3, 1917 One Penny.

THE ROLL-CALL OF HEROES—THE ROYAL INVESTITURE IN HYDE PARK.

Investiture of Pte J.H. Finn. (Bodmin Town Museum)

Basra War Memorial, Iraq. (David Harvey)

Lt E.K. Myles carrying a wounded officer under heavy fire. (Deeds that Thrill the Empire)

C.W. Train receiving his award from the King. (London Scottish)

Karanbahadur Rana. (Gurkha Museum)

Blaby Churchyard, Leicestershire, the resting place of Pte Robert Edward Cruickshank. (Donald C. Jennings)

S. KHAN

Near Beit Ayeesa, 12/13 April 1916

After the capture of Fallaniyah and Sannai-I-Yat on the River Tigris, Beit Ayeesa was the next objective that the 3rd (Indian) Division was going to try to capture on 12 April 1916. The following account is based on the war diary of the 89th Punjabis, who were in the area between 10 and 19 April. On 11/12 April they were involved in the advance against the Turkish-held positions at Beit Ayeesa. B and C Companies of the 89th Punjabis arrived at Rohde's Picquet, and part of A Company together with HQ were to follow soon after 6 p.m on the 12th. The advanced line of the Punjabis was 1,000–1,200yd ahead.

At 5.30 p.m. the Indian troops were told to report if they had any difficulties in establishing contact with troops of the 37th Brigade when more troops would be sent up. At 6.30 p.m. the remainder of A Company went up to Rohde's Picquet. Three officers had become casualties, one of whom was dead. A Capt. James then took command of the frontline.

Much of the ground towards the west was flooded and a planned advance and establishment of picquet lines on 12 April by the 37th and 8th Brigades was delayed for several hours. At 7.30 p.m. the enemy launched an attack against the Punjabis' left, which was dealt with by rapid fire from the picquet. The 27th Punjabis moved up in support of the left. In addition, the 1st Connaught Rangers, having occupied a southern position on a former picquet line, were in contact with the left of the 27th Punjabis.

At 9 p.m. A Company reported that 36th Sikhs had retired and enemy patrols were 'feeling' for his right flank. About a hundred of the enemy were being held off by Punjabi machine-guns, in particular the one in the hands of Naik (Cpl) Shahamad Khan, who for five hours until midnight had repelled all efforts by an enemy breakthrough, his colleagues from his section having all been wounded. At 11.30 p.m. 100 men from the Connaught Rangers arrived at Rohde's Picquet and assisted in plugging the gap on the right. By now Shahamad Khan's machine-gun had finally been put out of action. Having been relieved, he was now able to withdraw. In all, by the end of the operations on the 12th, the 3rd Indian Division had gained almost a mile on the south side of the Tigris. This was despite the flooded state of the river and ground which had affected both sides.

Not surprisingly, Shahamad Khan, Naik, No. 1605, 89th Punjabis was awarded the VC for his heroic five-hour stand, the details of which were published in the *London Gazette* of 26 September 1916 as follows:

> His Majesty the King has been graciously pleased to confer the Victoria Cross on No. 1605 Naik Shahamad Khan, Punjabis, for most conspicuous bravery. He was in charge of a machine gun section in an exposed position in front of and covering a gap in our new line within 150yds of the enemy's entrenched position. He beat off three counter-attacks, and worked his gun single-handed after all his men, except two belt-fillers, had become casualties. For three hours he held the gap under very heavy fire while it was being made secure. When his gun was knocked out by hostile fire he and his two belt-fillers held their ground with rifles till ordered to withdraw. With three men sent to assist him he then brought back his gun, ammunition, and one severely wounded man unable to walk. Finally he himself returned and removed all remaining arms and equipment except two shovels. But for his great gallantry and determination our line must have been penetrated by the enemy.

General Townsend was forced to surrender the besieged town of Kut-el-Amara on 29 April 1916, with 13,309 men, including 3,248 non-combatants, laying down their weapons. Once back in the city the Turks killed 250 civilians and the ill-fated Townsend force began its march into captivity, from which 4,818 did not survive. Mere words are not strong enough to describe the terrible suffering that the force endured, and all the time Townsend lived in comfort in Turkey. His troops had truly become a forgotten army.

Shahamad Khan, a son of Fayal Khan, was born on 1 July 1879, in the village of Takhti, Rawalpindi, Tehsil and District. He joined the Army on 1 December 1904 and, nearly ten years later on the outbreak of war, his regiment, the 1/89th Punjabis, were stationed at Dinapore. The regiment was composed of two companies of Punjabi Mussalmans, one of Sikhs, one of Rajputana Hindus, together with other men who were Rajputs, Jats or Mers.

In the previous weeks the regiment had already provided large drafts for other units, and those who remained received orders to leave in October 1914, embarking from Karachi as part of 29th Brigade. Together with half of the 69th Punjabis Battalion, they made a forced landing in South-West Arabia at Shaikh Saad, captured Fort Turba and relieved the island of Perim. After these operations they landed at Suez in the Canal Zone and left by rail for Port Said on 17 November where the regiment took over the defences of salt works as well as the northern section of the canal. Later the 29th Brigade concentrated at Kantara where the 89th Punjabis held the outpost line and in February 1915 they were attacked by Turkish forces. Two months later, the regiment was dispatched to the Gallipoli Peninsula, but only remained there for fifteen days as the authorities were concerned at the consequences of the possibility of Muslims serving in the Indian Army fighting against Muslims serving with the Turkish forces. The troops were annoyed on learning of this decision as they had already put in some good work.

Once back in Egypt at Alexandria, the regiment was ordered to France, and in early June became part of the Ferozepore Brigade of the Indian Corps. The next five months were spent in and out of the trenches, including a period at the Battle of Loos. The Indian Corps left France in December 1915 and the battalion was united with its former brigade in February 1916 in Mesopotamia at Pannah, having marched up from Basra. The brigade crossed the River Tigris and the regiment took part in many of the subsequent operations on the right bank of the river with the aim of relieving the besieged town of Kut.

In August the regiment returned to India, as it was considered that it had 'done its bit in the war'. Once again it was plundered by other units, especially for officers and NCOs. The regiment also provided troops for short periods on the Mohmand Blockade, and overall it had been very much depleted in numbers. In August 1917 the Punjabis were ordered to travel to Chitral as escort to reliefs, and a short time later they were ordered to return to Mesopotamia once more, where they landed on 7 December. In 1918 the regiment was active in the spring, and in November/December found themselves in Salonika, but did not take part in the fighting.

In the following month the Punjabis were sent to Batum in the Caucasus, where they were responsible for guarding a 200-mile line of railway and its bridges and stations between the town and Tiflis. Later these guarding duties were much extended, and when the British forces pulled out of Georgia and the Caucasus the 89th Punjabis, in addition to two other units, were left behind to carry on with garrison duties at Batum. Eventually, in July 1920, the battalion was sent to Turkey and returned home to India three months later.

It is highly likely that Shahamad Khan took part in almost all of the above operations of this much-used regiment. He was presented with his VC on 13 November 1919 by the King at Buckingham Palace and promoted to Jemadar (junior officer) in January 1920. In 1922 the 89th Punjab Regiment was changed to the 1st Battalion 8th Punjab Regiment. Shahamad Khan, whose name is sometimes spelt Shahmad Khan, died on 28 July 1947 at Takhti village in Pakistan, where he was buried in the village cemetery, Reference 8. Apart from his VC his decorations included the 1914–15 Star, BWM, VM (1914–19), King George V Silver Jubilee Medal (1935), King George VI Coronation Medal (1937) and Cross of St George (2nd Class) (Russia). They are part of the Lord Ashcroft Collection in the Imperal War Museum.

E.E.D. HENDERSON

West Bank of the River Hai, near Kut, 25 January 1917

On 12/13 April 1916 Shahamad Khan won the VC near Beit Ayeesa in one of the operations to move forward and relieve Kut-el-Amara. It hardly comes as a surprise to learn that no Victoria Crosses were awarded in connection with the surrender of Gen. Townsend's besieged force a fortnight later. For the rest of the year, the Mesopotamia Expeditionary Force was to spend time in building up a force strong enough to resume the offensive towards Baghdad and to finally drive the Turkish Army out of the country. In August the force was revitalised by the arrival of Gen. Sir Frederick Maude, who took over as commander-in-chief.

In fact, it was nine months before the next VC was gained in the Mesopotamia Campaign, and then there were two awarded for actions on the same day, 25 January 1917. This was at Hai Salient to the south-west of Kut and was to be the beginning of a new British offensive, which became known as the Second Battle of Kut-el-Amara. The attack was to be made by the 13th (Western) Division under Gen. Cayley, with battalions drawn from the 40th and 39th Brigades. The 40th Brigade had about 350yd of ground to cover before reaching the frontline of the enemy, while the 39th had slightly more.

The two brigades began their attack at 9.40 a.m. and the battalions chosen from the 39th to advance were the 9th (S) Worcestershires

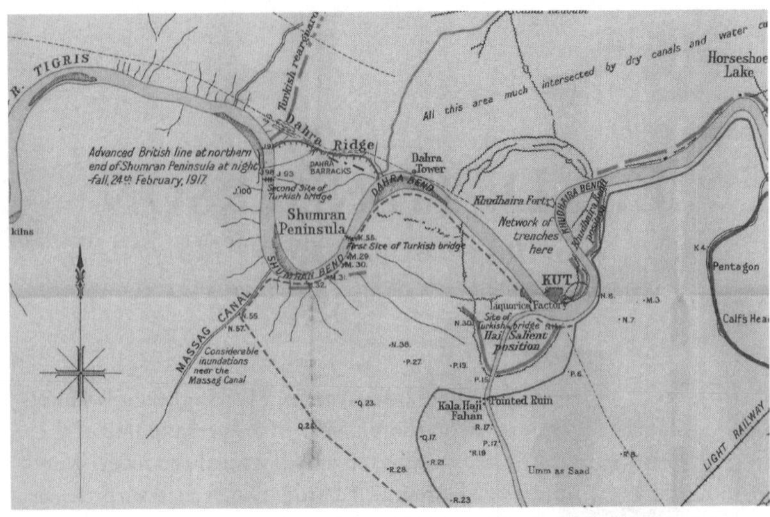

West bank of the River Hai near Kut, 25 January 1917.

on the right and the 7th (S) North Staffordshires. The battalions got within 50yd of the enemy front and were protected by artillery fire. After the bombardment lifted, they entered the enemy lines and, although the 7th North Staffordshires suffered heavy casualties, they still managed to achieve their objectives. However, the Turks made a series of strong counter-attacks from a northerly direction and they were well supported by shrapnel fire, trench mortars and a plentiful supply of bombs, which forced the Staffordshires back to where the Worcestershire battalion were positioned.

It was at this point, around 11.30 p.m., that the 9th (S) Royal Warwicks were brought up from 39th Brigade reserve to make a counter-attack of their own. Col Edward Henderson personally led the leading troops through the retiring troops across 500yd of open ground in order to recapture the objectives lost by the North Staffords. Despite being shot through the arm, he continued to move forward well in advance of his battalion, waving his men on. Once again he was wounded, but was able to lead a bayonet attack which resulted in the lost objectives being recaptured. In organising the new positions he was hit twice more. Lying out wounded in the open he was rescued by his adjutant, Lt R.E. Phillips.

It came as no surprise that Henderson died soon afterwards from his wounds, probably knowing full well that, without his magnificent example, the success of the first part of the operation would not have been achieved. By noon the Turkish counter-attack had been driven back with heavy casualties. One of the subalterns belonging to the 9th Royal Warwicks, taking part in the same action, was the future Field Marshal Viscount Slim, who was destined to become one of the most successful British generals in the Second World War.

At 3 p.m. the enemy began a second counter-attack using communication trenches on the left; it was also well supported by artillery and trench howitzer fire. The sheer numbers of the enemy forced the Midland battalions to slowly retreat to their original lines. The 'retirement was carried out in an orderly manner in quick time in spite of heavy enemy rifle and artillery fire'.

Despite the great gallantry being shown on the day, it is clear that the attack failed, although the enemy also suffered heavy casualties, especially from the shelling by British artillery.

Edward Henderson's posthumous VC was published in the *London Gazette* on 8 June 1917 as follows:

> Edward Elers Delavel Henderson, Major (Acting Lieut.-Colonel), late North Staffordshire Regt. For most conspicuous bravery, leadership and personal example when in command of his battalion. Lieut.-Colonel Henderson brought his battalion up to our two front-line trenches, which were under intense fire, and his battalion had suffered heavy casualties when the enemy made a heavy counter-attack, and succeeded in penetrating our line in several places, the situation becoming critical. Although shot through the arm, Lieut.-Colonel Henderson jumped up on the parapet, and advanced alone some distance in front of his battalion, cheering them on under the most intense fire over 500yds of open ground. Again wounded, he nevertheless continued to lead his men on in the most gallant manner, finally capturing the position by a bayonet charge. He was again twice wounded, and died when he was eventually brought in.

Henderson was buried at Amara War Cemetery, Iraq, 150 miles south of Baghdad, Plot XXIV, Row B, Grave 31. His name is also on a wall plaque in the cemetery. Other holders of the VC buried there include Lt Cdr Edgar Cookson and Cpl Sidney Ware. In 1933 the headstones in the cemetery had to be removed owing to the effect of salt in the soil and all the names of the men buried there were engraved on the wall of the cemetery.

Henderson's posthumous VC was presented to his widow at Buckingham Palace on 20 October 1917. Her home address was 'Tall Trees', Park Road, Camberley, Surrey.

Edward Elers Delavel Henderson was born in Simla, India, on 2 October 1878, son of Maj. Gen. P.D. Henderson CSI, formerly of the Madras Cavalry. He was educated at St Paul's School, London, and began his career as a tea planter in India. However, his ambition was to be a soldier and he joined the 5th (Militia) Battalion, the Worcestershire Regiment in May 1900, before moving to the West India Regiment as a second lieutenant on 13 December. He served in West Africa, taking part in minor operations against the forces of Bida and Kontagoro, for which he was awarded an African Service Medal (clasp). He was promoted to lieutenant on 10 February 1902 and continued to serve in West Africa (northern Nigeria) and this time was awarded a clasp for taking part in the operations at Arungu. In the following year he took part in the Kano-Sokuta Campaign in northern Nigeria, for which he was awarded a further African Service Medal (clasp). From July 1905 to February 1907 he served for nineteen months with his regiment in Jamaica.

On 20 May 1908 Henderson was transferred to the North Staffordshire Regiment on the disbandment of the West India Regiment and promoted to captain on 17 March 1909. In total he served in the West African Frontier Force for about nine and a half years (13 December 1900 to 28 June 1905 and 16 February 1907 to 10 September 1911). He then continued his service with the 2nd North Staffordshires in India.

Henderson married in 1910 and was back in England with the 3rd Battalion in 1914. He later served in the Great War with the newly formed 7th North Staffordshires, 39th Brigade, 13th (Western) Division, who sailed for Gallipoli from Avonmouth in June 1915, arriving on the Peninsula in July. Quoting from the history of the 7th North Staffordshire Regiment:

> The North Staffords remained in the line for a fortnight, during which time the Turks were very active. On the 19th of July they made a desperate attack, which was driven off. During this action the North Staffords sustained their first casualties, one officer being killed, Captain C.G. Grail, and 19 men and three officers wounded.

The wounded included Capt. Henderson. After they were relieved on 30 July the 39th Brigade moved down to the beach and embarked on lighters, proceeding to Mudros the following day for a short break. He was promoted to major on 1 September 1915 and later acting lieutenant colonel. On returning to the 13th Division he was given command of the 9th Worcestershires, who were also part of 39th Brigade. The division left Gallipoli for Egypt on 24 January 1916 and the Worcestershires moved to Mesopotamia in February/March. Shortly afterwards he was relieved by a senior officer from the Worcestershires who had returned from convalescence and left the 39th Brigade for the 38th Brigade for a period of just ten days in command of the 6th King's Own Royal Regiment. He then returned to the 39th Brigade where he took up command of the 9th Royal Warwickshires.

After the war, Henderson was commemorated in the garrison church of the Staffordshire Regiment at Whittington Barracks, Lichfield, Staffordshire, together with several other holders of the VC, all from the South Staffordshire Regiment. His decorations are held in the Lord Ashcroft Collection at the Imperial War Museum. Those not already mentioned include the 1914–15 Star, BWM, VM (1914–18) and MiD Oakleaf, and the Africa General Service Medal (1902) and their clasps. The Imperial War Museum also holds a portrait of him in their collection.

R.E. Phillips

Near Kut, 25 January 1917

According to the war diary of the 9th (S) Royal Warwickshires, 39th Infantry Brigade, 13th (Western) Division, to which Lt Robert Phillips was attached from the 13th (Reserve) Battalion, on 25 January 1917 they:

> ... took up positions in Kala Haji Fahan nullah (Deep Nullah) at 9.30 a.m. in immediate support of assaulting battalions. After intensive artillery bombardment Worcesters on right and N. Staffords on left stormed and secured enemy front line trench ... and began consolidation.... About noon a strong Turkish counter attack chiefly bombers supported by minenwerfers was launched. Battalion was ordered to advance and support the Worcester and North Staffordshires who were being gradually overwhelmed. Under the personal leadership of Lieut. Col. Henderson who had been killed, the battalion recaptured the trench driving the enemy back to his second line. At 3.00 p.m. enemy commenced big counter-attack working down communication trenches on the left supported by trench howitzer and artillery fire.

The sheer numbers of the enemy forced the Royal Warwickshires to withdraw. The attack had been a failure, but not through lack of tremendous courage and gallantry expended by the men involved in the day's fighting. The human cost in casualties of the 9th (S) Worcestershires and 7th (S) North Staffordshires had been very high and the 9th (S) Royal Warwickshires' war diary of 28 January reported a final tally of four officers killed, including Lt Col Henderson, as well as 2/Lt E.L. Moor, who died of wounds. Six officers were also wounded. Forty-five other ranks were killed or died of wounds, 118 were wounded, and eighteen missing. In addition, names who were forwarded for 'immediate recognition for valour' included Lt R.E. Phillips, Cpl J. Scott, Pte A. Kershaw and Sgt J. Goodfellow.

Lieutenant R.E. Phillips was awarded the VC for his deeds on 25 January, which was published in the *London Gazette* of 8 June 1917 as follows:

> Robert Edwin Phillips, Temporary Lieut. and Adjutant, Royal Warwickshire Regt. For most conspicuous bravery and devotion to duty. After his Commanding Officer had been mortally wounded in leading a counter-attack and eventually, with the help of a comrade, succeeded in bringing him back to our lines. Lieut. Phillips had in the first instance tried to get a telephone wire across the open, following the battalion in their counter-attack. This was impossible when the signallers were killed. His Commanding Officer lay wounded in the open, and as the counter-attack had succeeded, he turned all his energies on getting him in. He showed sustained courage in its very highest form, and throughout he had but little chance of ever getting back alive.

Phillips' commanding officer, Lt Col E.F.D. Henderson, whom he brought in, but who died shortly afterwards, was also awarded the Victoria Cross, and the comrade who helped Lt Phillips, Cpl J. Scott, was awarded the DCM.

A witness to Phillips winning his VC, an NCO from Leamington, described what he saw and his account was quoted in the *Midland Chronicle* of 15 June 1917:

> The enemy rushed a part of the line we were holding, and the Royal Warwicks were ordered up to set matters right. The Colonel was knocked out while leading the counter-attack in person. The enemy were sending a terrific barrage across, which for the time being severed communications between our advancing troops and the headquarters.
>
> It was then, that Lieutenant Phillips volunteered to re-open communication by means of a field telephone. The wire was paid out, and under the leadership of Lieutenant Phillips, who walked amid the torrents of fire as though he were without fear, the line was carried half-way across. Then the operators were wiped out, and the enemy's fire got worse than ever.
>
> Asking one of our chaps to go with him, Lieutenant Phillips made a rush towards the spot where the colonel lay wounded. The two men

> were forced back by the heavy fire, but later they had another try, and after four attempts Lieutenant Phillips managed to get to the side of the colonel. He rendered first aid, and moved the wounded officer to a place of greater safety. Then the man who had volunteered to come with him managed to rush through the enemy barrage and the two started to get the colonel back to our lines.
>
> In spite of the furious Turksih shell fire the little party got through, being hidden frequently in great clouds of dust and earth. 'The men worship him,' added the speaker of Lieutenant Phillips.

Field Marshal Lord Slim was a young subaltern of the 9th Royal Warwickshires and wrote of Robert Phillips, his senior officer, in the following amusing account:

> Long ago, in the First World War, when I was a bit more irresponsible, I served under an officer of vivid imagination. He was always fussing about dangers that usually didn't exist. Once after a day and half a night of his constant alarms, I was so fed up that I disconnected the telephone in the advance post I was holding. I wanted some sleep. I didn't get it. Within half an hour his imagination had painted the most frightful pictures of my position overrun by the enemy. He arrived with the reserve company to retake it. As he was my commanding officer I had some rather difficult explaining to do! I thought he was just windy. A few days later he won the VC by a superb example of leadership.

Phillips was promoted the day after he won the VC and was made battalion adjutant from 9 July 1917 to 9 May 1918 when he obtained a transfer to the Royal Air Force (RAF) to train for a pilot's certificate, but this aim was interrupted by home leave in October 1918 and the subsequent signing of the Armistice.

Phillips was presented with his VC by the King at Buckingham Palace on 9 November and was demobilised on 13 February 1919.

Robert Edwin Phillips was born at 12 Queen Street, Hill Top, West Bromwich, Staffordshire, on 11 April 1895, a son and one of six children of Alfred Phillips. From the age of 5 he was educated at

St James' Elementary School, Hill Top, not far from the family home, and later at King Edward VI's Grammar School, Aston, Birmingham (1907–11). He had gained a scholarship to the school and his family therefore did not have to pay school fees. The family lived at the same address until 1906 when they moved to a recently built house called 'Holyhead House' (54b), Hill Top. Several sources state incorrectly that this is where he was born. After leaving school in March 1911, Phillips entered the Civil Service as a boy recruit nine months later and worked as a tax surveyor for the Inland Revenue in Worcester. Over the next two years he also worked in Birmingham, Carmarthen and London.

Phillips enlisted in the Army on 17 March 1914 as a private in the 1/15th Company of the London Regiment (Civil Service Corps of the London Regiment (Territorial)) and was called up on the outbreak of war. A few months later, on 3 December, he was commissioned in the 9th (S) Battalion Royal Warwickshire Regiment. He arrived at Suvla Bay, Gallipoli, on 6 October 1915 and remained there until wounded on 17 November six weeks later. After he had recovered he was invalided to Egypt.

On 16 February his battalion embarked at Suez, arriving in Basra in Mesopotamia on 28 February 1916, and as part of Royal Warwickshires, 39th Brigade, 13th (Western) Division, he remained in the country for more than two years. Phillips rejoined his regiment in Mesopotamia at the time of the fall of Kut-el-Amara, and served with them until 9 May 1918. He was promoted to lieutenant on 10 April 1916, captain on 26 January 1917 and adjutant on 9 July 1917.

On 13 June 1917, a few days after his VC was published in the *London Gazette*, Aston Grammar Schools were given the day off in honour of the distinction gained by their former student.

The young officer arrived back at his parents' home on 26 October 1918 and somehow escaped the usual public reception given to a new VC holder on their return home. He was on a month's leave, the first that he had had in three years. However, he did not escape the public gaze for long, and on 4 November a meeting was organised to take place in West Bromwich Town Hall, where he was introduced to a very large audience by the Mayor, who was presenting medals to fifty local men who were serving in the war. Phillips, being the only VC holder in West Bromwich, was presented with his Borough Medal first. He was given a warm reception and in his reply to the Mayor's speech said that, although he was not serving with the local regiment, he was a member of the Royal Warwickshires from a neighbouring county. In that regiment were many men serving from the borough. The *Midland Chronicle* of 8 November mentioned:

> He is of a retiring disposition, and it was his desire, as well as that of his friends, that the knowledge of his return home should not be immediately made public. His family is very well known in the district, his father having for many years occupied a responsible position with Messrs C. Akrill and Co., Golds Green Foundry.

On 9 November Phillips attended an investiture in the ballroom of Buckingham Palace where the King presented him with his VC. On the 13th he attended a presentation ceremony at his old school, King Edward VI's Grammar, Aston, where he was given an enthusiastic reception from teachers and scholars alike, and on their behalf was presented with a silver casket 'as a small token of our thankfulness for what you and others have done, and as a token of our intense pride that one of our body should have risen to the greatest heights of courage and self-sacrifice'. In his expression of thanks, Phillips mentioned that at least two men with whom he served at Gallipoli were not only from the school but were form mates as well. He requested that the boys be given the rest of the day off as a holiday.

Phillips had one more function to attend, which was a reception on 15 November at Hill Top Council School, where local residents had gathered to greet their hero. The event was arranged by the Hill Top Patriotic Committee, which wanted to present gold hunter watches to eleven local servicemen and to celebrate the recent signing of the Armistice.

When Capt. Phillips left the Army in 1919, he returned to his job with the Inland Revenue, and during his working life served as assistant commissioner of taxes in Britain, Malaya and Swaziland. On 19 May 1920 Phillips married Beatrice Amy Brockhouse at St James's Church, Hill Top. Beatrice was a 24-year-old domestic science teacher. The couple lived at Barnt Green, Birmingham, and were to have two children, Michael and Rachel. In 1927 Alfred Phillips died and left Holyhead House to Elizabeth, his wife.

On 9 November 1929 Robert Phillips attended the House of Lords' VC Dinner hosted by the Prince of Wales.

When the equestrian statue to Field Marshal Earl Haig was unveiled in Whitehall in November 1937, Capt. Phillips was one of four VCs from the Birmingham District who was a member of the VC guard of honour. Eighteen months later in May 1939, his mother Elizabeth died.

In 1954 Phillips took the salute at the Hill Top British Legion's Armistice Day parade at St Paul's Church and two years later he took part in the VC centenary celebrations in London. In 1960 he retired from the Civil Service and moved to Cornwall with his second wife, Margaret Mary Ford. Six years later he attended the VC memorial service at St Martin-in-the-Fields on 13 July 1966 and a special dinner the following day.

Two years later, at the age of 73, Robert Phillips died in hospital on 23 September 1968 at St Veep, Lostwithiel, and was buried in St Veep Parish churchyard. In his will he left £3,452 and had presented his decorations to the Royal Warwickshire Regiment Museum, St John's House, Warwick. Apart from the VC they included the 1914–15 Star, BWM, VM (1914–19) and MiD Oakleaf, King George VI Coronation Medal (1937), Queen Elizabeth II Coronation Medal (1953) and Knight, *Legion D'Honneur* (5th Class) (France). Capt. Phillips was Mentioned in Despatches by Gen. Sir Frederick Maude on 31 March 1917, and in Lt Gen. W.R. Marshall's of 31 March 1918 for distinguished service in Mesopotamia.

The Phillips family home at Hill Top no longer exists and has been replaced by a modern housing development. However, a blue plaque to his memory was unveiled at Holyhead House in January 2008.

T. STEELE

Near Sannai-I-Yat, 22 February 1917

Four weeks after two men attached to the 9th Royal Warwickshire Regiment gained VCs on 25 January 1917, the slow advance towards the town of Kut-el-Amara had reached Sannai-I-Yat by 22 February. On this day, according to the war diary of the 1st Seaforths, 19th Infantry Brigade, 7th (Meerut) Division, the battalion stood to arms at 5.30 a.m. and, at daybreak, the 21st Brigade could be seen about a mile away to the right and moving towards Suwaikiya Marsh. At 6.30 a.m. British artillery began to bombard the enemy's camp behind their trench lines, and guns of the 7th Division also shelled the enemy frontline trenches. In addition, machine-guns swept the area. All this activity drew little response, although enemy aircraft did come over and drop a few bombs on the Allied camp.

The war diary entry is pretty matter-of-fact and does not reflect what happened later in the day when, after no fewer than five counter-attacks, the enemy made the decision to retire. During the afternoon, Indian troops to the right of the Seaforths moved forward, but later had to give ground. Seeing what was happening, Sgt Thomas Steele, the machine-gun sergeant, and Pte Joseph Winder, both of the Seaforths, rushed out to rally the Indians and to help save the situation. Doubling across the open landscape they seized a machine-gun which the Indians had carried back, took it to the right of a gap in the lines and brought it into action just in time to prevent a Turkish advance. During the evening the Seaforths sent patrols out as far as the fourth line, which was found to be empty, although a few stray

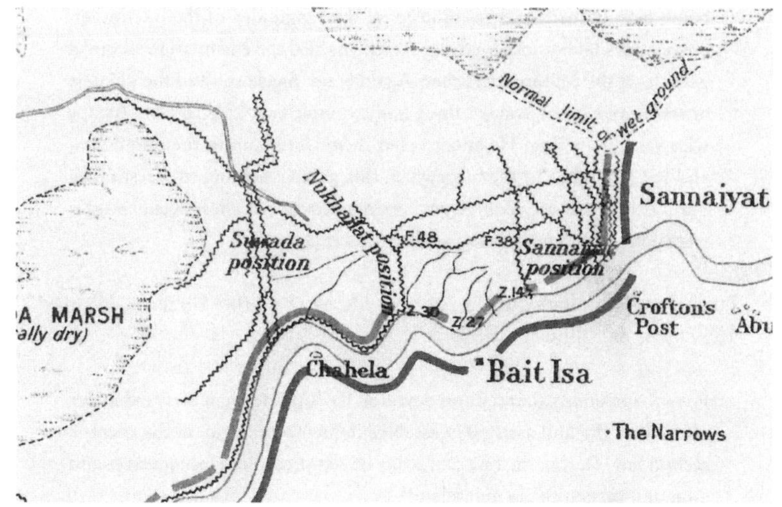

Sannai-I-Yat, 22 February 1917.

Turkish troops were rounded up. On the following day, the Seaforths' advance continued to beyond the Smada position, where it halted, leaving the rest of the division to move as quickly as possible in order to try to cut off the enemy.

The smashed Turkish trenches were full of heaps of dead and wounded, and were described as in a 'beastly mess'. The Turkish forces never seemed to have had much regard for their dead, preferring to leave unburied bodies to rot down on the battlefield.

For the prompt saving of the situation, Sgt Thomas Steele was awarded a VC, and Winder, whose role was no different, the DCM and *Médaille Militaire*. Steele's VC citation was published in the *London Gazette* of 8 June 1917 as follows:

> Thomas Steele, Sergt., No. 811, Seaforth Highlanders. For most conspicuous bravery and devotion to duty. At a critical moment, when a strong enemy counter-attack had temporarily regained some of the captured trenches, Sergt. Steele rushed forward and assisted a comrade to carry a machine gun into position. He kept the gun in action till relieved,

> being mainly instrumental in keeping the remainder of the line intact. Some hours later another strong attack enabled the enemy to reoccupy a portion of the captured trenches. Again Sergt. Steele showed the greatest bravery, and by personal valour and example was able to rally troops who were wavering. He encouraged them to remain in their trenches, and led a number of them forward, this greatly helping to re-establish our line. On this occasion he was severely wounded. These acts of valour were performed under heavy artillery and rifle fire.

Pte Joseph Winder's citation for his DCM (*London Gazette*, 18 June 1917) was as follows:

> For conspicuous gallantry and devotion to duty. He went forward under very heavy fire and assisted in establishing a machine-gun in the enemy's second line. During the rest of the day he repeatedly carried messages and ammunition across 'no man's land'.

Private Winder, No. 200592 was later promoted to company sergeant major. Sadly, when serving with the 2nd Seaforth Highlanders, 10th Infantry Brigade, 4th Division, he died on 2 November 1918, a few days before the Armistice. He was first buried at Presaeu Communal Cemetery Extension, France, reference A. 23. The village is nearly 4 miles to the south-east of Valenciennes.

Thomas Steele, of Scottish descent, was born on 6 February 1891 at Claytons, Springhead, Saddleworth, Yorkshire. Saddleworth was an area consisting of several villages which formed an urban district within the West Riding. In 1974 it became part of the Oldham metropolitan borough.

Thomas Steele was the eldest of three sons of Elizabeth and Harry Steele, a motor contractor. The other sons were Sam, born in 1893, and William, born in 1898. There was also a daughter, Emily. Thomas was educated at Austerlands Day School, Yorkshire, and Shelderslow Sunday School. On leaving school Thomas began work as a bobbin carrier at the Rome Mill, close to his home at Springhead. Later, and tiring of working in a factory, he decided to enlist in the Army, which he did on 16 August 1911, becoming a private in the 1st Seaforth Highlanders on the 22nd.

After initial training and a month's leave, he was sent to serve in India and was stationed there from 19 December 1912. On the outbreak of the First World War he was with his battalion at Agra and left with the 7th (Meerut) Division on 20 September as a member of the Indian Expeditionary Force. They arrived at Marseilles on 12 October for service on the Western Front.

Steele took part in most of the battalion's earlier engagements at Ypres, La Bassée, Neuve Chapelle and Loos, and was appointed lance corporal on 10 October 1915. He was then given about 24 hours' leave before leaving France with the 7th (Meerut) Division for Mesopotamia on 26 November. The Seaforths, now part of 19th Indian Brigade, were sent there as part of the force which was endeavouring to relieve Gen. Townsend's force at Kut-el-Amara.

Steele was promoted to sergeant on 7 January 1917 and was not always fit after suffering bouts of malaria, but this did not prevent him from being 'recommended for something', which was his way of telling his people at home in spring 1917 about the possibility of being awarded the Victoria Cross. After being wounded in twelve places he convalesced in Malpa, India.

After his VC was announced in the *London Gazette* of 8 June 1917, the *Oldham Chronicle* wrote the following piece:

> The gallant sergeant is of a most retiring disposition and beyond telling his parents that he had been recommended for something many weeks ago, nothing was known at home of his exploits until about three weeks ago, when he sent word to his fiancee that he had been highly recommended for the V.C. ... his father received a telegram from the sergeant's battalion headquarters last evening telling him of the award and asking him to send at once a photograph of Thomas who by the way has been offered a commission.

Samuel Steele, Thomas's middle brother, served in the Royal Scots, and William, the youngest, was a member of the Highland Light Infantry. Samuel had been wounded and was in hospital in Cardiff at around the time of the publication of his elder brother's VC. In time he had to undergo six operations. He was visited by his mother and the family was very proud on hearing Thomas's news.

On 15 August 1917, nearly six months after winning the VC, Steele was Mentioned in Despatches by Gen. Sir Frederick Maude. Four months later he left the Persian Gulf in December 1917 and served in Egypt and Palestine from 1 January 1918 to 6 February 1919. He was transferred to Regular Army Reserve on 8 March, and on 10 April received his VC from the King in the ballroom of Buckingham Palace.

Though wounded during the war, Steele later recovered sufficiently to play professional rugby league with Broughton Rangers and various amateur teams for several seasons. Throughout the rest of his life he was a regular supporter of VC and later VC/GC functions beginning with the Buckingham Palace Garden Party in June 1920.

He rejoined the Army on 9 April 1921, only to be transferred again to Regular Army Reserve on 4 June. Steele's career in the 1920s has been difficult to track down, but in 1927 he probably moved to Leicestershire in search of employment, which he later found with a wholesale fruiterer.

In November 1929 he attended the House of Lords' VC Dinner and was discharged from the Army on completion of his engagement on 21 August 1931. At around this time he married a lady called Bertha. Keen to keep up with his military links he enlisted in the Leicester Regiment, Territorial Army, on 29 March 1932 and became a sergeant with C Company. This battalion then became a Searchlight Battalion and on 9 December 1936 Steele transferred to the Royal Artillery.

Steele was called up for service from 26 September to 8 October 1938, from 18 June to 16 July 1939 and on 22 August 1939. He was embodied on 2 September 1939 and, while still serving as a company sergeant major (CSM), was posted to Lincoln with his Searchlight Unit on the outbreak of war. In 1941 he was posted to Leicester, and on account of his age served with the Home Guard and ARP. By now he was in his early 50s and was discharged on 23 April 1942 as he was 'no longer required for the purpose for which enlisted'. When serving with the Territorials on one occasion, he attended a summer camp and as a consequence lost his job; however, he managed to get another position, this time as a telephone clerk with a firm of solicitors. His last job before retiring in 1956 was with a car sales firm.

After the war, when still living in Leicestershire, Steele was a member of the committee of the Leicester Section of the Seaforth Highlanders Regimental Association. He was an enthusiastic member and 'a good sportsman, especially cricket'. In 1946 he attended the VE Parade in London on 8 June. In 1947 he served as a captain in the Leicestershire Army Cadet Force, and in June 1956 he was present at the VC centenary celebrations in London. On 24 July 1958 he attended the first of four VC/GC dinners, a Mayor's banquet and Garden Party at Buckingham Palace in 1962, and a service of commemoration at St Martin-in-the-Fields on 15 July 1964. When being presented with his Jubilee Medal in 1977, he was asked by the Duke of Edinburgh 'How did a Yorkshireman who served with a Scottish Regiment come to live and work in Leicester?' His reply was that 'You have to follow a good cook [his wife].'

After the death of his wife, Bertha, Steele returned to his roots in December 1977 to live with his sister-in-law at 1a Walkers, Springhead, Saddleworth. Walkers was a row of cottages where he had previously lived at No. 2. At the end of January 1978 the chairman of Saddleworth Parish Council, himself a Springhead man, visited Steele on the occasion of his 87th birthday. Steele was in bed at the time of the visit and a picture of the two men with Steele's medals appeared in the *Evening Chronicle*, Oldham, on 30 January.

Steele, never a man to seek the limelight, and one who clearly struggled to get a reasonable job between the wars, for once broke his silence when speaking to the *Evening Chronicle* reporter:

> The division [Meerut] served only a limited period in the European theatre of the war which Mr Steele says was worse because of the shellfire, wet conditions and starvation: 'In Palestine it was heat and dysentery ... it was all rice and biscuits with chlorinated water'.

Six months after this visit, Thomas Steele died on 11 July 1978 at his home at Springhead, and was cremated on the 17th at Hollinwood Crematorium, Oldham. His ashes were buried in the family grave at St Anne's churchyard, Stockport Road, Lydgate, Oldham.

As is often the case, different places lay claim to the same VC holder. Thus with Thomas Steele, he could be considered as an Oldham VC, a Springhead VC or a Saddleworth VC. The advantage of being attached to a town having won the nation's highest military honour was often financial, and Steele missed out on these benefits. With hindsight he was the sort of man who was only really happy when serving in the Army and found making a living in peacetime quite challenging.

In 1978 a cup inscribed 'The Tommy Steele V.C. Challenge Cup' was presented at reunion rallies of the Seaforth Association in Leicestershire.

Steele's decorations, apart from the VC, included the 1914–15 Star with clasp, the BWM, VM (1914–19) and MiD Oakleaf, Defence Medal (1939–45), War Medal (1939–45), King George VI Coronation Medal (1937), Queen Elizabeth II Coronation Medal (1953) and Queen Elizabeth Silver Jubilee Medal (1977). They were in private hands until 2009 when they were acquired by Lord Ashcroft and are part of the VC collection in the Imperial War Museum.

G.C. WHEELER

Tigris at Shumran, 23 February 1917

In the early part of 1917, one of the tasks of the British troops was to clear the enemy from the important bends in the River Tigris in the progress towards Baghdad. Such an operation was mounted at Shumran Bend, which was about 5 miles north of Kut-el-Amara, when a boat bridge was constructed at a point where the Tigris, already swollen by floodwater, was approximately 350yd wide.

The operation was very well prepared, and on 22 February the division (14th) sent out the orders for a crossing to be made on the Tigris at the Shumran Bend at daybreak on the 23rd. Soon after midnight, carts brought up specially made pontoons which were then put under cover and the carts returned. Turkish picquets on the opposite bank were seemingly unaware of this preparation, as the night was very quiet and no enemy fire was heard. The crossing was organised with a beachmaster as well as a ferrymaster.

Knowing that the far bank of the river was well defended with a loop-holed bund (or man-made embankment), and by machine-guns and covered by artillery, it was essential to effect the element of surprise to draw away enemy forces, and dummy crossings were organised at other points on the Tigris opposite Magasis and Kut-el-Amara.

The main crossing was led by Maj. George Campbell Wheeler of the 2nd Battalion 9th Gurkha Rifles, Indian Army, when he took his D Company across the River Tigris. The regimental history of the 9th Gurkha Rifles stated that each tow was of thirteen pontoons, with five rowers each, 'nine pontoons were allocated to rank and file, ten men to

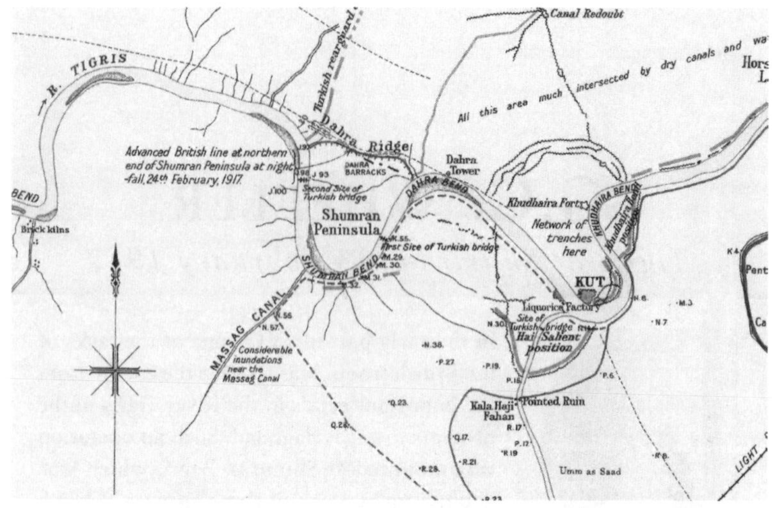

Shumran, north-west of Kut, 23 February 1917.

each boat; two were for Lewis guns and teams, and two for bombers'. Many of the rowers were Southampton watermen, members of the 1/3rd Hampshire Regiment. The first tow, led by Maj. Wheeler, had three other officers on board, 2/Lts Russell, Alington and Kerr, together with the regimental bombers and ammunition. The launch began at 5.30 a.m. on the 23rd and the first tow pushed off fifteen minutes later when the light was good enough for them just to see the far bank. When the pontoon was about halfway across, desultory fire broke out, which later became more intense and was accompanied by enemy shelling. Out of the initial group of thirteen boats, ten reached the opposite bank and three drifted downstream out of control. Once Wheeler's boat landed, the men were met with bomb and rifle fire from enemy trenches. The first enemy trench, which was only 15yd from the water, was quickly rushed and bombed to the left and right of the attackers. With the assistance of more regimental bombers then joining Wheeler, the front trenches were gradually cleared.

Kerr was wounded during the crossing and Alington shot dead on arrival at the first trench, but Lewis guns were sent off to cover the right and left flanks. One of the Lewis guns became jammed and this allowed an enemy counter-attack of thirty or forty men against Wheeler's party in the centre of the landing force. However, Wheeler and Russell, together with three Gurkhas, charged the approaching enemy with bombs and bayonets and dealt with most of them. It was at this point that Wheeler, 'who was leading a charmed life', was fired on at close quarters, but his assailant missed; another Turkish soldier then threw his rifle at the officer, which badly injured his scalp, leaving a 6in wound across his head. Despite this setback, Wheeler scrambled to his feet and, with four Gurkhas, broke up a bombing party of forty men and killed one man who was in the act of bayoneting Lt Russell in the shoulder. Wheeler kept the landing going, rallying as many men as possible and sending one party to the left to guard the flank among some ruins. With his small force he managed to occupy a trench nearly 200yd inland at a position named Liquorice Stack.

After each boat was emptied, it was quickly turned around to make its return journey to bring across more men, ammunition and other equipment. By then the boats were coming under much heavier fire and a few more began to drift downstream out of control, their crews either wounded or dead. However, they were collected up and a boat bridge 300yd long was finished by mid-afternoon. Columns from three battalions, the 2/9th Gurkhas, the 1/2nd Gurkhas and the 2nd Norfolks, managed to cross by use of the bridge at a point known as M.34 and they were followed by a reserve battalion. By late afternoon the remaining men from the 14th Division had crossed.

Two hundred prisoners were captured by the 9th Gurkhas during the day, and six officers and thirty-eight other ranks became casualties. The rowers, who had played such a vital part in the successful crossing, suffered forty-one casualties and at one point had to be replenished by reinforcements from the 13th Division. The Gurkhas were relieved during the night and bivouacked near the 'Hangar Pit', to the north-west of the Liquorice Stack and opposite point M.31. The next task for the Gurkhas was to clear the Shumran Peninsula of the enemy in order that a cavalry division could move through and attempt to prevent Turkish forces from using the Baghdad road. Also on 23 February a British force under the command of Gen. Maude finally retook Kut-el-Amara, which they held for the rest of the war.

Lt Russell received the DSO and Wheeler was awarded the VC for his leadership and gallantry, which was published in the *London Gazette* of 8 June 1917 as follows:

> George Campbell Wheeler, Major, 2/9th Gurkha Rifles, Indian Army. For most conspicuous bravery and determination. This officer, together with one Gurkha officer and eight men, crossed a river and immediately rushed the enemy's trench under heavy bombing, rifle, machine-gun and artillery fire. Having obtained a footing on the river bank, he was almost immediately afterwards counter-attacked by a strong enemy party with bombers. Major Campbell Wheeler at once led a charge with another officer and three men, receiving a severe bayonet wound in the head, but managed, in spite of this, to disperse the enemy. This bold action on his part undoubtedly saved the situation. In spite of his wound, he continued to consolidate his position.

George Campbell Wheeler was born on 7 April 1880 at Yokohama, Japan, a second son of Dr Edwin Wheeler. The Wheelers were an old Belfast family and Edwin was educated at Queen's College, Belfast, and after serving in the Royal Navy as fleet surgeon took up private practice in Japan. Wheeler was educated at Bedford School (1893–97) (formerly Bedford Grammar School) and represented the school at cricket and rugby. After deciding on a military career, he moved to Woolwich and then to Sandhurst.

He entered the Army with a commission on 20 January 1900 as a second lieutenant and joined the Indian Army on 18 April 1901. He was a linguist and was fluent in French, German, Japanese and Hindustani. He also had a fine baritone voice and was much in demand for operatic performances, especially in India. His first regiment was the East Yorkshire Regiment, then serving in India, which was composed mainly of men from Ireland. Wheeler joined the 2/9th Gurkhas in early 1902 and was promoted to lieutenant on 20 April 1902 and 'appointed a double company officer on 15th February, 1905, Captain on 20th January, 1909, and substantive Major, 1st September, 1915'.

The 2nd Battalion 9th Gurkha Rifles were part of 37th Infantry Brigade, 14th (Indian) Division and in 1916 Wheeler sailed with his regiment to Mesopotamia. He won his VC on 23 February 1917 when in action a few miles from Kut-el-Amara. He had become major/temporary lieutenant colonel from 24 December 1916, a rank he held until 18 June 1917.

After the war, Wheeler was presented with his VC by the King on 26 July 1919 at Buckingham Palace. He was later made acting lieutenant colonel from 5 December 1921 of the 1st Battalion 9th Gurkha Rifles when they proceeded on active service in operations against the Moplahs in Malabar in south India. He held this rank until 5 January 1922 and finished his military career as commandant of military police at Port Blair in the Andaman Islands, where he served for eighteen months.

Two other well-known soldiers who were also educated at Bedford Modern School were G.G.M. Wheeler VC (1873–1915) and Edgar Mobbs DSO (1882–1917). Commemorative tablets for the three men were unveiled at the school in 1923.

In 1930 Wheeler was present at the unveiling of the regimental war memorial. His colleague, the former Lt R.T. Russell, designed the plinth and was also present at the unveiling.

Wheeler later retired to Barton-on-Sea, Hampshire, where he lived at Maryville at the eastern end of Beech Avenue. He had a keen interest in various local affairs, including the annual Remembrance Day service, and was a member of the New Forest Players, the Conservative Club and a supporter of the National Fitness movement.

Wheeler died on 26 August 1938 at Grove Nursing Home of pneumonia after an operation and was buried at St Mary Magdalene churchyard, New Milton Cemetery. He was not given a military funeral, but his coffin was draped with a Union Jack. The local newspaper, the *Advertiser & Times*, reported Wheeler's death on the front page of the 3 September 1938 edition under the heading 'Death of a Gallant Soldier and Warm Hearted Gentleman'.

After his death, one of his three sons, Capt. D.E.B. Wheeler RAF, presented his father's VC to the National Army Museum, which was received on the museum's behalf by Field Marshal Sir Claude Auchinleck on 9 February 1958. Wheeler's other medals included the BWM (1914–20), VM (1914–19) and MiD Oakleaf, India General Service Medal (1903–35) with two clasps ('Waziristan 1919–21', 'Waziristan 1921–24') and King George VI Coronation Medal (1937). There is a portrait of him by Barbara Chamier.

By the late 1990s the headstone on his grave was in a dilapidated condition and the 9th Gurkha Rifles Regimental Association, partly supported by former members of Bedford Modern School, organised a replacement stone, which was blessed by the local rector, the Revd Andrew Bailey, on 3 September 1999. Eight retired Gurkha officers were present. In the 1980s Wheeler's very gallant action was still celebrated by the battalion in India as Shumran Day. The town of New Milton has another link with the Victoria Cross, as the late Charles Upham from New Zealand, who won a double VC in the Second World War, married his wife at the town's Roman Catholic church.

J. Readitt

Algayat-al-Gaharbigah Bend, 25 February 1917

The plan of action on 25 February 1917 from Gen. Maude, commander of the Mesopotamia Expeditionary Force, was for the cavalry to operate in the area around the northern flank of the enemy. Simultaneously, a division would move forward on the left bank of the Tigris. In addition, a senior naval officer was requested to assist the advance of I Corps with the use of his flotilla. The main task was to clear the battlefields on the banks of the Hai and the Tigris, while another division was to move forward when required.

On the day itself, the 13th (Western) Division moved forward from the Shumran Peninsula along the left bank of the Tigris while the cavalry division moved northwards. The cavalry managed to contain the Turkish rearguard posted in a canal which ran roughly north-east from the north-west corner of the Husaini Bend, and then a thirty-minute delay followed until the 38th Brigade from the 13th Division managed to reach positions at the Husaini Bend where they came under enemy shell fire. The British artillery replied in kind and the advance was duly assisted by support from the naval flotilla of five ships which had by then arrived on the scene. However, the enemy was not giving ground and, according to the *Official History*, at 12.30 p.m.:

> ... it was clear that the 38th Brigade's advanced line – 6th King's Own, 6th East Lancashire and 6th Loyal North Lancashire, in this order from the right – had been definitely checked by heavy rifle and machine-gun fire from some seven hundred yards from the enemy's trenches and was beginning to dig itself in. At this hour the Fourth Battalion of the Brigade, the 6th South Lancashire, was sent to the right to try and turn the enemy's flank. Passing through the line of the (dismounted) Hertfordshire Yeomanry, this battalion effected a lodgement in a section of the enemy's line about a mile and a half north of the Tigris bank, but found itself south of the enemy's left flank.

The South Lancashires came under very heavy machine-gun fire and the enemy was using a thick curtain of bombs and rifle grenades. The main obstacle was a hill and dried-up watercourse on the left of the Lancashires' front. According to the battalion war diary:

> A party led by 2nd Lt Jackson cleared [a] watercourse on left with bayonet in face of terrific machine-gun fire, rifle grenades and bombs. 2nd Lts Jackson and Jefferson killed, 2nd Lts Fletcher and Sharpley wounded, 21 men killed and 58 wounded.

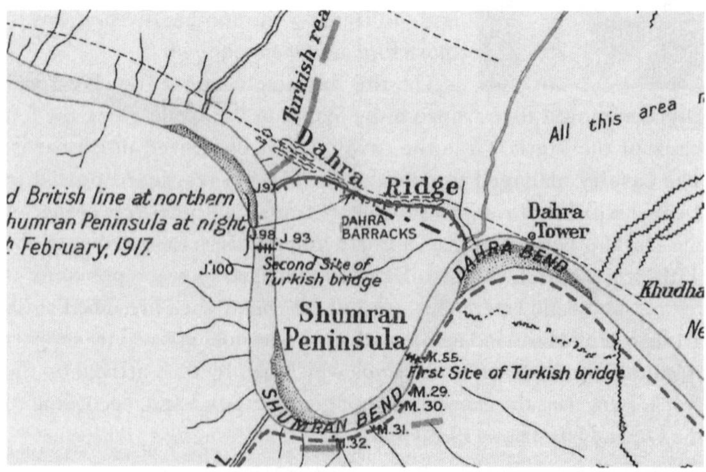

Shumran Peninsula, 25 February 1917.

It was during this action, after his officers had been killed or wounded, that Pte Readitt took command and, almost single-handedly, held the enemy at bay. The survivors of his party had reached a barricade which had been erected by the enemy in the watercourse. A counter-attack pushed them back, but Readitt, continuing to throw bombs, gave ground slowly. This deed, which gained him a VC, probably took place just to the west of the Dahra Ridge, to the north-west of the Shumran Peninsula, close to the Tigris. The citation for his VC, published in the *London Gazette* of 5 July 1917, reported the deed as follows:

> John Readitt, No. 18233, Private, 6th Battn. South Lancashire Regt. For most conspicuous bravery and devotion to duty when working down a broad, deep water-course. Five times he went forward in the face of very heavy machine-gun fire at very close range, being the sole survivor on each occasion. These advances drove back the enemy machine gun, and about 300yds of water-course was made good in an hour. After his officer had been killed Private Readitt, on his own initiative, organized and made several more advances. On reaching the enemy barricade, he was forced by a counter-attack to retire, giving ground slowly and continuing to throw bombs. On supports reaching him, he held a forward bend by bombing until the position was consolidated. The action of this gallant soldier saved the left flank and enabled his battalion to maintain its position.

A second account of the exceptional deeds of Pte Readitt was published in a copy of the *Empire News* of 8 July 1917:

> A Company, during the most critical stage of the Battle, recording that as the only survivor of the first four bombing raids along the watercourse he had fought on by himself until all his bombs were exhausted. During the fifth raid, Readitt had to rally the bombers who had scattered in the face of the enemy fire, and eventually he moved them up to the Turkish barricade, 'which formed the main enemy position and was the chief obstacle to the advance'.
>
> Here the enemy counter-attacked, but in spite of the fact that the enemy concentrated on him a deadly fire and every sniper in the Turkish ranks seemed to be shooting at him, Readitt never abandoned his do-as-you-please style of retirement. Whenever the enemy pressed him too closely

> he would just turn and let them have a bomb, which scattered them in all directions.
>
> Finally he was joined by another bombing party and then he made his most determined stand. Under his leadership, the bombers drove the enemy back once more, and after a fierce fight the whole position was captured and consolidated.
>
> The Turkish commander whom we captured later in the day, said he had never seen anything finer than the way that stripling had stood up to a whole army.

The 38th Brigade lay in their position and withdrew after dark; that day the British and Indian troops had been very successful, with the enemy retreating and being pursued by the cavalry.

John Readitt was born on 19 January 1897 at 34 Bamford Street, Clayton, Manchester, and was educated at the local St Cross Day School and also attended St Paul's Sunday School and Church. Always a keen footballer, he played full-back for a team in the Manchester Sunday School League. After leaving school he joined his father in his cobbling business in 600 Ashton New Road, Clayton, and on the eve of the start of the war he and his father signed a ten-year contract for repairing boots for Manchester United Football Club.

However, Readitt clearly wanted to 'do his bit' and at the age of 17 he volunteered for the Army on 12 April 1915, joining the 6th (S) South Lancashire Regiment (The Prince of Wales's Volunteers), who had been formed on the outbreak of war.

The battalion, part of 38th Infantry Brigade, 13th (Western) Division, sailed from Avonmouth for Gallipoli in June 1915. At some stage, Readitt suffered from severe frostbite. After the evacuation from the Peninsula his battalion moved to Egypt in February 1916 and then on to Mesopotamia after a short stay.

After winning his VC in February 1917, Readitt was unwell and spent some time in hospital at Kut-el-Amara. During the war he rose through the ranks to sergeant and after the Armistice was transferred to Z Reserve and discharged from the Army on 18 July 1919. Four months later he was presented with his VC by the King at Buckingham Palace on 26 November 1919. He then returned to work in the family business. In the following June he attended the VC Garden Party at Buckingham Palace.

In March 1921 John Readitt married Lily at St Paul's Church, Philips Park, Bradford, Manchester. The couple later had two sons, John and Frederick, as well as one daughter. In July Readitt was one of four local VCs introduced to the Prince of Wales when he was touring Lancashire; the others included George Evans, George Stringer and Harry Coverdale.

Three years later, on 12 July 1924, Readitt was one of the official guests at the unveiling of the war memorial at St Peter's Square, Manchester. The Portland stone war memorial was designed by Sir Edwin Lutyens.

Other VC holders present at the ceremony ouside the town hall, Albert Square, were John Thomas, Jack White, George Evans, George Stringer, Henry Kelly and Harry Coverdale. The group was greeted by the Earl of Derby.

In November 1929 Readitt was a member of the VC Honour Guard for the burial service for the Unknown Warrior in Westminster Abbey and also attended the House of Lords' VC Dinner.

After the Second World War, Readitt was a guest at the VE Parade celebrations in June 1946 and a VC Dinner the same day held at The Dorchester. A year later he was one of three VC holders who attended a dedication service at St Mary's Church, Droylsden, Manchester. In 1956 he took part in the VC centenary commemorations in London. Between 1958 and 1962 he attended three of the VC/GC Association dinners, as well as a special banquet held in 1962.

Always described as a quiet and unassuming man, John Readitt died after a long illness at 2 Bury Brow, Clayton Bridge, Manchester, on 9 June 1964, and his funeral took place four days later at St Cross Church, Clayton. The mourners included members of his family as well as representatives of the South Lancashire Regiment; standard bearers from the British Legion and buglers from the Ashton and Preston barracks were also present. Readitt was buried at Gorton Cemetery, Manchester, Section Z, Grave 223. The grave is shared by his widow, Lily, who died four years after her husband on 26 September 1968, and

John, one of their two sons, who died on 15 April 1968, aged 47. On 27 April 2000 Spinks sold Readitt's decorations to Lord Ashcroft for £40,000. Apart from the VC they included the 1914–15 Star, BWM, VM (1914–19), King George VI Coronation Medal (1937) and Queen Elizabeth II Coronation Medal (1953). In addition, he was awarded the Italian Medal, the *Al Valore Militare*, which was unnamed. The collection is on display in the Imperial War Museum.

J. WHITE

River Diyala, 7/8 March 1917

After Kut-el-Amara had been finally captured by Gen. Maude's force on 23 February, the Turkish Army retreated along the line of the River Tigris, pursued by the British Army and a naval flotilla.

In order to secure Baghdad the British needed to force a crossing of the River Diyala. It was during the first attempts at crossing this river that Pte Jack White won the VC on 7/8 March 1917 at a position about 8 miles from Baghdad. He was a member of the 6th (S) King's Own Royal Lancaster, 38th Brigade, 13th (Western) Division. Prior to the operation Diyala village needed to be cleared, and this was achieved on the 7th. The King's Own, together with the 71st Field Company RE and No. 2 Bridging Train, then moved into huts in the part of the village on the left bank of the Diyala. This site was chosen as the only suitable place to launch pontoons into the river and there were some bridge ramps which were chosen as suitable for the purpose. However, this was a fundamental error as it later emerged that the Turkish forces had this position very well covered with machine-guns. In addition, and owing to pressures of time, too little preparation had been carried out. The enemy were known to be occupying buildings on the far bank of the river and the orders for the battalion were to ferry men across the river, who on landing would drive the enemy out of their positions on the far side. Four pontoons, which had to be carried a considerable distance, were to provide cover for the sappers to build a bridge.

The King's Own were supported from right to left by the East Lancashires and Loyal North Lancashires respectively. The river was 50yd wide at this point and the moon was almost full. When the first pontoon was set down into the river it immediately attracted enemy fire, which led to heavy casualties and delayed the whole operation. A second attempt at working pontoons down the ramp was later made and this time the launching was sped up and artillery support was also laid on. However, one pontoon never made it into the river and the other three were quickly swept away by the current down the Tigris, all on board being either killed or wounded. Despite the extreme gallantry being displayed by the men involved, they were attempting the impossible.

It was when one of the pontoons was drifting out of control down river that Pte White, finding himself unhurt, called out to his comrades. There was only one response, from his officer 2/Lt Patterson (later captain), who, although badly wounded, had been protected by two men who had fallen on top of him. It was now that Jack White showed great ingenuity and common sense. Being a signaller, he had with him

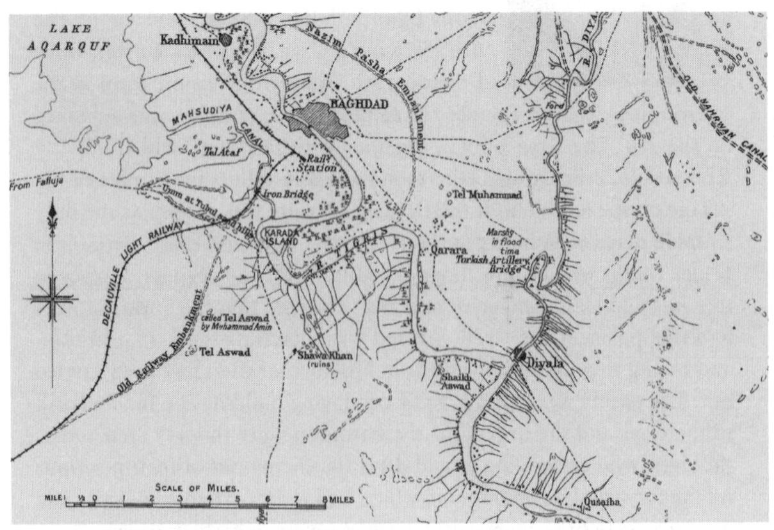

Diyala River, 7/8 March 1917.

a coil of telephone wire which he proceeded to attach to his boat and he dived overboard fully clothed. He managed to swim ashore while towing the boat to safety under constant and heavy machine-gun fire. The fire was so intense that seven of the men who rushed forward to help him were killed, but somehow he came through unscathed and his brave action certainly saved the life of his officer, 2/Lt S. Patterson, and several wounded men as well. Of the sixty men who had attempted the crossing, very few were still alive. Afterwards Pte White was sent down the line to the casualty clearing station (CCS) 'as it was thought he might have been suffering from shock, but after six hours he returned to the trenches and was in action again on the same day at the same spot'.

At midnight a third attempt at a crossing was made and again it was accompanied by an artillery barrage, but this attempt was abandoned and further attempts at a crossing were called off at 4 a.m. when casualties including the rowers had mounted to fifty. Later, when Pte White finally crossed the river as a member of a fatigue party of the King's Own, he came across the bodies of 300 Turkish troops who were buried in one huge trench.

For his gallantry Jack White was awarded a VC, which was published in the *London Gazette* of 27 June 1917 as follows:

> Jack White, No. 18105, Private, 6th Battn. Royal Lancaster Regt. For most conspicuous bravery and resource. This signaller during an attempt to cross a river saw the two pontoons ahead of him come under heavy machine-gun fire, with disastrous results. When his own pontoon had reached the midstream, with every man except himself either dead or wounded, finding that he was unable to control the pontoon, Private White promptly tied a telephone wire to the pontoon, jumped overboard and towed it to the shore, thereby saving an officer's life and bringing to land the rifles and equipment of the other men in the boat, who were either dead or dying.

Jack White was born Jacob Weiss of Russian Jewish parents, Isaac and Olga (née Braverman) Weiss, in Leeds on 23 December 1896. The Jewish family later moved to the Hightown district of Salford. Jacob attended Marlborough Road School, Garnet Street, Higher Broughton, and in 1907 joined the Jewish Lads' Brigade and Grove House Lads' Club. At some point the family name was anglicised to White and Jacob became Jack. Name changing was a common practice at this time as immigrants were often victimised, especially when it came to employment.

After leaving school and following in his father's footsteps, Jack entered the waterproofing industry, beginning work in his father's factory. He was on an export trade trip to Sweden in August 1914 when war broke out, so he hurried back to England in order to enlist, becoming a member of the King's Own (Royal Lancaster) Regiment. In the early part of his service he was booked to go to France, but missed the departure of the draft as he had been given two days' compassionate leave in order to attend his father's funeral; he had been killed when trying to escape from a burning factory building. White's battalion, the 6th (S) Battalion King's Own, left for Gallipoli in July 1915 and he was made a signaller; he was to spend most of the war in the Middle East.

After the war White returned home to a hero's welcome and was one of three Jewish men to win the VC, the others being Leonard Keysor, an Australian who moved to London, and Issy Smith, who moved to Australia. White visited his old school for a reunion on 19 March 1919, and on 30 April he was presented with his VC in the ballroom of Buckingham Palace by the King. In June 1920 he also attended the Garden Party at Buckingham Palace.

Soon after his return to Manchester White was given some money from a collection which he put into a firm that sold mackintoshes called White Bros (Manchester) Ltd. Unfortunately, 464 of his mackintoshes were stolen by a gang of Russian Jews. In April 1921 the case came to court and two of the criminals were given fifteen and twelve months' imprisonment respectively, together with a period of hard labour.

White moved to Broughton, Salford, and in 1921 he married May Daniels. The couple remained in Broughton and lived in 53 Devonshire Street. White then became a travelling salesman, specialising in antiques and Persian rugs, and kept an office and stockroom in central Manchester.

He was a founder member of the Jewish Ex-Servicemen's Association and spent a great deal of his spare time looking after the welfare of Jewish ex-servicemen. As a result of winning the VC he was much in demand for public appearances and talks, and was instrumental in organising events which would attract funds for this cause. He became an 'ambassador' for the cause of Jewish ex-servicemen and was invited to India where he became popular with the Jewish community in Calcutta.

He was a leading light in Jewish affairs and collaborated with Capt. Sydney Frankenburg, whose father had been mayor of Salford. The British Legion gave its permission for the two men to start up a sub-branch named after Capt. Frankenburg at Zion House, 97 Cheetham Road, Manchester, and White was made a life vice-president. The branch was not exclusive to Jewish ex-servicemen, but was a means of arranging social events and raising funds for the needy, who included Lancashire VC holders. It became an important part of Jack White's life.

At the unveiling of the cenotaph in St Peter's Square, Manchester, in July 1924, White was one of five holders of the VC who were specially invited and were welcomed by Lord Derby. The other VC holders with him were Henry Kelly, George Evans, John Readitt and John Thomas. White also regularly attended local annual Armistice Day parades.

Jack White attended the House of Lords' VC Dinner in 1929, where he met Capt. S. Patterson, the officer whose life he had saved, at a West End hotel. It was the first time the two men had met since March 1917. They had a long talk about old times and vowed to have an annual reunion from then on.

On 7 November 1937 White took part in a parade of Jewish ex-servicemen on Horse Guards Parade. Maj. Gen. the Earl of Athlone was accompanied by the Secretary for War, Leslie Hore-Belisha. Some 7,000 men wearing their medals were drawn up in eight ranks and at 'the front of the parade ranged the standards of the Jewish branches of the British Legion and other associations'. The band of the Scots Guards played for the inspection and, during the service of prayers and commemoration, banners were dipped for the *Last Post* and the National Anthem. Later the parade, led by Maj. Gen. the Earl of Athlone and the Chief Rabbi, Joseph Herman Hertz, marched past the Cenotaph in Whitehall. Jack White was given the honour of placing a wreath at the foot of the Cenotaph, and Mr M. Harris MM also laid a wreath on behalf of Leonard Keysor VC who was ill. Later a tea was held at the Albert Hall for those who had taken part. In the following year Keysor was again not well enough to turn out and the same two men laid wreaths at the Cenotaph on 6 November 1938.

During the build-up to the Second World War there were often outbreaks of anti-Semitism in some of Britain's largest cities, and a branch of Sir Oswald Mosley's British Union of Fascists set up its offices close to Manchester's Jewish quarter. On the outbreak of war Jack White applied to become a member of the Manchester Local Defence Volunteers (later Home Guard), which was predominantly for men who had served in the First World War and were now too old for active service or the very young waiting to join up. He was quickly made a group commander, but was later told that he wasn't eligible for such a position as his father had not been a naturalised British citizen. White was deeply upset by this slight against his father's memory, and rightly so. This was not an isolated case and Parliament was lobbied, but to no avail. Instead he worked as a volunteer ARP officer.

Never a man to give up easily, Jack White tried another tactic when he wrote a heartfelt plea to *The Times* on 11 September 1942, from 5 Bentley Road, Salford, in which he called for the formation of a separate Army to be drawn up from British Jews willing to fight the Nazis:

> Up to now they are eligible only for labour battalions. They are entrusted with shovels, but not with guns, with which to fight their bitterest enemy. This is clearly no answer to a proud and legitimate demand. What is needed is a specially Jewish army, fighting alongside the allied armies of the other United Nations on any and every battlefront. I am confident that whenever the Jewish army comes face to face with the Nazis they will prefer to die rather than surrender.

After the end of the Second World War White attended the VE Parade in June 1946, followed by the dinner at The Dorchester the same evening. On the welfare front there was much work to do in assisting refugees who had managed to escape the Nazi menace with their lives. Some had served with the Polish Army and White helped them with training and employment.

Jack White, who was surely as much of a hero in times of peace as in war, died on 27 November 1949 at the early age of 53 at his home at 5 Bentley Road, Salford. He was buried with full military honours the following day at the Jewish Cemetery, Blackley, Section F, Grave 341.

A small plaque to commemorate this Jewish VC, together with other Leeds associated VC winners, was unveiled in 1992 in the Memorial Gardens in central Leeds. There is also a memorial plaque to him in the Priory, Lancaster. Although the whereabouts of Jack White's VC is unknown, the King's Own Royal Regiment Museum does have an album compiled by a Mr Dobkin in October 1991 which includes copies of various items, including the *Victor* comic in which White was featured and other newspaper clippings. Cuttings from the Second World War are also included. This album can be inspected by appointment. His decorations are not publicly held and, apart from the VC, they would include the 1914–15 Star, BWM, VM (1914–19), King George VI Coronation Medal (1937) and *Medaglia Al Valore Militare* (Bronze).

In the spring of 2014, an exhibition entitled 'From Street to Trench: A War that Shaped a Region' opened at the Imperial War Museum North. It was supported by the Manchester-based clothing manufacturer Private White VC.

O.A. REID

River Diyala, 8/10 March 1917

On 9 March 1917, the day after Pte Jack White had won the VC in the attempt to cross the River Diyala, 13th (Western) Divisional orders were given to the 38th Brigade to attempt another crossing. This time it was the turn of the 6th Battalion Loyal North Lancs to carry out the task. According to the brigade diary:

> ... excellent arrangements were made by the O.C. North Lancs Major Harrison for the organization of his battalion.... The artillery barrage was more arranged to give the enemy the impression that the second attempt would be made in much the same place as the previous night. All preparations were complete by 11.30 p.m. and at 12 M.N. the artillery opened accompanied by heavy fire from our machine guns, Lewis guns and rifles. The crossing was being made in 4 columns called from the right, A, B, C and D. As soon as the barrage opened boats were launched at each of the crossings. A & B were successful immediately but C and D crossings failed, the boats being swept down the river. Ferrying went on, the two ferries which had succeeded but after about 3 trips ferry B had to be abandoned and only ferry A was left. This ferry managed to get through 11 trips taking men across. The troops that got across at first held about 300yds of the opposite bank.... The Turks counter attacked heavily with bombs from the wood on the right and gradually drove the men who had got across the river down to the left where they finally collected in a small bend in the bund just opposite crossing D and there held on.

Orders were then issued for the King's Own, East Lancs, North Lancs and South Lancs to combine in holding the bund and no more ferrying was attempted as pontoons had run out.

C Column under Capt. Oswald Reid was reduced in strength from fifty to fifteen men and therefore joined up with B Column. During the night the enemy continuously attacked from a neighbouring wood and tried to bomb the Lancashire men out of their defensive positions, but all these attacks were repulsed.

Again, according to the brigade diary, the following day (the 10th) was mostly quiet, although the enemy did shell the D Crossing and the bund. The main problem was one of ammunition supply to the North Lancs, who were on the right bank, and all efforts failed. Later orders said that the crossing was to be completed during the night. The East Lancs were selected to make the crossing and a second crossing was to be made by the Wiltshires 1,000yd further up the Diyala. These two crossings were to be run in tandem with a landing from the Tigris at Diyala village.

The crossings began at 4 a.m. on the 10th and this time were successful. This greatly relieved the troops on the far bank who by now were almost out of ammunition, as more troops from the brigade got across together with ammunition and stores:

> ... the North Lancs who under Captain Read [*sic*] of the King's Liverpool Regt had hung on so gallantly for about 30 hours to the right bank. This party had practically run out of bombs and ammunition and things were very critical. When resistance was at an end the crossing carried on without interruption...

After this success the division received orders to press on and the 39th Brigade was to act as the advance guard on its way to the Diyala–Baghdad road, having passed through the picquet lines. On the 11th the 38th Brigade was ready to push forward towards Baghdad, which was entered unopposed on the same day.

According to the King's Own regimental history:

> The heroism of those men who attempted to force the passage is still remembered in the name of the permanent bridge that spans the Diyala at that spot, for it is known as Lancashire Bridge. On the memorial which

> stands nearby are the following words: 'To The Glorious Memory of the Heroic Dead who are buried near this spot who gave their lives to carry out a brilliant feat of arms which resulted in the crossing of the Diyala [*sic*] River on 10th March 1917 in face of a strongly entrenched enemy. *Pro Patria.*'

Reid was wounded on 8 March, but probably had little choice but to remain on duty. On the 10th he suffered gunshot wounds to his neck and was discharged from duty three days later, rejoining the following day. The citation for his VC was published in the *London Gazette* of 8 June 1917 as follows:

> Oswald Austin Reid 1st Battn. King's (Liverpool Regt.). attached 1st Battn. Loyal North Lancashire Regt. For most conspicuous bravery in the face of desperate circumstances. By his dauntless courage and gallant leadership he was able to consolidate a small post with the advanced troops on the opposite side of a river to the main body, after his line of communications had been cut by the sinking of the pontoons. He maintained this position for thirty hours against constant attacks by bombs, machine-gun fire, with the full knowledge that repeated attempts at relief had failed, and that his ammunition was all but exhausted. It was greatly due to his tenacity that the passage of the river was effected on the following night. During the operations he was wounded.

On 24 April 1917 Capt. Reid was made second-in-command of his battalion and on 10 May he was promoted to acting major. On 14 May 1917 he left Basra and was invalided home to recover from his wounds, then given a month's leave in South Africa. On 10 June he relinquished his acting rank and on 22 July was given a hero's welcome in Johannesburg, where he was formally greeted by the Deputy Mayor and a member of the local recruiting committee. He left South Africa on 13 August and was Mentioned in Despatches on 15 or 18 August by Sir Frederick Maude. He rejoined his battalion on 11 October and was wounded shortly after he had assumed command of C Company, a position that he had to relinquish four days later as he was suffering from an inflammation of the knee. He was invalided to India, leaving Basra on 18 November 1917 to have his knee cartilage replaced. He was then Mentioned in Despatches a second time in December in connection with the capture of Baghdad.

Back in Johannesburg and on the fourth anniversary of the outbreak of the war in 1914, a 15,000-strong crowd showed up in front of the city hall in order to witness a unique ceremony at which Reid's father was presented with a special 'Sword of Honour', a presentation by the Mayor made to him for his son being the first locally born man to win the VC. The gold scabbard was suitably engraved and bore the badge of his regiment. It had cost £60 and was subscribed to by 600 people. The crowd called on Reid senior to draw the sword's blade and show them. Oswald was unable to be there as he was still serving in Mesopotamia. In April 1919 he left for service in Russia.

Oswald Reid, the third child in a family of seven, was born in Johannesburg on 2 November 1893. He was the eldest of three sons, the others being Victor and Clifford, and he also had four sisters. His father, Harry Austin Reid, was a pioneer architect of Johannesburg and formerly a captain in the commander-in-chief's bodyguard regiment (Lord Robert's Regiment). He had been awarded medals for the South African Wars of 1877, 1881 and 1899–1902. Oswald's mother, Alice Gertrude Reid, was also well connected, being a pioneer of both Johannesburg and Kimberley, daughter of George Bottomley JP, Mayor of Kimberley and a Member of the Legislative Council for Griqualand West.

Oswald was educated at the Diocesan College, Cape Town, and later at St John's College, Johannesburg and at Radley College, England. He arrived at Radley in 1910, and though he was only 17 he could be taken for 21. Quickly showing his leadership qualities and nicknamed 'Kaffir Reid', he was appointed captain of cricket and rugby football, and was a senior prefect. In 1913, at Lord's, he captained the Public Schools Eleven in their match against the Marylebone Cricket Club (MCC). He was also a colour sergeant in the college OTC.

Reid became an agricultural student and was later given a position in the Agricultural Department in South Africa. However, the outbreak of war put an end to this and he joined the Army on 14 August 1914 as a second lieutenant in the 4th Battalion King's Liverpool Regiment. He was promoted to full lieutenant on 5 March 1915 and his battalion left for Le Havre, arriving the next day, and he began his service as bombing officer. His battalion was part of Sirhind Brigade (Lahore Division). Reid described his early life on the Western Front in a letter to his father three weeks later, in which he gave details of his experiences in the Battle of Neuve Chapelle.

> I am still safe and sound. We arrived in the firing line just in time to take part in the battle of Neuve Chapelle, which I dare say you have read about. It was simply terrific and was a most severe baptism of fire. We are fighting in co-operation with all the Indians. We have just come back from the trenches for a bit of a rest.... The British successes cost us very dear. Over a hundred officers were killed or wounded at Neuve Chapelle. Our regiment got off comparatively lightly but my two best friends were both bowled over. One was killed by a shell which struck a house in which several of us were sheltering. It left the rest of us absolutely unharmed, but tore him about most dreadfully. The shell fire out here is terrific at times. When we went up into action the British were bombarding with 137 big guns and the Germans were by no means slow to reply either. The Germans have exceptionally good snipers located all over the place, and one is always liable to get picked off unexpectedly.

A month later Reid was wounded by a gunshot to his scalp and in the centre of his left cheek from a grenade during the Second Battle of Ypres on 27 April. After this incident he wrote to the headmaster of St John's College, the Revd J.O. Nash:

> ... my wound is only a slight one in the head, and in another month I shall be quite healed.... It was in the recent fighting at Ypres. Our regiment has been remarkably busy since we got out here. We took part in the battle of Neuve Chapelle and again at Ypres. We have only been out a little over two months and yet we only have seven officers and about 300 men left of our original 30 officers and 1000 men. I have had some narrow escapes. If the bullet that wounded me had struck me ever so little lower I would have been killed outright. Time and again shells have burst within a few yards of me, and left me untouched. I have even had my glasses whisked out of my hand by shrapnel without being touched myself. We had to march to Ypres in a tremendous hurry. One day we marched 12 hours on end. The men are wonderful in these marches. It must be remembered that they carry an enormous weight on their backs. The war

> here is simply colossal. The Germans are up to every vile trick. They were making great use of the poisonous gas at Ypres. It is much more painful than a wound and the men who get gassed are ghastly to see. Their shells have also got some poisonous gases in them. They nearly blind you if they burst near by. What has struck me most has been the marvellous imperturbability and cheerfulness of the British soldier. They face death as if it was a common occurrence. One cannot help keeping cool oneself when all the men behave like that. One soon becomes quite callous at the front and can easily bear to see a shell kill several men, and sometimes a best friend, without any undue emotion. The loss of life is quite terrible. Neuve Chapelle and the roads leading to it were a simple shambles.

Not surprisingly Reid suffered from headaches, but they gradually lessened and he appeared before medical boards on 3 and 26 May and 16 July 1915. On 28 August he was back in France, this time with the 1st Battalion, 6th Infantry Brigade, 2nd Division, and on 17 December was promoted to captain. On 15 February 1916 he wrote again to the Revd Nash:

> I feel quite proud to think that I am serving as a captain in the first battalion of the finest and oldest of British Regiments. Spring is stirring both armies to activity, just now and we all expect to have a go through the awful inferno of attacking or being attacked before long. It is unfortunate that one's intellect seems to become temporarily dulled on these occasions, otherwise it would be too terrifying for anything. It's just a regular tornado of every kind of death-dealing missile imaginable. The old methods of war must seem quite fairly peaceful – bullets, bayonets and some shells. But now-a-days there are also trench mortars, machine guns in plenty, rifle grenades. Mines, gas bomb and even liquid fire. Liquid fire isn't very common, but the others are often met with. So you can see that short hundred yards or so of ground between two trenches hold a ten to one chance of a wound in crossing them...
>
> The general opinion out here is that we really have got the upper hand of the Germans and we all hope to settle this matter this summer.

On 25 April 1916 Reid was wounded in the face at Arras and left France on 6 May, arriving back in England on the same day. By then he would probably have been Mentioned in Despatches on at least two occasions, but the death of his commanding officer prevented this. His address from 29 May 1916 to 3 July 1916 was a hospital at 27 Berkeley Square, London.

Reid was transferred to Peshawar, India on 21 August for service with the 2nd Battalion, who had been in India since the beginning of the war. He took part in the Mohmand operations against the hill tribes and served in India until he embarked at Karachi for Mesopotamia on 8 November and disembarked at Basra six days later. He was now attached to the 6th Loyal North Lancashire Regiment, 38th Infantry Brigade, 13th (Western) Division, and joined them in the field a week later on the 16th. His division was now part of the Mesopotamia Expeditionary Force and Reid was to take part in the operations at Kut-el-Amara, Baghdad and Samarrah.

On 4 December 1916 he wrote the following to his father:

> I have arrived out here safely and am attached to the above regiment [6th Bn. LNL]. I have a double company to command, and am first on the list for second-in-command of the battalion. This is a new young battalion. The country is all as flat as a pancake, absolutely devoid of trees; in fact it's nothing but a dry desert, and one gets awfully tired of looking at nothing at all. When I joined the battalion they were down the line refitting, now we are on our way up again with all sorts of rumours and desperate deeds to be done. Personally I think they are only rumours. In any case the Turk seems to be much more of a sportsman than the German.

It was almost a matter of time before such a natural leader of men as Oswald Reid won a Victoria Cross, which he duly achieved in the attempts to cross the Diyala River in March 1917. He arrived in Salonika on 20 December 1918 and was posted to the 2nd Gloucestershire Regiment, 82nd Infantry Brigade, 27th Division and left for the UK on 5 January 1919.

After the war Reid was decorated by the King in the ballroom of Buckingham Palace on 22 February 1919 and was accompanied by Victor, one of his younger brothers, who was training as a pilot with the RAF. On 1 November 1919 Reid attended an old boys' meeting at Radley College.

At some point he left for Russia as a member of the Slavo-British Legion Force to relieve the White Russians in their struggle against the Bolsheviks. On 6 February 1920 he was discharged from military embodiment when back in Johannesburg and became the Secretary of the Comrades of the Great War League. He resigned his commission, keeping the rank of captain. A few weeks later, on 1 April, he resigned from this position too and served in the Transvaal Scottish Regiment as a captain. He then decided to take up politics and in March stood unsuccessfully for the Troyeville constituency.

There is little doubt that his wounds and service in the First World War had undermined Reid's health and in the autumn be became ill with gastroenteritis and pneumonia. With little in the way of reserves of strength, he was unable to fight it off and died in hospital on 27 October 1920. At his military-style funeral four days later, the guard was formed by St John's College Cadets. The Revd Clement Thomson from St John's College officiated and at the graveside said: 'It was what we expected of him. His powers of leadership were the powers that come from a man who leads and does not order others to do what he is afraid to do himself.' Reid's Grave Number Reference in Braamfontein Cemetery is 22932, EC Section. Two years after his death on 31 July 1922, a special VC memorial was unveiled in the same cemetery by his aunt, Mrs W.K. Tucker. Once more cadets from St John's took part, together with other service personnel, relatives and friends. The SA Police band and Transvaal Scottish pipe band were also in attendance.

Reid's name is listed on the South African Memorial at Delville Wood Museum Somme area, which has a permanent exhibit on South Africans who won the VC during the First World War. His decorations are in the collection of the South African Military Museum, Johannesburg, as is his sword. Apart from the VC, his medals include the 1914–15 Star, BWM, VM (1914–1918), King of Italy's *Medaglia Al Valore Militare* (31 August 1917) and Mentioned in Despatches. He was the first Radleian VC to be commemorated at Radley College, Oxfordshire, where his name was included in the Book of Remembrance together with a raised map showing where he won his VC.

C. MELVIN

Istabulat, 21 April 1917

Six weeks after the crossings of the River Diyala on 8/10 March in which two VCs were won, followed by the British entrance into Baghdad, two more were gained over two days at Istabulat. The war diary of the 7th (Indian) Division gives a detailed account of the strongly defended Turkish positions at Istabulat and notes dryly:

> It was a difficult position to attack. A turning movement against the enemy's right flank was not considered practicable owing to the heat and want of water. A frontal attack south of the railway against such strong trenches and over such open ground was uninviting. The best chances of success appeared to lie in an attack north of the Dujail.

A brigade attack north of the River Dujail was decided upon, with another brigade in support to the south of the river, which would make a frontal attack once the attack to the north had cleared the enemy from the river banks.

The 21st Brigade was chosen to assemble on the north side of the river and was due to attack at 5 a.m. The other brigades involved were the 19th and the 28th. At 5.05 a.m. the 21st Brigade moved forward and one of their battalions, the 2nd Black Watch, moved along the north or left bank of the river with their left flank protected by a battalion from the 19th Brigade, the 28th Punjabis.

The objective were the redoubts to the extreme left of the enemy's position, and then the three battalions were to make an attack on the

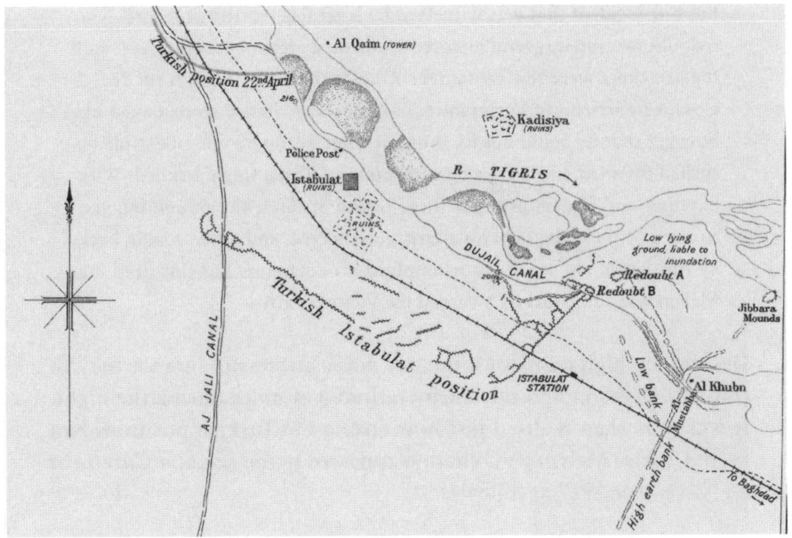

Istabulat, 21 April 1917.

redoubt at Dujail. Initial progress was very rapid, and by 7 a.m. the first redoubt had been captured and entered by the 8th Gurkhas and the 2nd Black Watch. However, these two battalions began to lose men when the Turkish resistance stiffened and the attackers were pushed back in a counter-attack by a determined enemy. They later recovered and managed to hang on to the eastern side of the redoubt for the rest of the day.

The Black Watch regimental history expanded on the role of the 2nd Black Watch in the recapture of the redoubt and noted: 'that what The Black Watch once had held, it should again hold and keep, and that the redoubt they had set forth to capture should be definitely theirs...'

A fresh assault was duly organised, but the losses of four company commanders, other officers and men were very high. Despite these losses there was little wavering in morale and within fifteen minutes the whole redoubt had been recaptured and its forward trenches occupied. Many of the enemy troops who had not become casualties were driven back in the face of intense fire. The battalion history commented:

> But one incident that was witnessed by several is worthy of record. The redoubt measured several hundred yards on its front and side faces, and the attackers were few in number. One of these, Pte Melvin (of No. 2 Coy), of Kirriemuir, Forfarshire, had by some chance so damaged his bayonet that he could not fix it on his rifle. Throwing his rifle aside he rushed forward and encountered a group of Turks single handed. With bayonet and fist he brought three to the ground; the remaining six, stunned by the violence of his attack, surrendered, and were brought back by this brave old soldier in triumph to his company. For this deed Pte Melvin was subsequently awarded the Victoria Cross.

Despite the high casualties, the day was a successful one for the 7th (Indian) Division and the enemy retired 3–4 miles during the night. It was only then realised just how strong the Turkish positions had been. Charles Melvin's VC citation appeared in the *London Gazette* of 26 November 1917 as follows:

> Charles Melvin, No. 871, Private, Royal Highlanders. For most conspicuous bravery, coolness and resource in action. Private Melvin's company had advanced to within fifty yards of the front-line trench of a redoubt, where, owing to the intensity of the enemy's fire, the men were obliged to lie down and wait for reinforcements. Private Melvin, however, rushed on by himself, over ground swept from end to end by rifle and machine-gun fire. On reaching the enemy trench, he halted and fired two or three shots into it, killing one or two enemy, but as the others in the trench continued to fire at him, he jumped into it, and attacked them with his bayonet in his hand, as owing to his rifle being damaged it was not 'fixed'. On being attacked in this resolute manner most of the enemy fled to their second line, but not before Private Melvin had killed two more and succeeded in disarming eight unwounded and one wounded. Private Melvin bound up the wounds of the wounded man, and, then driving his eight unwounded prisoners before him and supporting the wounded one, he hustled them out of the trench, marched them in and delivered them over to an officer. He then provided himself with a load of ammunition, and returned to the firing line, where he reported himself to his platoon sergeant. All this was done, not only under intense fire and machine-gun fire, but the whole way back Private Melvin and his party were exposed

> to a very heavy artillery barrage fire. Throughout the day Private Melvin greatly inspired those near him with confidence and courage.

The following addition to his entry in *The Victoria Cross 1856–1920* reads:

> Some of us would almost rather that Thrums had a V.C. than any other place whatever, and the fitting thing has happened. Charles Melvin, of the Black Watch, seems to be in other ways quite characteristic of the place. 'Ye see,' said his mother in an interview, 'he never tells me anything in his letters, and anything I heard about this was through some of his chums.' Thrums itself took the event with no less reticence. It hung out no flags; it rang no bells. And it probably thinks that Sir James Barrie, in sending a telegram to congratulate the hero, betrays an emotion only extenuated by his long residence in South Britain. 'One may note that the adjectival form of Kirriemuir is "Kirriemarian." Not "Kirriemuiran." As the London papers print it.' At least, the *Dundee Advertiser*, which ought to be the better authority, gives the former spelling to Sir James Barrie's telegram.

Charles Melvin was born in Boddin Craig, Montrose, Angus, Scotland, on 2 May 1885. He was the second son of three, together with two sisters, of James Melvin, a ploughman, and Mrs Melvin. Mrs Melvin was employed outdoors, but she later worked in a factory. Charles Melvin enlisted on 4 April 1907 at the age of 20, having previously worked in the Kirriemuir Linen Works factory. He was to serve for twelve years in the Army and half of those were spent in India before the war began, when by coincidence he was due for some leave. Instead, his division, the Meerut Division, left Karachi on 21 September 1914 and arrived at Marseilles on 12 October 1914 and was soon in action. On 5 December 1915 the division left for Mesopotamia, arriving at Basra on New Year's Eve. The 2nd Black Watch was now with the 21st Brigade of the 7th (Indian) Division. Melvin's two brothers also took part in the war: James, the eldest, served in France; and the youngest, David, in Macedonia.

After Melvin carried out the deed in April 1917 for which he was later awarded a VC, he wrote to his mother, who lived at 48 Glengate, Kirriemuir, saying that he had been given a gold watch by his commanding officer for his good work in the field, together with 'something else, but I don't know what yet'.

Melvin was wounded in France twice and once in Mesopotamia. At the end of January 1919 he returned home to a hero's welcome in his hometown of Kirriemuir and was met by a large crowd of well-wishers at the local railway station. The town Provost, together with members of the town council, greeted him as he stepped off the train amid considerable cheering. At the station entrance Melvin was met by a number of other soldiers who had been repatriated or were home on leave. A procession was then formed up and set off for number 48 Glengate to the sound of bagpipes. 'The Streets were thronged with people, and cheer after cheer was raised as he passed along.' A fund had been opened in Melvin's name and at some point he was presented with a number of War Bond Certificates. A few weeks later, on 25 February, Melvin got married in the South Parish Church manse (clergy house), Kirriemuir, to Miss Susan Irvine, third daughter of Mr David Irvine of Roselea, Kirriemuir.

After he left the Army as a private in 1919, Melvin was transferred to Class Z Army Reserve on 15 April and he was awarded his VC by the King at Buckingham Palace on 11 December. He also attended the House of Lords' VC Dinner in November 1929.

In civilian life Melvin worked as a caretaker. On 28 December 1930 he unveiled a memorial tablet to those men who belonged to South Church and who had served in the war. In November 1934 and 1936 he laid a wreath at the local war memorial. In 1936 he was interviewed by a reporter from the *Dundee Courier* at his home, and he came across as a very patriotic man who was only really at home when serving in the Army. When asked if people should fight in another war should one arise, he replied: 'If another country declared war on Britain I'd be the first to go again if I was able.' Another question was whether books reflected a true impression of war: 'No ... I've read many war novels. They're overdrawn. Too much hysteria and drinking. There were people whose nerves gave way, but that wasn't general. As for drinking in the frontline, it wasn't done. It wasn't as horrible as all that.' When pressed about winning his VC he replied:

> Well, you don't go out one day with the set intention in your mind to win one, you know. We were attacking a line of trenches in an open stretch of ground, and there was firing on us from three sides. Well, we got scattered a bit, and I found myself a few yards from the Turkish trenches. I looked round, and there wasn't a soul there beside me. I thought of going back. Then I thought if I went back I'd be copped in the back. Rather be copped in the front if I'm going to be copped at all, I thought.... I went on because it was the common sense thing to do. I threw my grenades into the trench, killing some men, and jumped in. There was a scuffle, of course, and the Turks, having seen my grenades, and thinking possibly I had more, surrendered. As a matter of fact, I had none, and my rifle was unloaded.

Melvin continued that he liked the Turkish troops and that he dressed the wounds of one of them before taking eight men as prisoners.

In the late 1930s Melvin was employed as a caretaker at the Barrie Sports Pavilion and camera obscura on the hill and was issued with a uniform. He was popular with visitors. Sir James Barrie had made a gift of the pavilion to his native town. Melvin was one of six townsmen who acted as pallbearers for Barrie's coffin at his funeral in June 1937.

Melvin didn't enjoy the best of health and in January 1937 he had a bad accident in the high street when he broke his leg. Probably delighted at the prospect of getting back into the Army, when the Second World War broke out he immediately joined the Home Defence at Dundee. He was one of a unit of ex-servicemen which formed the Home Defence Company and who were issued with full equipment. Wearing a uniform of khaki trousers and tunic, the 380 men who were between the ages of 45 and 55 were also issued with gas masks and rifles, and began their drill training in Bell Street, Dundee. Apart from Melvin holding the VC, about thirty of the others held the DCM or the MM. Some of the men had even fought in the Boer War.

At this time Melvin's home address was 7 St Colm's Close, Kirriemuir. In May 1940, when on duty, he discovered a fire which had broken out. When scaling a wall he was overcome by smoke and fell 30ft to the ground.

Four years later Melvin himself was buried in the same cemetery as his mentor, Sir James Barrie, on 21 July 1941, having died at the early age of 56. It is not clear whether his war service and wounds were linked to his early death, although he was unwell in the late 1930s. He died at

94 Roods, Kirriemuir, on 17 July. A large gathering of people took part in his funeral, including ex-servicemen, members of the forces home on leave, members of the British Legion and many other people from the town. His flag-draped coffin was carried to the graveside by a bearer party from the Black Watch under the command of Capt. Collins MC, and members of the Polish Military, who were also present, took the salute. After her death, Susan Melvin was buried next to her husband in 1961.

In May 1980 the Melvins' twin nephews, David and Nicoll, born in 1929, were invited to the Black Watch's Gordon barracks, Bridge of Don, Aberdeen, for a special ceremony to honour their late uncle. The two brothers presented a new trophy to a newly formed platoon which was named after the Kirriemuir hero. It was to be awarded to the best downhill skier in each year's new Melvin platoon. The 'Charles Melvin Challenge Cup' was later awarded to Cpl Guthrie, the then Junior Army Champion downhill skier. Melvin's medals are with the Black Watch Museum in Balhousie Castle, Perth, and apart from his VC include the 1914 Star and clasp (5 August–22 November 1914), BWM (1914–21), VM (1914–19) and MiD Oakleaf, and King George VI Coronation Medal (1937). Melvin's name is also included on the town war memorial and he also has a street named after him.

Kirriemuir has links to three local men who won the VC, and together their names are included in a stone set into a walk way in Cumberland Close in 2008. The other two men are Charles Lyell and Richard Burton. This form of commemoration pre-empts the British government's own idea of a design of paving stones to commemorate winners of the VC, and hopefully one will be placed in a suitable place in Kirriemuir in 2017.

J.R.N. GRAHAM

Istabulat, 22 April 1917

On 22 April 1917, the second day of operations at Istabulat, Turkish troops launched a heavy counter-attack on the 56th Rifles, Frontier Force of the Indian Army, in which Lt John Graham was serving with his 136th Machine Gun Company. He was instructed to move across open ground to a new firing position and his section suffered heavily from rifle and machine-gun fire. However, this did not deter him from directing his guns on the Turkish troops assembling for their attack.

Reduced to only one gun, he continued to keep it in action until he was wounded a second time. He was then forced to retreat and quickly rendered his gun useless to the enemy. After retiring from the position he acquired a Lewis gun, which he continued to use until he ran out of ammunition. By this time he had been wounded for a fourth time; he was weak from loss of blood and unable to take further part in the operation.

Graham is mentioned in *Surgery on Trestles* as he had come into the field ambulance:

> He had bullets through his legs and arms – eight in all; but the shot that knocked him out had passed through his neck from side to side. Miraculously, it had touched no vital structure. He was full of cheer, the life and soul of the officer's tent; afterwards, in India, he made a good recovery.

For his great gallantry Graham was awarded the VC, which was published in the *London Gazette* of 14 September 1917 as follows:

> John Reginald Noble Graham, Cap., Machine Gun Corps. For most conspicuous bravery, coolness and resource when in command of a Machine Gun Section. Lieut. Graham accompanied his gun across open ground under very heavy rifle and machine-gun fire, and when his men became casualties he assisted in carrying the ammunition. Although twice wounded he continued during the advance to control his guns, and was able with one gun to open an accurate fire on the enemy, who were massing for a counter-attack. This gun was put out of action by the enemy's rifle fire, and he was again wounded. The advancing enemy forced him to retire, but before doing so he further disabled his gun, rendering it useless. He then brought a Lewis gun into action with excellent effect till all the ammunition was expended. He was again severely wounded, and forced through loss of blood to retire. His valour and skilful handling of his guns held up a strong counter-attack, which threatened to roll up the left flank of the brigade, and this averted what might have been a critical situation.

In addition to the above citation, an entry in *The Victoria Cross 1856–1920* adds the following:

> This took place on 22 April, 1917, on the second day of the fighting near Istabulat, the culminating point in the operations which led to the fall of Samana, the railhead about 70 miles north of Baghdad. The brigade found the Turks hastily but fairly securely dug in about three or four miles from the position from which they had been driven out the previous day. The enemy's left rested on the Tigris, and their right stretched beyond the Baghdad–Samana Railway. It was from the railway embankment that they developed the counter-attack about five o'clock in the evening.

After recovering from his wounds in India, Graham returned as a company commander in Mesopotamia on 7 October 1917 with the rank of major. He remained there for three months before his company, the 136th, was transferred to Palestine. He returned to England in October 1918 and was soon demobilised.

Once Baghdad had been captured on 11 March 1917, the need for continuous action was reduced and, during the heat of the summer, Gen.

Maude left the Turkish Army undisturbed. Not surprisingly, the enemy had lost heart and was no longer willing to continue taking on the British. However, the German Gen. von Falkenhayn had by now taken command of the Turkish troops and was hoping to strike back at the British.

The remaining actions during 1917 mainly took place on the River Euphrates at Ramedi, where the Turkish Army had an outpost which was to be used as a point of concentration for a new attack against Baghdad. In September, a Turkish position at Tikrit was attacked.

Although his most important work had been done, the British force was dealt a severe blow on 18 November when their commander, Gen. Maude, died of cholera. He was buried at Baghdad (North Gate) War Cemetery where a special tomb was later erected. (At the time of writing, the cemetery has become a jungle of weeds and rubbish.) Ever popular with his troops, Maude had taken over command in August 1916 and was responsible for recapturing Kut-el-Amara and taking Baghdad.

On 26 March 1918 the British cavalry had great success at Khan Baghdadi. After achieving the impossible during an arduous cross-country advance in very rough terrain, they managed to encircle the enemy and capture 5,000 prisoners. The remainder of the enemy force fled towards Aleppo.

In August 1918 a small Anglo-Indian force reached Baku on the northern frontier of Persia and Afghanistan, where the Germans were trying to raise Muslim support for an attack towards the Khyber Pass and into India. Two months later, the last battle of the Mesopotamian Campaign took place near the ruins of the ancient city of Assyria, where the enemy held strong forward positions in the mountains. Clearly a frontal attack was not possible and, as they lacked essential transport, the British were forced to attack along the line of the River Tigris. The British plan was to make a series of raids which were strong enough to convince the enemy to concentrate his forces in the wrong positions. Simultaneously, and despite the appalling terrain, the British carried out a successful encircling movement and managed to force the Turkish forces to abandon their stronghold.

The war in Mesopotamia was now at an end. It was a clear victory for the Anglo-Indian force, which had endured four years of fighting a determined foe in very trying conditions. It is inevitable that the historical memory of this 'sideshow' is dominated by the tragic events of the five-month period in Kut-el-Amara when Gen. Townsend's force was locked up with ever dwindling supplies, followed by the 1,200-mile death march into captivity. Of the 11,800 men who left Kut-el-Amara with their escort on 6 May 1916, 4,250 either died during the march or in the Turkish camps which awaited them. During the march the British and Indian troops had been brutally treated, while Gen. Townsend, together with his officers, were excluded from this indignity and were catered for separately.

Having driven the Allied invasion force from the Gallipoli Peninsula in January 1916, from November 1916 to April 1917 the Turkish Army kept a whole Anglo-Indian division trapped inside the walls of Kut-el-Amara, which was a real shock for the British population. This shock deepened when news of the barbaric Turkish treatment of the remnants of the 6th (Indian) Division, who had become prisoners of war, was made public. It was therefore not at all surprising that a parliamentary inquiry into the running of the Mesopotamia Campaign was set up. In particular, a subsequent government report highlighted the utterly appalling conditions of the wounded when travelling in hospital ships bound for Basra.

Once Kut-el-Amara had been recaptured and Baghdad taken without opposition in the spring of 1917, the British command ran a sensible and well-organised campaign for the remainder of the war.

John Reginald Noble Graham was born at 1 Alipore Lane, Calcutta, on 17 September 1892, the eldest of three sons of Sir John Frederick Noble Graham, 2nd Baronet of Larbert and Dunipace in the County of Stirling and an East India merchant, and his wife, Irene Maud Graham (née Campbell). 'Reggie', as he was known, was educated at Cheam School, Eton, and Trinity College, Cambridge, and steered the Trial Eights boat race at Eton (1910) and Cambridge (1911).

The young man joined the 9th Argyll and Sutherland Highlanders at Dumbarton Castle on 15 January 1915 as a second lieutenant and was seconded to the Machine Gun Corps on 22 June 1916. He was soon promoted to captain on 13 July. After serving with the 9th Argyll and Sutherland Highlanders for nearly two years at home, he left for Mesopotamia in September and remained there until 22 April 1917. He was in command of a section of the 136th Machine Gun Company, which was operating with the 56th Rifles (Frontier Force), Indian Army.

Graham was decorated with the VC by the King in the ballroom of Buckingham Palace on 13 December 1918, a few weeks after the Armistice. On his return home to Cardross, he was met at the railway station by a large crowd and was immediately 'chaired' (carried on a chair) to a waiting car to take him to an official welcome.

On 11 January 1919 Graham ceased to be a member of the Machine Gun Corps and his name was listed with the Reserve of Officers on 23 November 1921. He relinquished his commission on 30 September 1921, but retained the rank of major. On 22 April 1922 he received a commission in the Calcutta Light Horse.

Between the wars Graham joined the family business of William Graham & Co., East India merchants in Calcutta. In November 1920 he married Rachel Septima, daughter of Col Sir Alexander Sprott Bt, CMG (Order of St Michael and St George), in Bombay and the couple had two children: Lesley, born in 1921, and John, born in 1926.

On 10 May 1925 Graham was one of four holders of the VC who attended the unveiling of the Machine Gun Corps Memorial in London by the Duke of Connaught. The other VCs were Lt A.E. Ker, Lt W.A. White and L/Cpl H. Mugford. In November 1929 he also attended the House of Lords' VC Dinner. Seven years later Graham succeeded to the baronetcy on the death of his father on 25 November 1936; his family motto was 'Forget not'.

On the outbreak of the Second World War, Graham received a temporary commission in the Argyll and Sutherland Highlanders. Holding the rank of lieutenant colonel he served on the War Office staff, Essex Division and Scottish Command 1942–46, and his final appointment was A/Q Movement HQ. He was made an OBE (Order of the British Empire) in 1946.

By 1959 Graham had matured into a very distinguished-looking man with white hair and moustache, and was often pictured wearing a bowler hat at various functions and gatherings. In the late 1950s he was made Gentleman Usher of the Green Rod to the Most Noble Order of the Thistle, a position that he held until 1979. One of his duties was to escort the Queen at the Order's annual service held in St Giles Cathedral. His son and heir, Sir John Alexander Noble Graham KCMG, was British Ambassador to Teheran in the late 1970s during the Iranian Revolution.

Graham was keen on outdoor pursuits such as fishing, riding and shooting, and his other activities included watercolour painting and compiling doggerel verse. His home was 38 Findhorn Place, Edinburgh, and he died in the city after an operation on 6 December 1980. His funeral service was held in St John's Church, Princes Street, on 11 December, followed by cremation at Morton Hall Crematorium. His ashes were buried at the foot of a large memorial cross in the grounds of the crematorium. His decorations and medals are held by the Museum of the Argyll and Sutherland Highlanders in Stirling Castle. Apart from the VC and OBE, they include the BWM, VM (1914–19), Defence Medal (1939–45), War Medal (1939–45), King George V Silver Jubilee Medal (1935), King George VI Coronation Medal (1937), Queen Elizabeth II Coronation Medal (1953) and Queen Elizabeth II Silver Jubilee Medal (1977). A diary which covers part of his war service is kept in the Imperial War Museum's archives.

PALESTINE

J.M. Craig

Near Gaza, 5 June 1917

The Suez Canal in Egypt, gateway to India and the Far East, was opened in 1869. Towards the end of the nineteenth century, Britain's Consul General virtually governed Egypt as a colony of the British Empire. On 18 December 1914, after hostilities had been formalised, the country was confirmed as a British Protectorate. However, not everyone was happy with this arrangement and there were increasing demands for the establishment of a regional United Arabia. In addition, and not to be outdone, Jewish interests were focused on Palestine, with hopes of establishing a new state within its borders. In 1908 the discovery of oil at the head of the Persian Gulf renewed political interest in the Middle East. It was also during this same period that the Royal Navy was busily making the changeover from coal to oil-fired ships and would very soon need a regular and large supply of oil.

The 500-year-old Turkish-based Ottoman Empire was keen to keep a hold on the region, but Britain, France and Germany also had interests in the area. A German–Turkish alliance would help her to push Britain out of the region, which in turn would threaten Britain's interests in India. The first German initiative was to build a railway which would run from Berlin to Baghdad; by August 1914, the line was only 400 miles short of completion. The Kaiser had also made strong overtures to Turkey and discussed the possibility of combining their two armies in the region, with the Germans supplying the brains, cash and leadership, and the Turks providing the greater part of the manpower.

When two ships being built for the Turkish Navy by the British were confiscated by the Allies, the Kaiser quickly offered the Turkish Navy two replacements, namely the battle cruisers *Goeben* and *Breslau*. These two ships wasted no time and anchored in the Dardanelles on 10 August 1914.

On 1 November Turkey, which had initially been politically neutral, declared war on Britain and France, and the action was reciprocated by the Allies four days later. The Ottoman Empire, of which Turkey was an integral part, was determined to conduct a Muslim holy war (*jihad*) against France, Russia and Britain. The Ottoman/Turkish Army consisted of 600,000 troops, and together with Germany would provide the Allies with a considerable threat.

In 1914 Egypt was desperately needed as a base for the Allies to use in the Middle East Campaign, and, in particular, the Suez Canal, Port Said and the town of Alexandria, north-west of Cairo. In effect,

South-west of Gaza, 5 June 1917.

Port Said guarded the Suez Canal and, in turn, controlled the supply of troops and men to the Middle East, particularly to Gallipoli.

In early February 1915 the Turkish Army launched what was a weak attack against the British defences on the Suez Canal between Lake Timsah and the Great Bitter Lake. The intention was to breach the canal defences and move deeper into Egypt, where, once in control, they would proclaim an Islamic revolt against the occupying powers. However, they did not succeed and Indian troops pushed them back towards Palestine. After the Allies had completed their evacuation from the Gallipoli Peninsula in January 1916, Turkey was able to release many of its troops to reinforce their presence in Mesopotamia, Palestine and Syria.

A second Turkish attempt to invade the Protectorate of Egypt took place in Easter 1916, but again without success. In the spring of 1916 the Egyptian Expeditionary Force was formed under the command of Lt Gen. Sir Archibald ('Archie') Murray, who had served on the staff at Mons in August 1914 and in later battles. From his orders it would have been made quite clear that he was to carry out any operations with the minimum of personnel, as the Western Front was the main theatre of war and where the final outcome would be decided. Not content with just 'sitting around' on the banks of the Suez Canal, he drew up a plan for using a mobile force which would eventually be based in the town of El Arish.

The British were seemingly not in a hurry to make an advance of their own, and several factors would have contributed to this inertia. In particular, the summer weather would make conditions very difficult to fight in. The problems of how to maintain a continuous supply of water for both horse and man also had to be addressed, as well as a railway line which would need to keep up with any military advance. It was considered, therefore, that the winter months would be a far better time to attack the outposts of the Turkish Army.

Meanwhile, during the summer the Turkish Army had increased its strength, and in August made an attack against British positions at Rumani, 20 miles to the east of the Suez Canal. But once again the Turkish troops were soundly defeated. With the failure of the enemy attacks, the British decided to try to clear the Turks out of the Sinai Peninsula between the Gulf of Suez and Palestine, an area which was part of the Turkish Empire. By December 1916 the British Army, which included a strong yeomanry element, with the assistance of ANZAC (Australia and New Zealand Army Corps) cavalry, had made steady progress, capturing El Arish and getting as far as Magdhaba to the south-west of Gaza. Although the Turkish defences were strong, they appear to have been taken by surprise by the Allied troops. In spite of hard fighting, the Turkish troops were surrounded and captured.

By January the British were 20 miles from Gaza as they reached the outskirts of the coastal town of Rafah. Here were based the only remains of the Turkish force in the Sinai Desert. After a bitter struggle the town was captured, which led to the surrender of the local Turkish forces. As a result, the whole of the Sinai was now in Allied hands and the threat to Egypt and the Suez Canal was removed.

During progress on the eastern boundaries of Egypt, the Allies had also been fighting Senussi tribesmen on Egypt's western frontier. The tribesmen had no quarrel with the British, but by December 1915 had been persuaded by the Turkish Army to attack the small British force. Taking up yeomanry and infantry who could be better employed on other fronts, this 'sideshow within a sideshow' eventually petered out in February 1917 when the power of the tribesmen was broken after a retreat.

On the eastern side of Egypt in early 1917, the next task for the Allied forces was to capture Palestine. The simplest plan seemed to be to make an advance along the line of the coast and then to fan out and eventually aim for Jerusalem. The key to initial progress in southern Palestine would be the capture of the ancient city of Gaza, which was likely to be much more of a challenge. The landscape was undulating, cultivated, cut by watercourses and included olive groves and cactus hedges, all of which would provide the Turks with strong natural defences.

The first attempt to capture Gaza was on 26/27 March 1917, and the advance was made by a small force of mounted troops and infantry. The force, under the command of Lt Gen. Sir Charles Dobell, advanced from Rafah along the coast and made an attack on the town from three different positions. Infantry made an attempt on Turkish positions from the south, while ANZAC infantry and cavalry attacked from the north and east. Simultaneously, a thick fog rolled in from the sea and created confusion before it lifted later on in the day. ANZAC troops did manage to enter the town, but were driven out as a result of a strong defence. In addition, enemy reinforcements had come from the rear of the British positions, so Dobell had no choice but to withdraw his troops at the southern end of the city. During the Allied assault, a vital problem was the constant lack of water for the British horses. The attempt on Gaza had been at a cost of nearly 4,000 casualties.

Although some lessons would have been learnt from this battle for control of Gaza, the next attempt was a real disaster for the Allies, partly as the Turkish defenders were now fully aware of a probable second attempt, which duly took place three weeks later. On 19 April, and despite the assistance of tanks, the British were beaten off again, this time with the loss of about 7,000 troops. The men were exhausted from fighting in a hot climate without adequate water supplies, and ammunition was also running short. At nightfall the attack was called off, and soon after Lt Gen. Dobell was relieved of his command. The days of Sir Archibald Murray were also numbered and he was duly replaced on 28/29 June 1917 by Gen. Edmund Allenby, previously commander of the Third Army in France.

However, it could not be said that Sir Archibald Murray was leaving in disgrace. His main legacy to Gen. Allenby was to lay the foundations of what was eventually to be a very successful British campaign in Palestine, something which Allenby fully recognised. The main concern for the campaign in Palestine was the difficulties of supply, so the pushing forward of a railway system was the first priority.

It will not come as any surprise to learn that no VCs were won during this period, and the first award was gained between the Second and Third Battles of Gaza by a young second lieutenant, J.M. Craig, from the 1/4th (T) Royal Scots Fusiliers, attached to the 1/5th battalion, on 5 June.

The 1/4th (T) Battalion Royal Scots Fusiliers and the 1/5th Battalion were both part of the 155th Infantry Brigade, 52nd (Lowland) Division. The division had served in Gallipoli and the crossing of the Sinai Desert from the Suez Canal, and had subsequently fought in the First and Second Battles of Gaza in March and April respectively. While plans were laid for a third attempt on Gaza, the destruction of a strong Turkish redoubt to the west of Gaza, named 'Sea Post' by the

5th King's Own Scottish Borderers, had led to a series of successful raids which successfully harassed the enemy positions. This situation was to continue for four months, but in early June the exasperated Turkish troops decided to strike back. At 6.15 a.m. on 5 June 1917, Turkish troops attacked British advanced positions a few hundred yards north of Samson's Hill at a position on Umbrella Hill. According to the battalion war diary:

> ... the first warning of enemy activity was given by sentries in the Firing Line who saw one of our men in the trench bayonet-fighting a Turk on the parapet... Soon after a grenade fell on the position. The rushed raid on Day Post left three men dead, two seriously wounded and the capturing of three other men, who were possibly wounded. Immediately Sec Lt J.M. Craig under heavy fire had taken out a party to see off the enemy who had already cleared off and to try and bring in the wounded. However the enemy fired heavily upon them from Umbrella Hill with rifles and a machine gun, and latterly turned on his 'whiz-bang' battery which fired H.E. and shrapnel; but our men showed the utmost contempt of danger, and went cooly on with their work. There was no lack of willing helpers, and the conduct and gallantry was a thing to be proud of.

It seems that in their attempts to rescue the wounded under heavy fire, the rescuers became extremely exposed to injury and Craig rescued Sgt Walker and then the medical officer, Capt. Gardner DSO, RAMC, who had been shot in the leg and had his thigh broken. Craig, by now wounded himself, brought the doctor in under the cover of a fig tree, 'where he scooped with his hands shelter for both these wounded'. Soon after, the Turkish 'whiz-bang' was silenced by a British battery and the post was later rebuilt. For his bravery and devotion to duty Craig was awarded the VC, which was published in the *London Gazette* on 2 August 1917 as follows:

> John Manson Craig, Second Lieut., 1st/4th Battn., attached 1st/5th Battn., Royal Scots Fusiliers. For most conspicuous bravery on the occasion of an advanced post being rushed by a large party of the enemy. This officer immediately organized a rescue party, and the enemy was tracked over broken country back to his trenches. Second Lieut. Craig

> then sent out his party to work removing the dead and wounded. During the course of this operation his men came under heavy rifle and machine-gun fire. An N.C.O. was wounded, and the medical officer who went out to his aid was also severely wounded. Second Lieut. Craig at once went out to their assistance, and succeeded in taking the N.C.O. under cover. He then returned for the medical officer, and whilst taking him to shelter was himself wounded. Nevertheless by great perseverance, he succeeded in rescuing him also. As the enemy continued in a heavy fire, and, in addition, turned on shrapnel and high explosives, Second Lieut. Craig scooped for cover for the wounded, and thus was the means of saving their lives. These later acts of bravery occurred in broad daylight, under full observation of the enemy and within close range. On three previous occasions this officer has behaved in a conspicuously brave manner, and has shown an exceptional example of courage and resource.

In a copy of the *Boy Scouts Headquarters Gazette* of October 1917, one of the men whose life had been saved by Craig's prompt actions told the story of what happened:

> The enemy rushed one of our posts. Word was passed on to Lieutenant Craig, who immediately went to relieve the post. After a hard fight the enemy were driven out and most of the prisoners released. We harassed the enemy right back to their trenches. Then Lieutenant Craig set about removing the wounded and the dead. It was while on this work that the enemy opened heavy fire from machine guns and from some of their batteries in the rear. For over an hour we were on the job of collecting wounded, with high exploding shells bursting all around. Every minute we were liable to be flung into the air with our stretchers and wounded by the violent explosions. The enemy also put snipers on to us. Lieutenant Craig didn't seem to mind in the least. He moved about under fire picking out the worst cases and having them removed. When the shell fire became hottest, he went into the thick of it and scooped out shelters for the wounded. Still under heavy fire he assisted to remove the wounded to these shelters. Had it not been for the way he stuck to us, every man would have been killed, for you can't lie wounded under shell-fire for very long without being finished off. I have never seen a braver officer than Lieutenant Craig. He was simply

> splendid, moving about there under heavy fire, all the time, and never thinking of himself.

John Manson Craig was born 5 March 1896 at Innergeldie, Comrie, Perthshire (now Tayside). He was the son of John Craig of Craigdarroch, Ayrshire, and Margaret Eleanora McCosh. Most of his schooling was spent at Morrison's Academy, Crieff (1905–14). During this period he became a boy scout with the 5th Perthshire Troop, Crieff. At the end of the summer term of 1914 he left for Trinity College, Cambridge, where he gained a science degree and became a member of the OTC. Eight months after the war began, he joined the Cameron Highlanders on 6 April 1915. After training he served with the 6th Battalion in France and saw action at Loos in September. He was then commissioned in the spring of 1916 and posted to the Royal Scots Fusiliers, serving in Egypt and Palestine. During the voyage he was placed in charge of a draft of men on board the *Ivernia* when it was torpedoed and sank.

In May 1917 Craig was wounded and, shortly after he had recovered, he rejoined his regiment and was awarded the VC for the deed near Gaza. Towards the end of the war he transferred to the RAF and was discharged from the services with the rank of lieutenant in 1919. He was presented with his VC by the King at Buckingham Palace on 10 December 1919.

Between the wars Craig spent seventeen years as an inspector with the Sudan Plantation Syndicate growing cotton in the Blue Nile Province. In 1931 he married Elizabeth Melville Henderson. In 1940 he returned home on leave and joined the RAF Police, serving for five years with the rank of wing commander, though he did not fly. After the war he retired to Comrie, where his hobbies included golf and gardening, and he also took an active interest in local affairs. At one point he was presented with a book of signatures of all the villagers in Comrie, a souvenir of which he was very proud.

During his life Craig was able to attend most of the VC functions, including the Buckingham Palace Garden Party on 26 June 1920, and the Cenotaph and Unknown Warrior services on 11 November 1920.

He also attended the House of Lords' VC Dinner in November 1929 and the VC centenary commemorations in London in 1956.

After a long illness John Craig died at Crieff Cottage Hospital on 19 February 1970 and was cremated at Perth Crematorium three days later. His ashes were buried in the family plot at Comrie Cemetery, reference 4489. He was survived by his wife and twin sons, John and Ronald, born in 1936, and a daughter, Nora, born in 1940. The family home was at Coneyhill, Comrie, and the VC is still in the family. His other medals included the 1914–15 Star, BWM, VM (1914–19), Defence Medal (1939–45), War Medal (1939–45), King George VI Coronation Medal (1937) and Queen Elizabeth II Coronation Medal (1953).

A.M. LAFONE

Beersheba, 27 October 1917

Taking over from Gen. Sir Archibald Murray, Gen. Allenby arrived in Cairo on 27 June 1917 after an unsuccessful command of the Third Army on the Western Front in the Battle of Arras in April. He took over the Egyptian Expeditionary Force on 28/29 June. Such was the swiftness of his becoming acquainted with the nature of his new command that within a week he had stamped his personality and authority on the seasoned but badly demoralised forces in the region. One of his first decisions was to move his HQ from Cairo to Umm el Kelab, close to Rafah and the border with Palestine. He became instantly popular with officers and other ranks, and, using a contemporary description of his methods, 'he was a man you could do business with'. Within a very short time he visited members of his forces, which consisted of a desert mounted corps and two infantry corps. His method was to make a whistle-stop tour of his forces to cast an expert eye over man, horse, transport and weaponry, pointing out any obvious deficiencies, and also to listen to the men on the ground. A major offensive was soon planned and the scheme presented to the British War Cabinet in July. It became known that Prime Minister David Lloyd George famously wanted to make a present of the capture of Jerusalem to the British people in 1917.

During the Egyptian and Palestine Campaigns, there were two fundamental problems which had to be addressed and solved, namely transport and the need for a constant supply of water. A railway had been constructed for the movement of troops and supplies in the crossing of the Sinai Desert, and water was taken by train. Later, a supply of water was drawn from Kantara on the Suez Canal to positions close to Beersheba, south-west of Gaza.

In order to break the deadlock over the vital capture of Gaza, a change of tactical thinking was required. The main Turkish defences in the southern part of Palestine stretched for 25 miles in a south-easterly direction from Gaza to Beersheba. With this length of line there were bound to be weak spots, including Beersheba itself, and Allenby was keen to identify them. In addition, considerable time and great ingenuity was spent in confusing the enemy about what would be the Allies' next move. This included the deliberate planting of misinformation. The final plan was for Gaza to be attacked, but for Beersheba to be the main objective.

The Yeomanry Division had served as detached brigades from 1915 and, together with the Desert Column, took part in the advance across the Sinai Peninsula from the Suez Canal. It was reorganised in August 1917 when, as the Yeomanry Mounted Division, it joined the Desert Mounted Corps. By October the Allied force, under its new commander, had been in entrenched positions on the Gaza–Beersheba road for several months. On 26 October, the 8th Mounted Brigade, on loan to the Australian Division, held a 12-mile outpost line from El Buggar to Point 510. The right of the line was held by the 1st County of London (Middlesex) Yeomanry, with the 3rd County of London Yeomanry on the left and the City of London Yeomanry in reserve. B Squadron were ordered to hold these trenches, but an enemy aeroplane observed their positions, and presumably the Turkish plan would have been to push the cavalry off the line El Buggar–Points 720–630–510 and make the Allied infantry fight for the ridge.

With the aim of occupying two hills at Points 720 and 630, a Turkish force, wearing slouch hats, made a bold surprise attack, after what had been a quiet night, against the Middlesex Yeomanry at 4.15 a.m. on 27 October. They were driven off twice and then made a dismounted attack and captured the post. Although the Yeomanry had put up a most gallant defence against an estimated force of 3–4,000 men, it was only a matter of time before they were overwhelmed. According to the war diary, their commanding officer, Maj. Alexander Lafone:

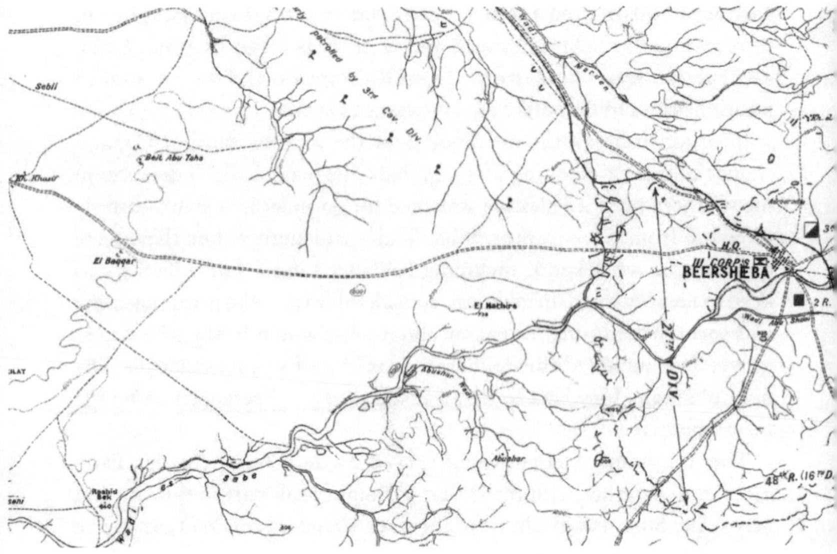

Beersheba, 27 October 1917.

… held 720 with two troops and put one troop on El Buggar Road and the other troop in close support between 720 and the El Buggar Road. This troop was sent to support Major Lafone and got as far as his led [*sic*] horses when they received a message from Major Lafone that they were to remain where they were for the present owing to heavy M.G. rifle and shell fire. At 6.30 the guns at Kasif were ordered to retire, as the Turks were working round the right flank, and there were no troops acting as escort. In the meanwhile a message was received from Major Lafone at 0640 saying 'Enemy estimated at 6 troops moving South East from Bir Imleh. There is also increased enemy activity on my East. I should like to be reinforced.' This was followed by another message received at 0720. 'I have driven off party of enemy, strength unknown at 0515; there appears to be considerable activity … I have only two troops here and two machine guns, no means of communicating with you except by despatch rider.' [Note: despatch riders and Very lights were the only means of communication.]

Two extra troops, which were the only reserves spare, were then sent to support him from the City of London Yeomanry, but they were held up by intense fire and never even reached Point 720. Meanwhile, the 1st County of London Yeomanry were being attacked on almost all sides and were being shelled heavily by high explosives and shrapnel:

> At 10.10 Major Lafone's last message was received: 'My casualties are heavy. Twelve stretcher-bearers required. I shall hold on to the last as I cannot get my wounded away.' At 11.15 a mass of horsemen were seen surging up upon 720, and it became obvious that the post had fallen, despite the extraordinarily gallant resistance put up by the garrison, of whom only four unwounded men escaped from the position. At 11.40, 2nd Lt. John observing that 720 was in the enemy's hands and that he was in imminent danger of being surrounded and entirely cut off, withdrew his troop via *Khasif* to *Imsiri*.

B Squadron casualties were two officers and eight other ranks killed, eight wounded and missing.

After Lafone's death, the few remaining men from the garrison withdrew, but several were hit as they ran back and at 11.15 a.m. the enemy swarmed over the British positions. However, the yeomanry had managed to delay the enemy progress sufficiently to allow for a relief by members of 158th Infantry Brigade and the 3rd Light Horse Brigade, which was organised later that evening when the line was reoccupied and the enemy forced to withdraw. As a consequence, the vital extensions being prepared for the Battle of Beersheba (Third Battle of Gaza) of railways, a pipeline and signal communications were saved from destruction by the enemy.

Not surprisingly, Maj. Lafone was awarded a posthumous VC, and in a letter his colonel later said of him:

> He held a post until only three unwounded men remained against vastly superior odds, and was one of the last to fall, but not before he had shown a magnificent example that he was able to hold his post from 3.45 in the morning until 11.30 ... He is deeply mourned by officers and men, and his squadron is inconsolable. Everybody loved him, and his loss is one it is quite impossible to replace.

Another who knew Lafone wrote:

> He was one of the most selfless men that ever lived, and had his life not been what it was he would not have been able to show the enduring bravery and absolute self-sacrifice which won for him the Victoria Cross. It was not won by one swift deed of courage in the heat of a charge.

After Lafone's death and according to his National Archive file, he was initially buried at 'Esani 1/20,000 T 13 about 150yds SSW of House on Hill 720 by a chaplain of the 2/4th R.W. Kents and later in Beersheba War Cemetery, Palestine, 25 miles south-east of Gaza and south-west of Beersheba'. The grave reference is Row Q, Grave 7. Also in the same cemetery are the graves of Capt. John Fox Russell VC and Lt Col Leslie Maygar VC.

The citation for Lafone's VC was published in the *London Gazette* on 18 December 1917 as follows:

> For most conspicuous bravery, leadership and self-sacrifice, when holding position for over seven hours against vastly superior forces. All this time the enemy were shelling his position heavily, making it very difficult to see. In one attack, when the enemy cavalry charged his flank, he drove them back with heavy losses, in another charge they left fifteen casualties within twenty yards of his trench, one man, who reached his trench, being bayoneted by Major Lafone himself. When all his men, with the exception of three, had been hit, and the trench which he was holding was so full of wounded that it was difficult to move and fire, he ordered those who could to move to a trench slightly in the rear, and from his own position maintained a most heroic resistance. When finally surrounded and charged by the enemy, he stepped into the open and continued the fight until he was mortally wounded and fell unconscious. His cheerfulness and courage were a splendid inspiration to his men, and by his leadership and devotion he was enabled to maintain his position, which he had been ordered to hold at all costs.

The Lafone family came from France and settled in England in the 1740s. Alexander Malins Lafone, one of several children, was born on 19 August 1870 at Cressfield, Crosby Road South, in the district of Waterloo, Liverpool. He was the eldest son of Henry Lafone of Knockholt, Kent, and his second wife, Lucy, daughter of David Malins of Edgbaston, Birmingham. His father was a hide and leather merchant and a partner in the family business. When business interests moved from Liverpool to London, the family moved to Court Lodge, Knockholt, Kent, in the 1870s. Alexander was educated at Dulwich College and became a member of the 3rd XV rugby team (1888–89 and 1889). From Dulwich he passed the entrance for Cooper's Hill, a Royal Engineering College based at Runnymede, and attended City and Guild's College, London. After studying engineering for two years at the Electrical Engineering Institute, South Kensington, and spending a year and a half at Messrs Marshall & Sons, Gainsborough, Lincolnshire, working in the workshops, Lafone was appointed assistant manager and engineer to the Jokai Tea Co., Assam, in 1894. Three years later in 1897, he joined his father in business at Butler's Wharf Ltd. He later became a director of several companies.

On 28 December 1899 Lafone changed course in his career when he joined the Montgomeryshire Yeomanry with the rank of sergeant, and in the following year served in the Second Boer War in South Africa. He took part in operations in the Transvaal, west of Pretoria, and was wounded in the right eye on 18 August. He later received the Queen's Medal and three clasps, sailing for England on 12 December. He was offered a commission, which was to be his second, when he became a member of the Middlesex Yeomanry on 14 August 1901.

The Middlesex Yeomanry had been raised in 1797 and served in mounted roles in the South African and First World Wars, and Lafone was promoted captain on 14 July 1902. He had previously held a commission as a second lieutenant in the Hertfordshire Imperial Yeomanry from 25 April 1901 until 19 June when he resigned.

Throughout his service years Lafone continued to hold onto his several directorships. However, in 1903 he left his father's business when he joined the Colonial Service and took up a post in Nigeria, West Africa. Unfortunately he was dogged by bouts of malaria and his Colonial Service career came to an early end; he returned home to Knockholt in order to recover from malaria. While back at the family home at Court Lodge, his mother died on 22 November 1910 and was buried in St Katherine's Church graveyard. Meanwhile, Lafone had become a partner in the firm of F.A. Roberts & Co., of Leadenhall Street in 1910/11.

A day before war broke out on 4 August 1914, the Middlesex Yeomanry were mobilised at Moulsford Camp in Berkshire. Lafone was now a major and the Middlesex Yeomanry, who had been renamed 1st County of London Yeomanry (Middlesex, Duke of Cambridge's Hussars, TF), assembled in Churn, Wiltshire, and they became part of the 2nd Mounted Division. In November they left for further training in Norfolk, and Lafone's regiment received orders to leave for the Middle East. They embarked at Avonmouth on 14 April 1915, arriving at Alexandria two weeks later. After service in Egypt, Lafone (known as 'Laffy') served in the Dardanelles, the Balkans and Palestine. He left for Gallipoli with his regiment and served in a dismounted capacity. At the end of the year the regiment returned to Alexandria, where their horses were returned. On 3 February 1916 Lafone left Port Said for leave in England, and on 4 March he returned to duty at the Suez Canal defences after his regiment had become part of the 8th Mounted Brigade. He embarked at Alexandria on board HT *Nitonian* on 12 November 1916 for Salonika, where he arrived five days later. Although his regiment returned to Egypt in June 1917, Lafone was at home from then until October, rejoining his colleagues in Palestine after they had finished their service in Salonika. Lafone was then drafted into the Yeomanry Mounted Division of the Desert Mounted Corps, but was killed in action in Palestine on 27 October 1917 during the action that won him the VC.

In his will, dated 17 August 1917, Lafone left £30,955 15*s* 8*d* and the grantees were his brother, the Ven. Henry Pownall Malins Lafone, Archdeacon of Furness, and Walter Erskine Stuart Menteth. His VC was presented to his brother on 2 March 1918. Henry lived at Cartmel Vicarage, Grange-over-Sands, Barrow-in-Furness, and at one time had been vicar of St George's Church in the same town.

In 1920 the Middlesex Yeomanry became a Territorial Army (TA) unit of the Royal Signals. In 1963 Lt Col S.J. Williams, in command of 47 Signal Regiment (Middlesex Yeomanry) TA, in talking about Lafone's action at the Supreme Headquarters Allied Powers Europe (SHAPE) with the then military representative of the Turkish Army, agreed with him that 'in recognition of the gallant stand of a brave soldier' the Turkish government would present a 'Cavalry lance to the Regiment at its Annual Camp' in 1964. However, this was not possible and the presentation was made in the following year by Maj. Gen. E. Alpkaya to the regiment, then in camp in France at Camp de Frileuse, on 10 July 1965. In return, Lt Col Williams presented a sword on behalf of the regiment, which was inscribed 'Presented by the Middlesex Yeomanry to the Turkish Cavalry with mutual respect for the bravery of Major A.M. Lafone VC on 27th October, 1917'.

In 1966 a Turkish flag was also presented to the Middlesex Yeomanry, which is used to commemorate the life of Maj. Lafone with an annual *In Memoriam* notice, as well as an annual Lafone Day. A service is also held in the crypt of St Paul's Cathedral.

Lafone's decorations apart from his VC and South African Medals included the 1914–15 Star, BWM and VM (1914–19). His VC is held in Dulwich College, where he is commemorated, and his name is also listed on the Regimental Memorial in St Paul's Cathedral, together with that of Lt Col Oliver Watson VC. Lafone's name is also commemorated on the village war memorial (1923) and with a memorial plaque in St Katherine's Church. The wording includes two very apt lines by Thomas Macaulay:

For how can man die better
Than facing fearful odds?

J. COLLINS

Wadi Saba, Beersheba, 31 October 1917

On 31 October 1917, in what became known as the Third Battle of Gaza, the Allies attacked the town of Beersheba on the Wadi Saba. They deliberately chose its weakest point of defence, namely the high ground from the south-west, as it would allow the attackers to look down over the town. As is so often the case in the Palestine Campaign, a regular water supply for both horses and men was a major problem, as too was transport. The name of Beersheba, a town of plentiful water, was a corruption of the Arabic for 'Seven Wells'.

The town was indeed successfully captured and 1,800 prisoners, together with nine guns, were taken. The final part of the capture was a dramatic charge by an Australian cavalry brigade brandishing bayonets. The good news was that, of the town's principal seventeen wells, thirteen were still intact.

At the other end of the Turkish defence line, 30 miles to the north-west at Gaza, which was heavily entrenched and wired, the Allies were also to be successful on the following day when they captured the outer defence of the town, a front of some 5,000yd. Assistance had been called for the day before from the Royal Navy, which bombarded the town on 30 October. Overall, fighting continued for six more days before Gaza was completely in Allied hands.

Preparation for the attack had been very thorough and every effort had been made to avoid detection of any signs of the extension of pipelines, railway lines, signal communications and all other signs of an impending attack. The Desert Mounted Corps, together with XX

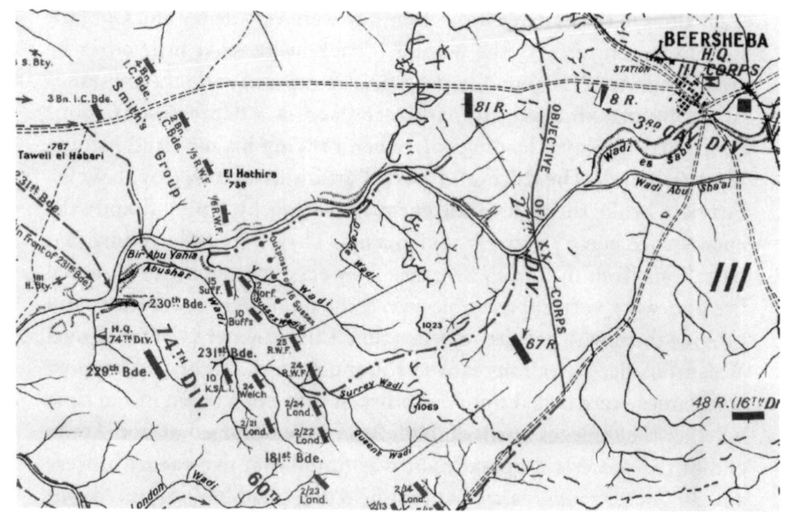

Wadi Saba, Beersheba, 31 October 1917.

Corps, were positioned on the right flank, and by 29 October the 74th (Yeomanry) Division, one of four divisions serving with the Desert Mounted Corps, had moved from the area behind Gaza and had taken up positions at Gamli before moving out to Khasif. The other three divisions were the 10th (Irish), 53rd (Welsh) and 60th (London). The 74th Division, together with the 60th, attacked positions on the south-west of the town between the Wadi Saba and the Khalasa–Beersheba road. Having taken on the main Turkish defence line, they then consolidated positions between the Wadi at points H.29. D.4. 8 and Wadi Saba. The Camel Brigade, assisted by two infantry battalions from the 53rd Division, were to attack to the north of Wadi Saba, and the remains of the 53rd were to cover the possibility of Turkish interference on the northern flank from their positions around Hareira.

The 25th Royal Welsh Fusiliers, 74th Division, advanced across a plain and were pinned down by machine-gun fire each time they breasted a rise. By 10.40 a.m. they were forced to lie out in the open, when 600yd from enemy lines, while the Allied artillery set about trying to destroy the enemy wire through an intense bombardment.

Casualties in the extreme heat of the day were very heavy and Cpl Jack Collins began to carry the wounded back using what little cover he could find. At 12.30 p.m. the attackers rose up and, with the assistance of strong machine-gun fire, advanced across a depression. Collins continued to play a leading role when rallying his men and leading his command. The 24th and 25th Battalions of the Royal Welsh Fusiliers broke through to the enemy positions by 1 p.m. despite the enemy wire being relatively undamaged. They were followed by two battalions from the 230th Brigade. They encountered heavy shrapnel fire and were very exposed; however, the numerous small wadis did provide them with a degee of protection. Unfortunately, the two Royal Welsh Fusilier Battalions moved too much to the right and support companies were called upon to assist. It was not known at the time whether the trenches north of Wadi Saba were occupied or not. At the end of the successful operation it was found that five enemy officers and 307 other ranks, as well as four field guns, had been captured, but the Allied cost was also high.

Cpl Collins deservedly won a VC not only for saving the lives of many of his comrades, but also in leading others to the attack and personally accounting for fifteen of the enemy with a Lewis gun. His citation was published in the *London Gazette* of 18 December 1917 as follows:

> 355652 ... Acting Corpl., Royal Welsh Fusiliers. For most conspicuous bravery, resource and leadership, when, after deployment, prior to an attack, his battalion was forced to lie out in the open under heavy shell and machine-gun fire, which caused many casualties. This gallant non-commissioned officer repeatedly went out under heavy fire and brought wounded back to cover, thus saving many lives. In subsequent operations throughout the day Corpl. Collins was conspicuous in rallying and leading his command. He led the final assault with the utmost skill, in spite of heavy fire at close range and uncut wire. He bayoneted 15 of the enemy, and with a Lewis gun section pressed on beyond the objective and covered the reorganization and consolidation most effectively, although isolated and under fire from snipers and guns. He showed throughout a magnificent example of initiative and fearlessness.

It has proved very difficult to pin down the actual birthplace of John (always known as Jack) Collins, who was a son of Thomas, a collier, and Mary Ann Collins. However, it was probably in the West Hatch, Bickenhall, Ashill, area south-west of Taunton. He was probably born on 10 September 1877, but this date is uncertain. John attended the village school at West Hatch and later the family moved a short distance to Wood Marsh, Windmill Hill, Ashill. When he was about 10 to 13 years old in the late 1880s his family moved to Merthyr, where they lived at 54 High Street, Penydarren, Glamorgan. After he finished his schooling, John was probably involved in the local mining industry. At the age of 18 he enlisted with the Royal Horse Artillery as a driver on 18 November 1895, and his service number was 12118.

Collins took part in the Boer War and was one of the first troops into Ladysmith. Later he served in India, before leaving the Army, possibly in 1907, after twelve years' service. Three of his brothers also served in the Boer War and their parents received congratulations from Queen Victoria. From then on the family were known as 'the fighting family of Penydarren'. John then worked as a tip labourer in Bedlinog Colliery, Penydarren.

When the war began, Collins was in his mid- to late 30s and enlisted in the Welsh Horse Yeomanry with the service number 340, being the second man from Penydarren to do so. In early 1915 the Welsh Horse were part of the North Midland Brigade of the 1st Mounted Division, training in the Diss area of Norfolk. They were soon transferred to the 1/1st Eastern Mounted Brigade and continued training in the Woodbridge area of Suffolk. On 25 September, the brigade sailed for Mudros from Liverpool on board the Olympic.

On 10 October they landed at ANZAC Cove and their brigade was attached to the 54th (East Anglian) Division in the role of dismounted cavalry. Their duties were to hold the extreme left of the ANZAC Front. Collins took part in the Gallipoli Campaign until December 1915, and later served in Egypt as a member of the Suez Canal Force, where his regiment was part of 3rd Dismounted Brigade. He had been promoted to sergeant on 31 October.

On 4 March 1917 the 1/1st Welsh Horse Yeomanry amalgamated with the Montgomeryshire Yeomanry and formed the 25th Royal Welsh Fusiliers, 231st Brigade. Collins later saw action in Palestine in the Second Battle of Gaza in April 1917, and he was awarded the DCM for his gallantry in action at Foka on 30 November (*London Gazette*, 1 May 1918). He was also Mentioned in Despatches by Gen. Sir Edmund Allenby on 16 January 1918. The DCM citation read as follows:

> For conspicuous gallantry and devotion to duty. As soon as the enemy opened fire at point blank range, he rallied all the men near him, took control of a portion of the line, and brought every available rifle to bear on the enemy. During the consolidation he did exceptionally good work, and later when the enemy counter attacked, went under heavy fire from post to post to see that they were being held to the best advantage. His ability and devotion to duty were of the highest order.

During a battalion parade at Ramallah, Collins was presented with the ribbons for the DCM and VC by Gen. Allenby. In May the 231st Brigade, 74th (Yeomanry) Division, left for France and Collins was presented with his VC by the King at Buckingham Palace on 1 June. He was later wounded in France on 8 October and promoted to acting quarter master sergeant. He was discharged from the Army for the second time on 20 February 1919.

Prior to the war Collins had married Mary Ellen O'Brien, daughter of John and Mary O'Brien, at St Illtyd's Roman Catholic Church, Dowlais, on 17 March 1910. They lived at 21 Caerhendy Street, Penydarren, Merthyr Tydfil, Glamorgan, and the couple had six sons and two daughters.

After his discharge from the Army, Collins worked as a security guard at the Dowlais Steelworks. In June 1920 he attended the VCs Garden Party at Buckingham Palace and the service at the Cenotaph on 11 November, followed by the burial of the Unknown Warrior in Westminster Abbey. In November 1929 he also attended the House of Lords' VC Dinner.

During the Second World War Collins served as a sergeant major in the Home Guard at Dowlais from 15 August 1940 to 20 September 1942.

After the war he attended the VE Parade on 8 June 1946 and the subsequent VC dinner at The Dorchester.

Jack Collins died at the age of 70 on 3 September 1951 in St Tydfil's Hospital, Merthyr, and was buried in the Roman Catholic section of Pant Cemetery, Merthyr Tydfil, Mid Glamorgan. A service was held at his home and his funeral was slightly delayed by an overtime ban by grave diggers, which led to many mourners being prevented from attending the service on 8 September. However, those who did attend the military funeral included his family, the Mayor of Merthyr, representatives of the British Legion and other ex-servicemen's organisations, as well as members of the Royal Welsh Fusiliers, who sounded the *Last Post* and fired a salute at the graveside. The reference of his grave is Plot XE, Grave 44, and the grave was unmarked for six years as his wife Mary couldn't afford the cost of a headstone. However, news of her plight leaked out and, with the financial assistance of the town and the British Legion, a stone was put in place in 1957.

Jack's wife was later buried alongside him, having died on 7 December 1968 at the age of 76.

The Royal Welsh Fusiliers Museum in Caernarfon Castle holds Collins' VC and his other decorations, which include the DCM, Queen's South Africa Medal (1899–1902) with five clasps ('Belfast', 'Diamond Hill', 'Johannesburg', 'Orange Free State' and 'Cape Colony'), King's South Africa Medal (1901–02) with two clasps ('South Africa 1901' and 'South Africa 1902'), 1914–15 Star, BWM, VM (1914–19) and King George VI Coronation Medal (1937).

Collins Court in Wrexham commemorates the sergeant's memory, as do the Memorial Gardens in Merthyr.

J.F. Russell

Tel-el-Khuweilfeh, north-west of Beersheba, 6 November 1917

Using troops from XX Corps to the west and the Desert Mounted Corps to the east, Gen. Allenby's planned capture of Beersheba, 25 miles south-east of Gaza, was successfully carried out on 31 October 1917. The day ended with the 4th Australian Light Horse Brigade charging through the Turkish defences into the town and capturing 1,800 Turkish prisoners. The following day the British also made progress near Gaza when they captured some of the town's outer defences. On 2 November there was further progress to the north of Beersheba, and on the 5th the main Turkish defence line between Gaza and Beersheba was broken by the Allied forces. On the 6th Khuweilfeh, 11 miles north of Beersheba, was taken; Gaza fell the following day and the British pushed 8 miles further northwards. The Turkish Army had suffered a major defeat and retreated towards Hebron and Jerusalem.

Capt. John Fox Russell, a medical officer attached to the 1/6th Royal Welsh Fusiliers, 158th Brigade, was involved in much of this period of fighting, especially when tending the wounded on 5/6 November during the fighting for possession of the flat-topped hill known as Tel-el-Khuweilfeh, which was very strongly contested. For a time, ownership was denied equally to each side and at one point on the 6th members of the 1/1st Hertfordshire Regiment and the 1/6th Royal Welsh Fusiliers, when on the hill, were mistaken for Turkish troops and were fired upon by Allied artillery, thus forcing them to return. The subsequent line held by the 1/6th Royal Welsh Fusiliers on the same day was a thin one and was enfiladed in several places; the battalion was under continuous strain. It was in this situation that Russell was to win his posthumous VC when he tended the wounded in extremely precarious and exposed positions, constantly going out to deal with men whose wounds had been caused by enemy snipers or machine-gun fire. He was eventually killed while undertaking these duties.

However, the hill-top position was finally taken, but at a cost of high Allied casualties. Turkish casualties were even higher. No fewer than seventeen British officers were killed and nineteen wounded, and six of those killed were from the 1/6th Royal Welsh Fusiliers.

The brief account above makes Allenby's plan look as though it went like clockwork and takes little note of the terrible conditions in which these actions took place. Access to a regular water supply for both man and horse was, as always, vital in the blistering heat, and the unsanitary landscape, which had been occupied by Turkish forces, was covered in fog and clouds of flies.

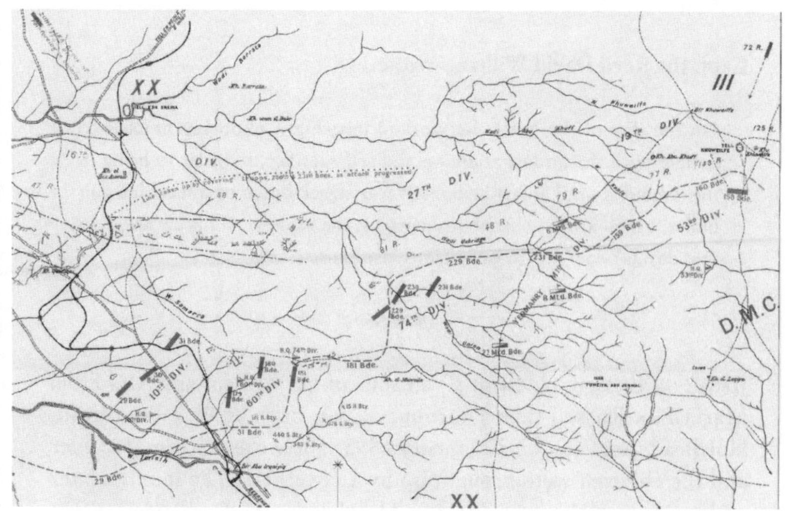

Tel-el-Khuweilfeh, 6 November 1917.

The citation for Russell's VC was published in the *London Gazette* of 11 January 1918 as follows:

> John Fox Russell, M.C. Capt., Royal Army Medical Corps, attached 1/6th Battn. Royal Welsh Fusiliers. For most conspicuous bravery displayed in action until he was killed. Capt. Russell repeatedly went out to attend the wounded under murderous fire from snipers and machine guns, and in many cases where no other means were at hand carried them in himself, although almost exhausted. He showed the highest possible degree of valour.

After his death, according to an account published in a local newspaper dated 22 June 1956, CSM Owen Thomas of Holyhead wrote:

> It is impossible to describe our feelings and how we miss him as every man in our battalion would have gladly laid down our lives for him. I am proud to say that his conduct during the great battle was in every way magnificent. As usual, his first care was for the wounded. It was while on such duty that he lost his life. He went through a hail of bullets to attend to a wounded man and thus fell one of the noblest and best of Britain's sons.

Capt. the Revd David Williams wrote:

> On the day of the battle he worked untiringly, exposing himself to danger with the utmost abandon and self-sacrifice, in order to bring in the wounded until at last he himself was struck down by a machine-gun bullet. I shall always cherish his memory, the memory of his devotion on that day as one of my most precious inspirations.

John Fox Russell, eldest of seven sons of Dr William and Mrs Ethel Maria Fox Russell (née Thornbury), was born at Plas Tanalltran, Holyhead, Anglesey, on 27 January 1893. There was also one daughter and the children were brought up by a governess. The family's later address was 5 Victoria Terrace, Holyhead, and Dr Russell was a general practitioner. For a short time John attended the local National and County Schools, and after taking a chorister examination he attended Magdalen College School, Oxford (1904–07). When his voice broke after a few years, he left for St Bees School, Cumberland (1908–09), where he sat for the entrance examination to the Royal College of Surgeons in Ireland. He also served in the school OTC. However, instead of studying in Dublin he began his medical studies at the London School of Medicine from October 1909. At the same time he joined the London University OTC.

John became associated with the Royal Welsh Fusiliers (TF) when he was commissioned on 5 December 1913. In August of the following year he attended a camp at Aberystwyth, during which time his battalion was mobilised and he was put in command of H Company of the 6th Battalion (TF), which mainly consisted of young men from Holyhead. Henry, one of his brothers, was a second lieutenant in the company and also his deputy. In 1895 his father had commanded a volunteer company before him. The company carried out their initial training at Caernarvon, Northampton and Bedford. John was soon promoted to lieutenant on 2 September 1914 and temporary captain on 27 January 1915.

Although he volunteered for overseas service his battalion was not sent abroad and he requested that the War Office relieve him so he could continue his medical studies at the Middlesex Hospital (a move that his father was anxious for him to do) in early 1915, as his studies still had eighteen months to run. In March 1916 he was awarded his diploma and transferred to the RAMC on 22 May 1916 with the rank of captain. He was then attached to a battery of the Royal Field Artillery in France on 10 October 1916. Wishing to return to the Royal Welsh Fusiliers he arranged for a transfer to the 6th Royal Welsh Fusiliers (TF), who were then in Egypt, and having arrived there in December 1915 he became their medical officer. On his voyage out his ship passed another in the Mediterranean which was carrying his brother, Henry, who had by then left the Royal Welsh Fusiliers, having served with them in Gallipoli and contracted frostbite. Henry was then in the process of being transferred to the Royal Flying Corps (RFC).

John married Alma G. Taylor at St Mark's Church, Tunbridge Wells, on 23 September 1916, and they set up home at Court Royal, Tunbridge Wells. Soon after his marriage he embarked at Devonport on 10 October, arriving in Salonika on 22 October. As he had wished, he was duly attached to the 1/6th Royal Welsh Fusiliers on the 24th. They were one of four battalions of the 158th Brigade, 53rd Welsh Division. He saw service in Palestine and took part in the first battle which attempted to capture the fortified town of Gaza, 2 miles from the Mediterranean Sea. The 158th Brigade was to advance against the part of the Ali Muntar Ridge, which was south of the town and overlooked an open plain. However, the advance of the attackers was slowed not just by the enemy, who were entrenched with numerous machine-guns as well as artillery, but also by 10ft cactus hedges which were more impenetrable than barbed wire. From that point onwards, and under heavy fire, the advance was slow and casualties on both sides were heavy.

However, by early evening the 53rd (Welsh) Division had managed to capture the Ali Muntar Ridge, but it was of no use as, based on the information he had to hand, the commander-in-chief, Gen. Dobell, decided that a withdrawal was necessary, which took place the following morning. British casualties were close to 4,000, including more than 500 killed. Capt. Russell tended the wounded under fire and was later awarded the MC, which was published in the *London Gazette* of 16 August as follows:

> For conspicuous gallantry and devotion to duty. He showed the greatest courage and skill in collecting wounded of all regiments, and in dressing them, under continuous shell and rifle fire.

The inconclusive Second Battle of Gaza took place on 17 April when the division fought at Samsons Ridge, to the south-west of the town, although it was mostly a 54th (East Anglian) Division affair with the 53rd playing a secondary role.

Records show that Russell was ill in Cairo in June 1917, and in the same month Gen. Allenby became commander-in-chief of the Egyptian Expeditionary Force, bringing a fresh approach to the Gaza problem and planning a third battle to take place at the end of October. Allenby was determined to learn from the experiences of the two previous failed attempts to capture Gaza. The secret would involve a well-planned period of preparation and training. It was in this battle that Capt. Russell was to win a posthumous VC at Tel-el-Khuweilfeh, north of the small town of Beersheba, on 6 November. He was later buried near where he fell, before being transferred to Beersheba War Cemetery, Row F, Grave 31. The inscription reads: 'He gave his life for others; greater love hath no man than this'. Two other holders of the VC are also buried there: Maj. Alexander Lafone and Lt Col Leslie Maygar, an Australian who had won his VC in South Africa in 1901 and was killed at Karm in Palestine, eleven days after Russell. In the following year, Alma Russell was presented with her husband's VC by the King at Buckingham Palace on 2 March 1918.

John's younger brother, Henry, born in 1897, who had joined the RFC after serving at Gallipoli with the Army and had become a captain, was killed during an air display at Hooton, near Liverpool, two days after the end of the war. He had gained the MC and was Mentioned in Despatches. A third brother, William, died during a bathing accident in 1940.

John Fox Russell was subsequently commemorated in several places, including: St Peter & St Paul Church, Aldeburgh, Suffolk; County Secondary School, Holyhead; Holyhead War Memorial; Students' Common Room, Middlesex Hospital, London; RAMC HQ Millbank; RAMC Memorial, Chapel Cloisters, Magdalen College, Oxford; Royal British Legion Club, Holyhead; St Bees School, Cumbria; 5 Victoria Terrace, Holyhead (the family home); and the 'Dr John Fox Russell VC Scholarship', Holyhead. He is also commemorated on the North Wales Heroes' Memorial in Bangor, North Wales, and the former Cybi Hall in Holyhead, which is now the J.E. O'Toole Centre. There are further commemorations to him in the form of a plaque on his parents' grave and a Commonwealth War Graves Commission (CWGC) headstone. The link with Aldeburgh was not because he lived in the Suffolk town, but rather because he was a friend of the Garrett family who lived locally and to whom his mother was related. As for St Bees, two other First World War VCs are also remembered there: William Leefe Robinson and Richard Wain. Henry is listed on the Holyhead War Memorial and also shares the plaque at 5 Victoria Terrace, Holyhead with his brother.

A portrait of John Fox Russell, which recreated his VC action of tending the wounded of the RWF in terrible conditions, was commissioned.

Alma Russell remarried in 1919 and became Mrs Whitehouse; later she became Mrs Thomas and moved to New Zealand. In June 1956 she and one of her late husband's sisters, Mrs F.G.J. Manning, were two of the guests invited to the VC centenary commemorations at Hyde Park, a service at Westminster Abbey and a Garden Party given by the Queen Mother in the grounds of Marlborough House. As well as the VC and MC, John Fox Russell's decorations included the BWM (1914–20), VM (1914–19) and MiD Oakleaf, and Territorial Force War Medal (1914–19). They were donated to the RAMC Museum (now the Army Medical Services Museum in Mytchett, Surrey) by Alma, who died in 1990.

A.D. Borton

Sheria, 7 November 1917

The 60th (London) Division, consisting of the 179th, 180th and 181st Infantry Brigades, served on the Macedonian Front after it arrived in Salonika in late December 1916. After taking part in the Battle of Doiran the division was transferred to Egypt in June 1917. The division was composed entirely of London Territorial battalions who had previously served in France in the second half of 1916. In June the division was transferred to Egypt and concentrated on the Suez Canal in early July. On 5 July it moved to the front, 10 miles south-west of Gaza. It became part of XX Corps in August. The 181st Brigade, consisting of County of London battalions, was under the command of T/Brig. Gen. E.C. da Costa.

Since his arrival in Egypt, Gen. Allenby, commander-in-chief of the Egyptian Expeditionary Force, had been preparing his troops to capture Beersheba and Gaza, and by mid-September Lt Col Arthur Borton of the 2/22nd (County of London) Battalion would have been aware of the role that his battalion was to play in these offensive operations. A month later, without giving too much away, he wrote home to his family on 21 October: 'I cannot write as fully as I should like to but I can tell you that I've got the biggest chance I could have hoped for!!'

On 30 October the 60th Division were concentrated in an area 6 miles south-west of the town of Beersheba, near the Wadi Mirtaba. The 181st Brigade, together with the 179th, made an attack on the Beersheba defences on the following day on the right of the 74th Division, and by early afternoon all the objectives had been taken.

On 1 November Borton wrote home to report these stirring events:

> We took our hill, and the men did far better than I ever dreamt they would.... They got to within 500yds of the enemy and then lay for two

> hours in the open under a very heavy fire waiting for the artillery to cut the wire, their casualties being about 15%... The Brigadier then got a message to me to know whether we could go without the gaps being cut? It was the one thing I had been hoping for, as I felt that no wire was going to stop us ... I'd got a flag with 'The Queen's' badge on it, in my pocket, and when the time (8.15 a.m.) arrived I tied it to my walking stick, and away we went. I've never felt so damn proud in my life. The Flag was a surprise to the men, and tickled them to death! – We got in practically without loss. We cut the wire 25yds behind our own barrage. This of course meant a few hits from our own guns, but not a soul in the trenches dared show his head, and the moment the guns lifted we were into them with bomb and bayonet and scuppered the whole garrison ... Everyone is longing for the next whack. I thought I'd got over any longings in this direction by this time, but the men are so wonderful that it is impossible even to feel frightened, which I always have up to the present, but never no more.

A few days later on 6 November, as a necessary preliminary to an advance beyond the Wadi Sheria, the 60th Division made an attack on the Kauwukah and Rushdi systems at 12.30 p.m. This time the 179th and 180th Brigades broke through and occupied Sheria Station after two hours of heavy fighting. On the next day, the 7th, the Turkish forces were still holding out at north-east Tel-el-Sheria. The London attackers began their advance soon after 3.30 a.m. and the 181st Brigade war diary described progress as slow as they moved over unknown country. It was not until daybreak at 5.30 a.m. that the 2/22nd London Regiment actually reached the Wadi Sheria.

The battalion war diary continues:

> [The battalion] pressed forward with the greatest gallantry coming under heavy rifle and machine gun fire, from the high ground immediately to the north of the Wadi ... and the battalion continued the advance northwards against successive ridges which were stubbornly contested by the enemy, until it had gained its final objective on the ridge running east and west through G. 10 & 11.

The Turkish forces were only dislodged after a fierce bayonet charge by the London troops, and after later repelling several counter-attacks the line was established 1 mile to the north of Tel-el-Sheria. The battalion also captured four field guns and two machine-guns. The human cost of this success to the 2/22nd (County of London) Battalion was five officer casualties, including two second lieutenants, and nineteen other ranks killed together with ninety-nine wounded.

A strong bridgehead had by now been made across the Wadi Sheria and the way was now clear for the Australian Light Horse to make an attempt on the station east of Kh. Um Ameidat, 4½ miles to the north of Tel-el-Sheria.

The following day, 7 November, was the day that the coastal town of Gaza was finally captured, with the assistance of Allied warships operating off the coast. It was probably also the best day in Arthur Borton's life as he won the Victoria Cross through his dashing leadership. After the operation he again wrote home about the attack and explained just how close they were to failure:

> As the light grew better I found we were in a devilish awkward fix; we were swept by machine-gun fire from both flanks, and behind their artillery put down a barrage on top of us; and if it had not been the light was still so bad we should have been wiped out in matter of minutes. It was impossible to stay where we were and hopeless to go back, so to go forward was the only thing to do and we went. One of the men had a football: how it got there, goodness knows. Anyway we kicked off and rushed the first guns, dribbling the ball with us. I take it the Turks thought we were dangerous lunatics, but we stopped for nothing, not even to shoot, and the bayonet had its day. For 3,000yds we swept up everything, finally capturing a field battery and its entire gun crews. The battery fired its last round at us at 25yds.

The citation for Borton's VC was published in the *London Gazette* of 18 December 1917, yet from his father's diary it is clear that his son was not aware of the high honour until early February:

> For most conspicuous bravery and leadership. Under the most difficult conditions in darkness and in an unknown country, he deployed his battalion for attack, and at dawn led his attacking companies against a strongly held position. When the leading waves were checked by a withering machine-gun fire, Lieut.-Colonel Borton showed an utter

> contempt of danger, and moved freely up and down his lines under heavy fire. Reorganizing his command, he led his men forward, and captured the position. At a later stage of the fight he led a party of volunteers against a battery of field guns in action at point-blank range, capturing the guns and detachments. His fearless leadership was an inspiring example to the whole brigade.

On 18 November the 60th Division was concentrated in the Gaza area and marched forward on the following day. Between the 24th and 27th they relieved 232nd Brigade of the 75th Division and the 52nd (Lowland) Division in the Judaean Hills.

The 60th Division continued to distinguish itself during operations in Palestine, which later led to the fall of Jerusalem in early December when the divisional commander, Maj. Gen. Sir J.S.M. Shea, accepted its surrender. For his role in these operations and some which involved him in 1918, Borton was awarded the CMG for Palestine (Despatches) and the Order of the Nile (Egypt).

In mid-February 1918 Borton arrived home from Palestine to a most enthusiastic welcome when he returned to the village of Yalding. The progress of his car was stopped by people wanting speeches and to offer general congratulations. They then drove to the family home in Cheveney where he was received by a guard of honour made up of Boy Scouts and wounded soldiers from Cheveney Hospital. A week later on the 23rd, accompanied by his wife, he received his VC and the DSO at Buckingham Palace from the King. A month later on 16 March Borton left England to return to Palestine.

After he had won his VC and the Turkish forces surrendered, Borton tried hard to return to service in France, but the authorities sent him to north Russia instead, where he arrived in February 1919. He remained there for three months, during which time he was awarded the Order of St Vladimir of Russia, before returning home to Newcastle from Archangel on 28 May. He was demobilised on 12 June.

Arthur Drummond Borton, known as 'Bosky', was born on 1 July 1883, the eldest of three children of Lt Col A.C. Borton DL, JP and Mrs A.C. Borton (née Drummond, daughter of Gen. Henry Drummond) of

Cheveney House, Yalding, Kent, and grandson of the late Sir Arthur Borton, GCB, GCMG, former soldier and Governor of Malta. Arthur junior was educated at Eton, where he was a member of Mr A.C. Ainger's house, and the RMA Sandhurst, from which he passed into the 60th Rifles as a second lieutenant in 1902. He served in the last months of the Boer War, taking part in operations in the Transvaal from March to 31 May, and was awarded the Queen's Medal with three clasps. He later served in Bermuda and Ireland, and was stationed in India for four years. Borton became a lieutenant on 9 May 1906, but was invalided from the Army two years later as being unfit for general service. He returned to England in 1910.

Borton then took up fruit farming in the United States, where he was living on the outbreak of war in August 1914. He quickly returned to England in mid-October and rejoined the 60th Rifles. However, finding that there was no speedy prospect of his getting to the front, he switched services to the RFC and become an observer. In December he teamed up briefly with his brother, Amyas, known as 'Biffy', at Brooklands Aerodrome and at Christmas the two brothers flew home for the festivities, landing at an airstrip recently made at Hatch End, the family estate. In January 1915 Borton left for France as an observer with No. 3 Squadron. Two months later, on 5 March, the aeroplane in which he was flying crashed badly while on an air reconnaissance mission. The pilot broke both his legs, while Borton's neck was broken in two places and he suffered from concussion. At the same time, Amyas was suffering from a bout of jaundice and the two brothers convalesced at home together. On his return to active flying, Amyas was wounded and later awarded the DSO. Borton left for France to bring his brother back from Boulogne to London. For a second time Borton was pronounced unfit for service by the Army medical authorities. But he was undeterred and managed to obtain a position in the Royal Naval Volunteer Reserve (RNVR). On the eve of leaving for the Dardanelles he married his fiancée, Lorna. He left for Gallipoli as a lieutenant commander in charge of two squadrons of Motor Machine Guns Armoured Cars, Royal Naval Air Service (RNAS), and took part in the Suvla Bay landings, arriving on 7 August 1915 and remaining in the frontline until the later evacuation from the Peninsula. He was awarded the DSO for these services (*London Gazette*, 31 May 1916): 'In recognition of most valuable services in command of a detachment of Royal Marine machine-guns in difficult and dangerous parts of the line in the Gallipoli Peninsula.' He was often unwell while serving on the Peninsula and particularly suffered from dental problems.

In June 1916, after passing an Army medical board, Borton was appointed second in command of the 2/22nd Battalion London Regiment. He soon left for France and was there for only a short time before returning home because of a technical point about his postings. Once the problem was sorted out he returned to France in September for several weeks. His division, the 60th, escaped the Battle of the Somme and in November was transferred to Salonika via Marseilles. The 2/22nd Battalion served continuously at the front and, in the following May, Borton was made temporary lieutenant colonel after his colonel was declared unfit. Now Borton had a battalion of his own to command, but according to his letters home he was not very well at this time and his moods swung from one extreme to another. In particular his teeth were still giving him problems. In his obituary notice in *The Times* one of his letters home was quoted:

> I have at last realised my ambition to command my own battalion and am the proudest man on earth. My only fear is that I shan't last, as my general health isn't too good. Have also been very unlucky in having two very heavy falls in the last week, which have shaken me up a bit; I took the most infernal toss last evening and it hasn't done my neck any good.

In June 1917 Borton arrived in Egypt and the two brothers met up briefly in Cairo in early July. In another letter Borton talks of being in a camp in Alexandria.

After being released by the Army in June 1919, Borton tried to obtain a position in the Colonial Service, and a note in his service file (WO 374/7727) records that the Army gave him a recommendation and stated 'we have nothing against him'. A few weeks later he made a journey to Spitzbergen, travelling as a civilian with the idea of joining Gen. Ironside's British force in northern Russia. However, the Bolsheviks triumphed and the British force was withdrawn. Borton did meet up with Ernest Shackleton, the explorer, who gave him a job in Spitzbergen. However, it didn't work out and Lorna, his long-suffering wife, journeyed out to be with him and the couple returned home two months later.

From 1919 Borton's life took a turn for the worse, as he was unable to hold down a job, ran up large debts and began to drink heavily. Although the eldest son, he was unable to succeed to the family estate on the death of his father and instead he and Lorna went to live in 3 Park Road, Southwold on a small private allowance. In June 1920 he attended the VC Garden Party at Buckingham Palace, and the services in November 1920 at the Cenotaph and at Westminster Abbey where he acted as one of the pallbearers for the coffin of the Unknown Warrior. In the same year on 31 October he unveiled the Yalding War Memorial at the Parish Church of St Peter & St Paul. In November 1929 he attended the House of Lords' VC Dinner.

On 5 January 1933 Arthur became ill at about midday when he was leaving his home in Southwold. It seems that he suffered a stroke and was taken to hospital by ambulance, but he died seven hours later after never having regained consciousness. Borton's body was taken by road on the following Sunday for his funeral and burial on the 9th at Hunton churchyard extension (St Mary's), Yalding. The burial party was made up of members of the 2nd London Regiment, who also supplied two buglers to play *Last Post* and *Reveille*. The guard of honour was drawn from members of the Boy Scouts and wounded soldiers from Cheveney Hospital. His coffin was draped with a Union Jack.

On the Sunday evening a memorial service was organised at Southwold Parish Church. The Mayor and council officials left the town hall in a procession to the church headed by a large body of ex-servicemen. Prior to the evening service a muffled peal was rung on the church bells. In his address the vicar of Southwold spoke of Borton being a great Englishman whose life was 'a wonderful story of heroism, culminating in the award of the highest honour a British soldier could attain'. The collection at the church was given to the Earl Haig Fund for ex-servicemen.

Borton had certainly fully entered into the life of the Suffolk coastal town and was respected by all those with whom he came into contact. He was president of the local British Legion and used to preside over the local ex-servicemen's dinner in the Constitution Club. At one town meeting, and despite having had a recent operation on his foot, he attended in a bath chair in order to speak against a suggested plan for buildings to be erected on Southwold Common.

In his will Borton left £2,960. His younger brother had inherited the family home at Cheveney on the death of their father, Arthur Close

Borton, who died on 9 October 1927, aged 76. Their father had married Laura Devas of Pickhurst Manor, Hayes, Kent, in 1912.

Borton's name is commemorated on the KRRC Plaque in Winchester Cathederal and his decorations are with the Queen's Royal Surrey Regiment Museum, Clandon, Surrey. Apart from his VC, DSO and Queen's South African Medals with three clasps, they included the 1914–15 Star, BWM, VM (1914–19), Knight, Order of the Nile (Egypt) and Knight, Order of St Vladimir (Russia). As with many VC actions, a painting of Borton's VC action of 7 November 1917 in Palestine was also commissioned.

Amyas Eden Borton, Borton's younger brother, born 20 September 1886, was also educated at Eton and served in the Black Watch (Royal Highlanders). He had always been interested in flight and took up flying while on leave, becoming experienced in handling balloons before transferring to early aircraft and acquiring his pilot's licence (no. 170). On the outbreak of war he transferred to the RFC. He rose to the rank of air vice-marshal and, like his elder brother, was awarded the DSO and CMG. It was in June 1915 that he won his DSO when he was seriously wounded during a reconnaissance flight; he was shot through the neck and jaw, but still managed to get his aeroplane back safely. In 1917 and 1918 he served in Palestine and commanded the Palestine Brigade, RFC. He was later gazetted a brigadier general.

After the war Amyas became the first man to fly non-stop from England to India and he also took part in other long-distance flights and aerial survey work. In 1921 he was in command of the RAF in Iraq and was later awarded the CB for his work there. Returning home he became commandant of RAF College at Cranwell in 1923, the same year that he married Muriel Streatfield, daughter of Canon H.B. Streatfield from Chiddingstone, Kent. He continued to serve with the RAF before retiring in 1933 when he became a director of D. Napier & Son. He used to commute from Yalding to London in his own aeroplane and became a businessman, although he was mostly unsuccessful. After the war he had another business venture breeding turkeys.

He became a deputy lieutenant of Kent and was chairman of the Kent Territorial and Auxiliary Force Association from 1938 to 1949. During the Second World War he assisted in the formation of the local Home Guard.

In 1963 he was forced to sell the Cheveney Estate and move to a spacious cottage on the estate for his last six years, dying in hospital in 1969.

It would appear that the village of Yalding has taken precious little interest in the Borton family over the years and the grave of their 'local hero' has received very little attention. Even the Yalding village war memorial was allowed to be vandalised in the late 1970s, although it was later restored. Let us hope that the centenary of the Great War and the idea of a commemorative paving stone for every VC will go some way towards correcting this situation.

As for the two brothers, there is little to be gained in sitting in judgement over the way that they ran their lives, as they were very much of their era, in that both were only really happy when on active duty in the services and preferably in times of war. Never lacking in courage, it was peacetime that seemed to give them problems, and when it came to handling their finances they were seemingly unable to cope.

S.H.P. Boughey

El Burf, 1 December 1917

After the successful capture of the ancient city of Gaza on 7 November, Gen. Allenby's advance quickly reached Wadi Hesi to the north, while Allied warships were operating off the coast. On the 8th at Huj to the east of Gaza, 'the last British cavalry charge' took place where Austrian batteries, defending the retreating Turkish columns, were put to the sword by a detachment of the Warwickshire Yeomanry, who in turn lost nearly half of their men as well as 110 horses. The charge also led to eleven Austrian artillery guns being captured.

After the capture of Gaza at the third attempt, progress inland was made at Beersheba as well, when the British captured more ground to the north of the town. Overall Allied progress in Palestine under Gen. Allenby was now picking up pace and Hebron and Jerusalem were well within his sights. On 9 November the ANZAC Mounted Division joined XXI Corps from Gaza.

On the 10th, the coastal town of Askalon was occupied and fighting also took place near Esdud. On the following day the Turkish Army stiffened its resistance when it set up a new line of defence covering Hebron and Jerusalem. On the 12th the German Gen. Falkenhayn, recently appointed commander of the Turkish forces, managed to drive the ANZAC Mounted Division 4 miles back in the direction of Ramleh. The next day the Allied cavalry attacked towards Junction Station, stormed the El Mughar Ridge and managed to open up a gap in the

Turkish defences, which led to a further enemy retreat. On the 14th the 75th Division, which also had the use of armoured cars, captured Junction Station where the Beersheba rail line joined up with the Jaffa–Jerusalem line, giving them control of the main railway network. The next day the ANZAC Mounted Division occupied Ramleh and Ludd. By mid-November the Turkish Army had became split into two sections, which contributed to a considerable increase in the loss of their troops taken prisoner, with over 9,000 men on the 15th alone.

Meanwhile, the coastal town of Jaffa fell to the Allies when it was entered without opposition by a New Zealand brigade on the 16th. Inland and to the south-east, on the 18th the Allies moved eastwards into the Judaean Hills, which was to prove a very difficult landscape to fight in as it consisted of a series of ridges which were difficult to negotiate. It was also the beginning of the winter rainy season. On the same day, Gen. Falkenhayn moved his HQ from Jerusalem to Nablus. By the 20th the 75th Division, aided by mist, had managed to storm three ridges and was then only 5 miles from the Holy City. On the 21st the Allied plan was to move further eastwards and get behind the Turkish defences in order to cut the Jerusalem–Nablus road. It was thought this ploy would have the effect of saving Jerusalem from destruction. After a force had advanced northwards from Hebron, the advance on Jerusalem began in earnest. Its capture would not be the end of the Allied invasion of Palestine, but its fall would provide the Allies with a major political triumph.

A young second lieutenant, Stanley Boughey, joined the 1/4th Royal Scots Fusiliers, 155th Brigade, 52nd (Lowland) Division in Palestine in August 1917. In the second half of 1915 the 52nd Division, including the 155th, 156th and 157th Infantry Brigades, and made up entirely of Lowland Territorial Battalions, served in the Gallipoli Campaign, and after returning to Egypt took part in the advance from the Suez Canal across the Sinai Desert. It then took part in the first two unsuccessful attempts to capture Gaza in March and April 1917 as part of XXI Corps. At the beginning of November the division had captured a strong redoubt, Umbrella Hill, which was the key to the Gaza defences.

During the rest of the month the 52nd Division made slow progress in the advance towards Jerusalem, and on 19 November turned eastwards towards the Judaean Hills, occupying Annabeh and Kubab without much difficulty. Three days later, the 155th Brigade took Beit Izza and on the 24th the division attacked towards the Jerusalem–Nablus road, with the 155th Brigade attempting to capture El Jib, which they found too strongly held. In the last days of November the enemy made a series of strong counter-attacks of their own, and on the 28th a new defensive line had been established to the north-east of El Burf on a ridge which closed a gap in the divisional line. Fighting continued on the 29th and the 8th Australian Light Horse relieved all of the 155th Infantry Brigade except for three companies of the 1/4th Royal Scots Fusiliers who remained on the defence line south of Shilta at El Burf.

At 1.20 a.m. on 1 December the Royal Scots Fusiliers, supported by the Australians, were attacked by a Turkish assault battalion made up of German storm troopers. The attacking troops drove the Allied forces off the ridge north of El Burf, previously held by B, C and D Companies and the Australian cavalry, who had by now run out of grenades. The enemy, just 30yd away, threw stick grenades and also brought heavy rifle and machine-gun fire to focus on the position. According to the 1/4th Royal Scots Fusiliers war diary:

> 'D' Coy bombers were sent for and most gallantly and determinedly led by 2nd Lieut. S. Boughey, succeeded after a very hot encounter in bombing the enemy down the forward slope of the hill and eventually forcing the enemy on this part of the line to surrender. 2nd Lieut Boughey was shot in the head just as the enemy put up their first white flag. At dawn the enemy began to retire from the ridge on the right.

D Company, assisted by a party of grenadiers and some field artillery, had managed to take the enemy in the flank, virtually encircling them and pushing them back down the hill. It became a complete rout.

As a result of the failure of their attack, the enemy suffered between 200 and 300 casualties and the prisoners captured included a German battalion commander. The storm troopers were newly arrived from Galicia and this was their first action on the Palestine Front. The human cost to the 1/4th Royal Scots Fusiliers, apart from the mortally wounded 2/Lt Boughey, was three other ranks dead and six wounded.

Later in the day, 155th Brigade arrived at Ramleh and an entry in their war diary told the story of the day's events:

> Brig.-Gen J.G. Wilson praised 1/4 RSF whose men were armed with bombs which were of particular value in view of the existence of dead ground immediately in front of the main position. The action of 2nd Lieut Boughey, 1/4th R. S. Fusiliers was particularly prominent in leading bombing counter-attacks. I understand that this officer's name has been brought to the notice of Divl. Commander. By O.C. 1/4th Royal Scots Fusiliers for special recommendation.

It was at Ramleh that Boughey succumbed to his gunshot wounds at a casualty clearing station three days later; his file gives conflicting evidence about which one, but it was either CCS 35 or 45. The latter number was noted on his death certificate. He was buried at Deir Sineid, Peg 8, and later moved to Gaza War Cemetery, Plot XX, Row A, Grave 1, which is north-east of the town and now part of Israel. On the 5th the 155th Brigade marched out from Ramleh to take over the lines to the north of Jaffa.

Boughey's posthumous VC award was published ten weeks later in the *London Gazette* of 13 February 1918 as follows:

> For most conspicuous bravery. When the enemy in large numbers had managed to crawl up to within 30yds of our firing lines, and with bombs and automatic rifles were keeping down the fire of our machine guns, he rushed forward alone with bombs right up to the enemy, doing great execution and causing the surrender of a party of 30. As he turned to go back for more bombs he was mortally wounded at the moment when the enemy was surrendering.

On the announcement of the VC award, the Ayrshire County TA sent a congratulatory message to Mrs Boughey, expressing the hope that the great honour might help to alleviate the loss of her gallant son. He had been a member of the Ayrshire Yeomanry prior to the war. Mrs Lucy Boughey received her son's posthumous medal at Buckingham Palace on 2 March 1918, a day when eight other posthumous VCs were received by the relatives of Philip Bent, George Paton, John Fox Russell, John Harrison, Alexander Lafone, Walter Stone, William Clamp and George Clare.

Stanley Henry Parry Boughey, a son of James and Lucy Boughey, was born on 9 April 1896 at 3 Danube Street, Liverpool, although most references state he was born in Ayrshire, Scotland. His parents later lived at 37 Queen's Gate, Claremont Park, North Shore, Blackpool, having settled in the town in 1905 after moving from Yew Tree Farm, Hurleston, Nantwich, Cheshire, where a relative had a farm.

When living in Blackpool, Stanley attended Claremont Council School and Clifton College, North Shore. He was a founder member of the 1st Blackpool Scout Troop, and though only 5ft 3½in was a keen athlete and an esteemed member of the North Shore Cricket Club. He also won prizes for swimming. As a young man he joined the office of the solicitor Richard Banks of Abingdon Street. At this time he also took up ambulance work with the St John Ambulance/Red Cross, which was to stand him in good stead when he was called up at an hour's notice as a member of the RAMC on the outbreak of war in 1914. He worked with the Red Cross, having become a qualified first aider on 1 September. Initially he served in France from October, beginning work in Boulogne. Later he was attached to the Motor Transport when still serving in France, and he was at one time working with the Post Office Section. He was later invalided home with appendicitis and sinusitis to King's Lancashire Military Convalescent Hospital, Squires Gate, in December 1915 (later to be a Pontins Holiday Camp), where he remained for six months before being discharged from the Army.

While back in England, Stanley was a member of Claremont Congregational Church, Warley Road, North Shore, and regularly attended services there when convalescing. (This church, later United Reform, closed down in 1995.) Later he decided to try and rejoin the Army. After a medical on 10 May 1916 he was posted to the Ayrshire Yeomanry as a corporal, and after a period of training at Harwich he was ordered to report to Kimmel Park on 8 December.

The Ayrshire Yeomanry were later disbanded and its personnel transferred to the Royal Scots Fusiliers, with whom Boughey was granted a commission on 28 March 1917. He attended an officer's training course in April and was drafted out to Egypt, leaving on 12 July and disembarking at Alexandria on the 29th. He joined his battalion in the field on 11 August. Three weeks later he attended Trench Mortar School before moving to Palestine, and on 1 December took part in the fighting at El Burf which preceded the capture of Jerusalem. In forcing the surrender of thirty of the enemy he became the second man from Blackpool to gain the VC during the war, the first being Lt Victor Smith, who won his in Gallipoli.

When Mrs Boughey was told of the possibility of a high honour for her dead son, she said, according to a local reporter: 'it was better to have died a hero than lived a coward'. Boughey's commanding officer, Lt Col G. Stewart Richardson, wrote home to the bereaved parents and told them that it was mainly through their 'son's magnificent example and self-sacrifice that we managed so well'. He added:

> His work in the battalion has always been of a standard that deserved the highest praise. No matter how hard or difficult the work was, he was ever ready, always cheerful, and he was a most conscientious officer.

Boughey's effects were sent home in February 1918 and they included a valise and a tin box. His Commemorative Scroll was sent to his parents in May 1919.

After Boughey's death, a memorial service was held at Claremont Congregational Church, and in his address the Revd Ambrose Evans said:

> ... when Lieut. Boughey was at the King's Lancashire Military Convalescent Hospital he regularly attended his old church and Sunday School, and his blue-clad figure was familiar to all the congregation. When he went away Lieut. Boughey said he felt he would never return. It was a singular thing that he died near the place where Jesus Christ was crucified.

In 1918 a memorial to Boughey was unveiled by the Mayoress of Blackpool, Mrs A.L. Parkinson, which took the form of an endowed bed in Victoria Hospital with a bronze plaque to Boughey's memory above it. Other guests who attended the ceremony were the Mayor, Alderman A.L. Parkinson MP, Mr and Mrs Boughey and several hospital officials. After the Union Jack was removed to unveil the plaque, the Mayoress said that 'she appreciated the great privilege afforded to her to unveil the tablet in memory of a gallant and heroic resident. His act of heroism, which was recorded on the tablet, won their everlasting gratitude and admiration.'

The money required for the endowment was donated by the Corporation of Blackpool on behalf of the townspeople. The Tramways and Electricity Committee were to provide the money from the profits of manufacturing munitions. The Mayoress also:

> ... expressed the hope that those who had occasion to use the bed might benefit from the skill of the doctors and the care and attention of the nursing staff, and that the memorial would act as a stimulus to all to emulate the good example which the Lieutenant had bequeathed them.

The bed's first occupant was L/Cpl Hurst of the Lancashire Fusiliers, and after the ceremony the Mayor and Mayoress entertained the assembled company to tea. Mrs Boughey was keen that the memorial bed should be supplied with extra comforts and she and some of her relatives opened a small fund. The hospital was vacated by the hospital authorities in the 1930s and no longer exists.

After the war a memorial to Boughey and a Roll of Honour were unveiled at Claremont Congregational Church. The ceremony was performed by Mrs Higham of Fairhaven. Boughey's memorial took the form of a photograph set in a frame of unpolished dark wood and the Revd Ambrose Evans read out Boughey's full VC citation and tributes from his former commanding officers and comrades. Mrs Boughey was a member of the congregation. The church Roll of Honour, also unveiled by Mrs Higham, consisted of a picture frame of twenty young men from the church who served in the war, half of whom died as a consequence and others who were badly wounded. The Revd Evans had himself also served in France, working with the YMCA.

On 10 November 1923 the town war memorial was unveiled on the Princess Parade at the end of the Promenade and took the form of a 100ft-high obelisk made from Cornish granite. A crowd of 30,000 turned out for the ceremony and the mothers of two local VC winners were invited to unveil it, namely Mrs L. Boughey and Mrs Smith, mother of Lt A.V. Smith VC. The memorial includes the names of the two officers.

Boughey's decorations apart from the VC included the 1914–15 Star, BWM and VM (1914–19). The VC was sold at *Spinks* on 10 February 1986, but the whereabouts of the VC or his campaign medals is not publicly known. In 2008 the memorial plaque above the hospital bed in the Blackpool Hospital turned up at a car boot sale. It is hoped that it is in good hands.

C.W. TRAIN

Ain Karim, near Jerusalem,
8 December 1917

By 5 December 1917 British trains were now able to reach as far as Ramleh. It was only a matter of days before Jerusalem was captured by Allenby's forces and the concentration of the final attack towards the Holy City began on 4 December. The 53rd (Welsh), 60th (London) and 74th (Yeomanry) Divisions from XX Corps were the main infantry troops who were to take part in this historic event, and in order to minimise destruction it was planned that the Holy City would be encircled. The 60th and 74th Divisions were to attack eastwards from a front between Ain Karim and Beit Surik, and after gaining their objectives they were to move to the left and take up positions on the Jerusalem–Nablus road. Two brigades from Hebron, a town 17 miles to the south that had just been captured, were to move up and protect the right flank of the 60th Division.

The line of the British advance on 8 December lay along the western rough-terraced hillside of Jurahs above Ain Karim, across several watercourses and re-entrants through terraces, vineyards and olive groves. Owing to previous heavy rain the soil on the terraces had turned 'sodden and sticky'; the going became abominable and the soldiers' feet became as heavy as lead.

Cpl Charles Train, who was to win a VC during these operations, was an NCO with the 2/14th (County of London) Battalion of the

London Regiment (London Scottish), 179th Infantry Brigade, 60th Division; the war diary for the 179th Brigade entry for 7–10 December gives the following details:

> To reach their objective 2/14th Bn. had first to take Tumulus Hill which, owing to strong enemy resistance [met with] the 2/13th Bn. had been unable to do. Strong resistance was again met with from TUMULUS HILL, but 2/14 pressed on and gained the heights, before the true summit was reached. However, they were pulled up, confronted by 2 machine guns; but, on his own initiative Cpl. C.W. TRAIN 2/14 Bn. went forward and single handed took on the right gun, accounting for the machine gun and its team. Cpl. F.S. THORNHILL then came up and took on the left gun. Cpl TRAIN afterwards went to his assistance and these two N.C.O.s accounted for the second team and captured the gun. TUMULUS HILL thus captured, was the key to the situation.

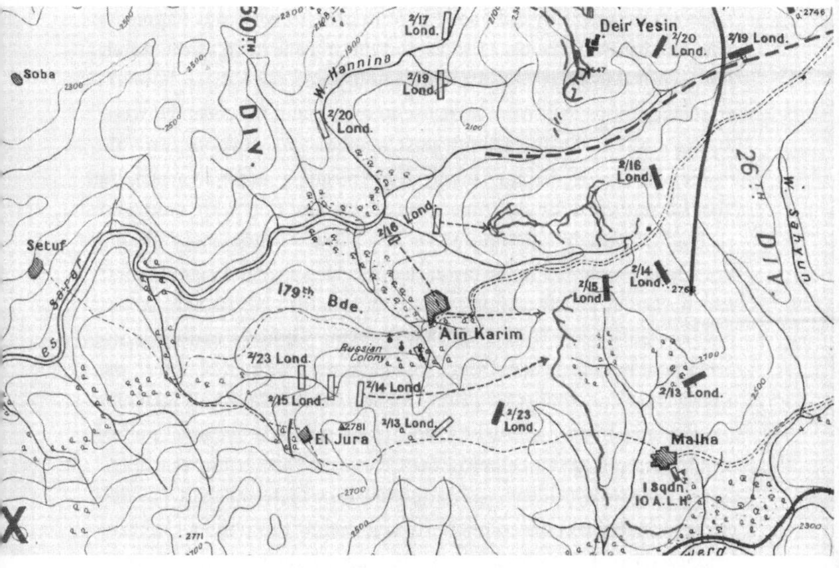

Ain Karim, 8 December 1917.

A much less dry account of the same action was published in chapter XIII of *Kilts Across the Jordan* by Bernard Blaser. After describing the terrain of hilltop villages over rocky ground, where the use of camels was severely limited as the ground was covered with sharp flints, he went on to describe the British attack. The objective was to clear some of the last defences before Jerusalem could be captured:

> The advance began at 8pm and the destination and point of deployment for 4am was a stone watch-tower half-way up a hill to the south-east of Ain Karim. Moving in single file and 'stumbling over rocks and boulders, down precipitous slopes' they reached the broad Wadi and after moving through well kept vineyards and round a rocky eminence in pale moonlight they came into sight of Ain Karim. However this did not last long as the moon was quickly obscured and it began to rain. It was a wretched night and it was thought that the enemy would not be expecting a surprise attack. Indeed a patrol belonging to the 13th Bn had already captured some advance Turkish posts and brought back a few prisoners without even raising the alarm.
>
> However the enemy did finally become alive to what was happening after the British force began to ascend the slope leading to the watch-tower and the Turks began to fire rapidly and for half an hour the attacking troops had to crouch close to the ground for cover. However during a lull in the Turkish fire the Companies managed to reach the tower and deployed round the deep re-entrant in order to attack the Turkish positions. By this time it was dawn and they were now quite visible to the enemy who opened up with a heavy machine gun and rifle fire which accounted for many casualties. However the main body of men pushed on slowly towards the objective only to be caught by several machine guns firing from a spur on the right. To make matters worse firing now began to come from a village to the rear as well. There was a momentary possibility of a catastrophe whereby the whole attacking force could be wiped out but the now much reduced companies pushed on up a steep slope and climbed the series of terraces before reaching a line of sangars which were sheltering the Turkish defenders. Once they engaged with the Turks no quarter was given. At this point a Company belonging to the 13th Bn captured the ridge on the right and cleared it of Turkish machine guns after repeated bayonet charges. These were

> the very guns which had previously given so much trouble. Guns in Ain Karim were also silenced.

After the first line of sangars (a stone breastwork or look-out post) had been passed, progress was again slowed by two machine-guns firing from the right and the whole battalion was now held up. It was at this point that Cpl Charles Train came to the rescue. The following extract is taken from a comrade's letter, and it gives a vivid description of the incident in which Cpl Train took such a leading part:

> We just lay there and pelted each other for about three quarters of an hour, when a chap in our platoon named Train made a dart forward of about twenty yards, and gradually crept up their barricade, let off one or two rifle grenades on the way, and dodged their bullets. He worked right up to the end of their barricade and enfiladed with his own rifle fire. A German officer in charge of the barricade let fire at Train with his revolver. Train flopped, and shot him, wounding him severely. That finished it! They all scooted out of the other end of the barricade, and as they came out so we brought them down. One of them cleared out of the back way, and tried to get his machine gun away, and had got it on his shoulders and gone about fifty yards, but Train got him tapped and brought down with a beauty between the shoulders, so, as you will see, it was his day out, as at the finish he had practically drove the Turks out of the trench on his own, and captured two machine-guns, which would undoubtedly have caused many casualties in our ranks later in the day. The sight of the barricade I shall never forget. The Turks were lying all over the shop, not one escaped, and they were nearly all dead. The German officer was dancing about holding his trousers and offering an orange for a field dressing. That was the finish of the spasm, and 'ot is not the word.

Having reached the top of Tumulus Hill, C Company were able to bring enfilading fire onto the Turkish trenches, and within a short time this success led to the enemy troops running away in the direction of Malhah.

Thus the main Turkish defences of Jerusalem were now in Allied possession, but as we have seen the city was not to be fought over and the 60th Division made a change of direction to the left and moved towards the north of the city. Although orders had been issued that no guns should be fired within a certain radius of Jerusalem, this created a problem as the Turkish Army had positioned its light calibre artillery batteries on the edge of the modern suburbs, and on gaining the last ridge the enemy intermittently fired at the advancing troops. However, within a few hours the plan to surround the city was accomplished and the Turkish forces were said to have been pouring through one gate while Allied troops came through another.

A much-repeated and humorous story later concerned the symbolic offering of the keys of the city to the victorious forces, and at first the Mayor offered them to Ptes Church and Andrewes, two mess cooks from the 60th Division, when they were in search of eggs and not keys to the Holy City. Eventually Maj. Gen. Shea of the 60th Division received them on behalf of Gen. Allenby. Two days later, Allenby himself was officially greeted by the city's Military Governor when he entered Jerusalem on foot through the ancient Jaffa gate. His entourage included Maj. T.E. Lawrence and Lt Col Archibald Wavell. Fighter aircraft circled overhead and volleys of machine-gun fire were heard in the street, but no Allied flags were flown. When the Kaiser visited the city in 1908 he entered on horseback.

A day after Train's VC citation was published in the *London Gazette*, the battalion war diary also announced the award 'for conspicuous gallantry at *Ain Karim* on 8 December 1917':

> C.W. Train, No. 510051, Corpl., 2/14th Battn. London Regt. For most conspicuous bravery, dash and initiative displayed under heavy fire when his company was unexpectedly engaged at close range by a party of the enemy with two machine guns and brought to a standstill. Corpl. Train, on his own initiative, rushed forward and engaged the enemy with rifle grenades, and succeeded in putting some of the team out of action with a direct hit. He then shot at and wounded an officer in command, and with bomb and rifle killed and wounded the remainder of the team. After this he went to the assistance of a comrade who was bombing the enemy from their front, and shot at and killed one of the enemy who was carrying the second gun out of action. His courage and devotion to duty undoubtedly saved his battalion heavy casualties and enabled them to advance to their objective at a time when the situation seemed critical.

After returning from Palestine, where he had been presented with his VC ribbon at a battalion parade by Lt Gen. Sir P.W. Chetwode, Train served for a third time in France and was decorated with his VC by the King at Blendecques, 3 miles south of St Omer, on 6 August 1918. The ceremony took place in the grounds of a château as the King was making one of his visits to his Army in France. Two other men received their VCs on the same day: John Crowe, an officer of the Worcestershire Regiment, and Cecil Knox from the Royal Engineers.

An article in the *London Scottish Regimental Gazette* of September 1918 described the scene when Maj. Whyte, representing the colonel who was on leave, and a body of men from Train's battalion was chosen to take part in the parade:

> Train motored to the function in a luxurious Daimler, and the rest sampled the old joys of the London General Omnibus Company! Rain, several times in the course of the day, threatened to spoil the proceedings, but at the hour of the ceremony the weather seemed to have definitely decided to amend.
>
> The day was naturally one of considerable excitement for Train. He was aroused by the Orderly Sergeant in the small hours of the morning, and received with somewhat 'mixed' feelings the news that the King was in the area, and would hold an investiture in the afternoon. He has been 'sweating' on the leave list – though one never knows what luck may yet befall distinguished men like Train – and, if less for his own sake than for the gratification of proud and interested home folks, there was possibly a tinge of disappointment at missing the Buckingham Palace experience, for since he has received the Cross just eight months after it was won, that was a reasonable hope. The investiture, in the secluded grounds of a château, occupied by the distinguished Army Commanders in the 'somewhere behind the line,' had all the brilliance that military pomp can lend it in the way of smart troops splendidly turned out, and the striking display of staff colours.

The kilted Train, the third man to be presented, was put at his ease by the King who preferred the name 'The London Scottish' to the 14th Battalion, London Regiment, and who knew that he was the first man in the regiment to win the VC. The King shook the sergeant's hand and congratulated him 'on the most gallant action which most undoubtedly saved your battalion many casualties'.

After his VC had been announced, a newspaper reported:

> Major-General Sir Newton Moore attended a meeting of the Islington Borough Council yesterday evening, at which an Islington V.C. Sergt. Train, was presented with an Illuminated Address and a parcel of War Bonds and Treasury Notes of the value of £216, as a tribute to his heroism, and the General added his own warm congratulations to those of the Council.

Sgt C.W. Train was also presented with a gold-knobbed walking stick by Mr E. Smallwood MP on behalf of the Highbury Patriotic Meeting.

Sgt Train was twice offered a commission, which he refused, preferring to stay in the ranks. He attended a school of musketry in September and remained in France until after the war, returning home on 17 February 1919. After the war Train was the recipient of a disability pension and was awarded 6*d* a day for 'Distinguished Conduct' for as long as the pension continued.

Charles William Train was born at 58 Chatterton Road, Finsbury Park, on 21 September 1890. He was educated at the Gillespie Road London County Council schools, attended St Thomas's Church and joined the church's football team. He was later briefly employed as a solicitor's clerk at Messrs Walker, Martineau & Co., of Gray's Inn.

Train came from fighting stock, for his father, a native of Midlothian who moved to London, was for many years a member of the Old Volunteers and was considered to be a crack shot. At the age of 18 Charles Train decided to enlist in the London Scottish for four years on 22 February 1909, and he joined A Company. He was fractionally over 5ft 7in tall and his service number was 55366. Between 1909 and 1913 he attended annual military training at Salisbury, Dover, Erith Hill and Abergavenny. He was still in the Army on the outbreak of war and left for France with 1/14th Battalion, arriving at Le Havre on 16 September. He took part in the fighting at Messines at the end of October, and on 2 November was made a lance corporal. In the following year he contracted diphtheria in France and was invalided home on 24 March. After becoming a member of the 3rd Battalion, he returned to France on 4 July.

In early September he was wounded and invalided home a second time, arriving on 9 September. He remained at home during this time; his medical records show that he was treated for a hernia and later employed drilling recruits in Hove until January when he was sent as one of a draft that reached the 2nd Battalion in Salonika in mid-January 1917. Remaining there for nearly seven months, he left Salonika for Egypt on 12 August where he served until 17 June 1918. In September 1917 he had been promoted to acting corporal, and then to sergeant on 30 March 1918. His records show that he was wounded on 1 May 1918 and returned to France on 23 June.

After he had returned from France in February 1919 he attended the VC Garden Party at Buckingham Palace in June 1920, and at some point in the early 1920s he decided to emigrate to Canada where he:

> ... became well known in Vancouver after he had joined the British Columbia Shipping Federation in 1926. He was appointed Secretary in 1935 and was later put in charge of longshoremen's pension and welfare funds and worked tirelessly on their behalf. For many years he was known as Mr Shipping Federation and even after his retirement did much work to further the causes which had been his life's work.

In 1929 Train was back in England in order to attend the House of Lords' VC Dinner in November. In 1956 he came over with the Canadian contingent to take part in the VC centenary commemorations in London, the Hyde Park parade and the Lord Mayor of London's reception at the Guildhall on 27 June 1956.

After making what was to be a final visit to England in October 1964 and returning home to British Columbia, he became ill and was taken to hospital. He died in hospital in Vancouver on 28 March 1965, aged 74.

A few days later, at the close of his funeral service, a Sgt Piper 'from "The Seaforths of Canada" played the casket to the coach with four holders of the Victoria Cross as escort'. Train's body was buried at Forest Lawn Memorial Park, Gilpin Street, Burnaby, British Columbia Field of Honour, Normandy Section, Lot 208, Grave 3. His decorations also included the 1914 star with clasp ('5th Aug.–22nd Nov. 1914'), BWM, VM (1914–19), King George VI Coronation Medal (1937), Queen Elizabeth II Coronation Medal (1953) and Territorial Efficiency Medal (1921). They are with the London Scottish Regiment in Horseferry Road, London, together with those of Robert Cruickshank VC.

J.A. CHRISTIE

Fejja, 21/22 December 1917

After Allenby's force had advanced 60 miles on a front of 30 miles and accepted the surrender of Jerusalem on 9 December 1917, the Turkish Army had withdrawn in the night to the Jordan Valley. The Ottoman Empire was beginning to collapse and when the Turkish Army was driven out of Palestine the plan was for the country to be run as a British Protectorate. However, for the time being British and ANZAC forces camped outside the Holy City.

By 21 December 1917 the extreme left of the British line was about 10 miles north-east of Jaffa and the 1/11th Battalion (County of London), London Regiment (Finsbury Rifles), 162nd Brigade, 54th Division was given orders to attack an enemy position called Bald Hill. During the ensuing fighting L/Cpl John Christie gained the Victoria Cross. The following account of the action is based on the battalion and brigade war diaries:

> From 10–15 [10.15 p.m.] a barrage was brought down on the Turkish held Bald Hill, a position of great natural strength, which the enemy had spent much effort in fortifying and putting up wire on its south-west side. The barrage was followed three hours later by a British advance from the south-east and Turkish positions were 'carried and held in spite of three very determined enemy counter attacks to retake the Hill, all of which were repulsed with severe enemy loss. The enemy had also showed great activity with Austrian Bombing Parties throughout the night, repeated attempts being made to bomb a way up the Communication Trenches, these also all failed and the Hill remained in our hands. Enemy artillery was also very active throughout the night. Bald Hill being heavily shelled.

L /Cpl Christie's deed was witnessed by an officer, who wrote:

> At a critical time in the darkness and confusion, L.-Cpl. Christie filled his pockets with bombs and quite alone got out of the trenches, and following the Turkish trench in the open, rained bombs on the Turkish bombers. We afterwards counted twenty-six dead Austrians in that particular trench.'

He was later sent for and congratulated in the presence of all the officers in the section.

Leaving one company to garrison the hill, the battalion moved forward at 8.30 a.m. with the assistance of the 1/4th Northants on the right and 161th Brigade to the left to attack the Turkish positions at Fejja, which were taken with little opposition. A new line was reconnoitred and consolidated by 10.45 a.m. During the afternoon, the battalion withdrew to a position 800yd south of Bald Hill and handed over the new line to the 1/4th Northants.

While at rest, the battalion scoured the battlefield and salvaged large quantities of material, including 200 rounds of small-arms ammunition. In addition, forty-two of the enemy, including two officers, were buried on Bald Hill. A few days later, on Christmas Day, when the weather conditions were very wet and cold, the battalion 'celebrated' with a meal of bully beef, biscuits and oranges. On the 29th the battalion moved to the Jewish colony of Mulebbis.

Just over two months later, Christie's VC citation was published in the *London Gazette* of 27 February 1918 as follows:

> No. 450685, John Alexander Christie, Rifleman (L.-Corpl.), London Regt. For most conspicuous bravery, when after a position had been captured, the enemy immediately made counter and bombing attacks up communication trenches. L.-Corpl. Christie realizing the position, took a supply of bombs over the top, proceeding alone about 50yds in the open along the communication trench, and bombed the enemy. He continued to do this alone, in spite of very heavy opposition, until a block had been established. Returning towards our lines, he heard voices behind him; he at once turned back and bombed another party moving up the trench, entirely breaking up a further bombing attack. By his prompt and effective action he undoubtedly cleared a difficult position at a most

critical time and saved many lives. Throughout he was subjected to heavy machine-gun fire and shell fire. He showed the greatest coolness and a total disregard for his own safety.

After the announcement of his VC, Christie was given a great welcome home when he returned to Islington and was presented with a testimonial from the Borough.

In March 1918, now back in Palestine, he was wounded in the wrist and knee at Medjelyaba, and later in the month, while still undergoing treatment, he was presented with a VC ribbon by the Duke of Connaught at Yezour, near Jaffa. Christie left for England in November 1918, and on the 16th he was decorated by the King at an investiture in the ballroom of Buckingham Palace.

John Alexander Christie was the son of Andrew and Sarah Christie, born in Edmonton, North London, on 14 May 1895, and his home address was 35 Fairbridge Road, Upper Holloway. He was of Scottish parentage and was always known as 'Jock'. After leaving school he moved to the Midlands for a short time before returning to London and living in Islington. He became a railway clerk in the Accounts Section of the Parcel Department, Euston station, with the London & North-Western Railway (LNWR) and continued with his education at the Working Men's College, Holloway. He was also a keen athlete and a member of St John's Holloway Football Team. On 1 September 1914 Christie, who was a fraction over 5ft tall, enlisted as a rifleman in the 1st/11th (County of London) Battalion, The London Regiment (Finsbury Rifles), a Territorial battalion which was part of the KRRC. The battalion had been formed four weeks earlier at 17 Penton Street, Pentonville, and was attached to the 3rd (London) Brigade, 1st (London) Division.

Christie remained in England, initially training in Crowborough, Sussex, and on 24 April the battalion was posted to East Midland Brigade, East Anglian Division, which was stationed at Norwich, Norfolk. On 7 May it became part of the 162nd Brigade, 54th (East Anglian) Division, and left for St Alban's, Hertfordshire, where it remained until 28 July 1915. The brigade then sailed from Plymouth to Mudros as part of the Mediterranean Expeditionary Force. Christie's 'Burnt File' states that he sailed on HMS *Aquitania* bound for Gallipoli. His battalion landed at Suvla Bay on 11 August, but he was wounded at Chocolate Hill within two weeks of his arrival. On 1 September 1915 he was admitted to hospital in Alexandria with gunshot wounds to his head and left knee. He returned home and was treated at St Bartholomew's Hospital and remained in England until he sailed from Devonport for Alexandria in Egypt, arriving there in mid-July 1916. He joined his battalion at a position named 'Manchester Post' and was temporarily attached to the 1/7th Essex Battalion, also of the East Anglian Division, but he returned to his own battalion on 24 August. On 27 November he was sent on a brigade bombing course and then rejoined his unit in the Canal Zone on 10 December 1916.

At the end of March and in mid-April he took part in the coastal advance towards Gaza, and was present at the unsuccessful attempts to capture Gaza. His file also notes that he was suffering from severe sunstroke. On 18 August 1917 he was admitted to hospital suffering from conjunctivitis and later returned to his battalion in the field. In the same month as he was made a lance corporal, he won the VC at Fejja, north-east of Jaffa, on 21/22 December 1917.

In January 1919, two months after the Armistice, Christie was presented with a bureau and a cheque from his Traffic Department Staff colleagues at Euston station. He had already been honoured by the Chairman and Board of Directors of the LNWR. The inscription in the bureau was as follows:

> Presented to Lance-Corporal J.A. Christie, V.C., by his colleagues in the Traffic Department at Euston Station to mark their admiration of his conspicuous bravery on the battlefield in Palestine on December 21–22, 1917, for which he received from the King's hands the coveted decoration of the V.C.

In his reply to this gift, Christie, having been greeted with cheers, said that:

> … he only did what he considered was his duty, and he would be ready to do the same again if circumstances required it; he expressed his great pleasure at meeting his colleagues, and thanked them warmly for their goodwill, and also for the handsome bureau and cheque. The bureau, he added, would always remind him of his friends at Euston Station, and he would treasure it as long as he lived.

Christie served in the Army at home until 11 February 1919, before being discharged and returning to work on the railways.

Christie attended many of the Victoria Cross gatherings, including the Garden Party at Buckingham Palace on 26 June 1920 and the ceremony for the Unknown Warrior in November 1920. In 1926 he drove food wagons in London during the General Strike. In November 1929 he was unable to attend the House of Lords' VC Dinner as he could not get time off from work; later he worked as a traveller for a Nottingham firm. An LNWR 'Patriot Class' locomotive was named after him, and another was named after Wilfred Wood VC. Christie married Muriel May Newton from Nottingham at Worleston, Cheshire, in December 1931, fourteen years after he won the VC, and they made their home in Bramhall, Stockport. Christie became a prominent local figure in the wine and catering trade in the Manchester area. The couple were to have two sons: John, who moved to Australia and became an airline pilot (he held his father's medals); and Kenneth, who had a career in the wine trade and lived in Devon.

At some point in the 1930s, he became Northern Area sales manager for Colmans of Norwich. Later in the 1930s he became a member of the executive committee of the Brands (Wines and Spirits) Protection Association and later became its vice-chairman.

During the Second World War he served as a special constable, then as a driver in the Auxiliary Fire Service and later transferred to the Special Constabulary. He became a director of Messrs Smallmans Ltd in the late 1940s and held the position until about 1964. In 1956 he became treasurer of the newly founded VC/GC Association and was a very active and popular member. He was actively involved with the arrangements of the various reunions and dinners that took place. It was his VC that was featured on the dust jacket of Sir John Smyth's book, *The Story of the Victoria Cross*. He attended the functions and

VE Parade in London on 8 June 1946 and the subsequent dinner at The Dorchester, and the ceremonies in London during June 1956, including the Hyde Park parade on 26 June.

Christie was an active Freemason and a founder member of Albatross Lodge. He was also president and captain of his local golf club. In 1961 the Kent and County of London Yeomanry (Sharpshooters) named the trophy for best all-round cadet of the year after him. In 1965 a small room was set aside for the exclusive use of members of the VC/GC Association at the HQ of the Association in Belgravia, London, and thirteen members greeted the prime minister, Harold Macmillan, who officially opened the room, although it was not large enough to hold the thirteen heroes. The VCs wore red carnations and the George Cross (GC) holders blue cornflowers. The members who attended included Jock Christie and Sir John Smyth. Tommy Gould VC said that when their members got together they never talked about their awards but 'about gardens and cricket, Test matches and politics'. At a dinner held in 1966 the toast was made by the prime minister, Sir Alec Douglas-Home, to 'absent friends' and Jock Christie made the response.

By this time Christie was living at 3 Bramley Close, Bramhall, Cheshire. In the spring of 1967 he was admitted to hospital after a stroke and died six months later at St Thomas's Hospital, Stockport, Greater Manchester, on 10 September 1967. He was cremated at Stockport Crematorium five days later. The funeral address was prepared by Sir John Smyth VC, who was also chairman of the VC/GC Association. The two men had first met in 1920 and had remained firm friends ever since. Three other VCs attended: R. Cain, J. Towers and W. Wood, as well as three holders of the GC. Smyth's address was read by the Revd Harold Woolley VC, since Smyth was unable to attend. In his very moving eulogy, Smyth listed some of Christie's qualities and ended by saying 'and as we leave this chapel our hearts should be filled with pride and thanksgiving for a life so nobly lived'.

After the service Christie's ashes were scattered in the First Garden of Remembrance. According to his widow, Christie was 'a man who hated any fuss whatsoever'. He was remembered by his local golf club at Bramhall, who displayed a picture of him together with a copy of his VC citation, as he had been captain of the club in 1950 and president in 1957. At some time he was also a member of the committee of the Davenport Rugby Club. On 6 September 2009 a Service of Thanksgiving for John Christie took place in Bramhall, which was followed by the dedication of a special park bench in Bramhall Park, and his son, Ken, and grandson were in attendance. Ken wore a set of his father's miniature medals for the ceremony, which, apart from the VC, included the 1914–15 Star, BWM, VM (1914–19), the King George VI Coronation Medal (1937), Defence Medal (1939–45), Queen Elizabeth II Coronation Medal (1953) and Constabulary Long Service Medal. They are not publicly held.

J. DUFFY

Kereina Peak, Corval Hill, 27 December 1917

After the 10th (Irish) Division had taken part in the successful Third Battle of Gaza in the first week of November 1917, it concentrated at Karm before moving a week later to Deir-el-Belah. This was followed by a march northwards via Beit Duras to Junction Station and then via Latron eastwards to the Judaean Hills. On 1 December the division was in position on the line Beit Dukka–Beit Ur et-Tahta–Suffa, north-west of Jerusalem. On their right were three divisions, the 53rd (Welsh) to the east of Jerusalem, the 60th (London) and the 74th (Yeomanry). Reaching north-westwards towards the sea to the north of Jaffa were the 75th, 54th and 52nd Divisions.

Owing to a severe decline in the weather over the Christmas period, a plan to advance into the southern portions of Mount Ephraim was abandoned and replaced with a new plan to move at dawn on the 27th. However, this was countered by the enemy who launched a successful attack against the outposts of the 60th Division at 11.30 p.m. on the 26th. Despite the enemy's success, six hours later the planned Allied advance began when the 29th and 30th Brigades pushed forward against strong opposition. The 6th Inniskilling Fusiliers, 31st Brigade, were involved in the attack and subsequent capture of Kereina Peak, which was about 10 miles to the north-west of Jerusalem.

The divisional war diary of 27 December noted the following:

> The whole operation met with resistance from small bodies of the enemy with murderous machine guns. The advance was considerably delayed owing to the extremely difficult and hilly nature of the country. Roads have to be made before guns etc can be moved forward and entailed very hard work and long hours for the Pioneers and Infantry.

And according to the battalion war diary's rather cryptic account:

> the Battalion left camp at 0400 and were in position at 'jumping-off' point at 0600 (The Battalion were ordered to take 1st KEREINA PEAK, while 29th Bde (on the left) were taking DEIR IBZIA & 5th Innis. Fus. on right THREE TREES. The Battalion were then to advance up the hill called THE ISLAND and occupy KH. EL HAFY, taking up and consolidating a line with their left resting on the WADI AIN ARIK and their right on KH. EL HAFY.)
>
> At 0645 advance was made from the jumping-off point, LOWER KEREINA being gained at 0730 and KEREINA PEAK at 0830. Little opposition was met with, until gaining the PEAK, where a strong party of the enemy were

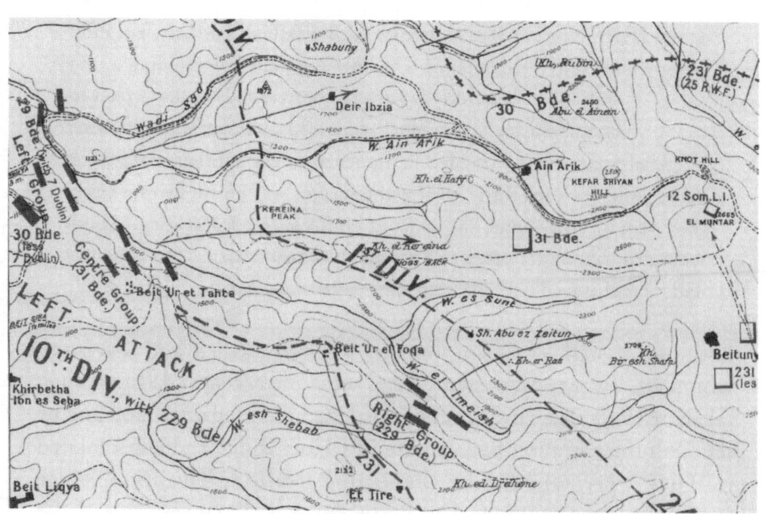

Kereina Peak, 27 December 1917.

> posted with Machine Guns. The two attacking companies, however, utilising dead ground, approached within assaulting distance of the guns, which they then charged, one gun being captured. The enemy then retired, but kept up a heavy fire, with Machine Guns & snipers, from THREE TREES (about 200 to 300yds away), until that position was taken by the 5th Innis. Fus. at about 0930.
>
> At 1230 the advance was continued from the PEAK to the ISLAND; as before two companies (A & D) attacking, one coy (B) in support and one coy (C) in reserve. Before the advance, the position was effectively shelled by the artillery, but while climbing the hill we came under heavy enfilading machine gun fire from the direction of AIN AINEIN. A line from P. 19. D. 9. 8 to KH. EL HAFY (inclusive) had been gained by 1500 & was then consolidated.

It was during this fighting that Pte James Duffy of the 6th Battalion Royal Inniskilling Fusiliers, 30th Brigade, won his VC when advancing under heavy fire from the enemy and rescuing several wounded men. The citation was published in the *London Gazette* of 28 February 1918 as follows:

> James Duffy. No. 17978, Private, Royal Inniskilling Fusiliers. For most conspicuous bravery displayed while his company was holding a very exposed position. Private Duffy (a stretcher-bearer) and another stretcher-bearer went out to bring in a seriously wounded comrade; when the other stretcher-bearer was wounded he returned to get another man; when again going forward the relief stretcher-bearer was killed. Private Duffy then went forward alone, and under heavy fire succeeded in bringing both wounded men under cover and attended to their injuries. His gallantry undoubtedly saved both men's lives.

Battalion casualties during the day were five killed and seventeen wounded. Twenty-five enemy dead were observed and fifteen men taken prisoner. The advance continued the following afternoon and by the 29th the battalion had captured El Tireh Ridge and consolidated it. They were relieved by the 16th Battalion, The Devonshire Regiment, that evening. The battalion war diary also noted the very fine weather after the previous cold and wet conditions, and also the difficulties which the transport endured in having to bring rations and ammunition by pack mule up over the hills. In addition, no blankets had been available for the men and sleep was almost impossible because of the cold nights. Six months later the 10th Division left for France, arriving at Marseilles on 1 June 1918, and Duffy was decorated a few weeks later by the King in the quadrangle of Buckingham Palace on 25 July 1918.

James Duffy's deed was later featured in a poem by Tom Kelly, 'Lines on the Irish V.C. Hero'. Duffy returned to Ireland for the first visit to his family home at Bonagee since he was awarded the VC in 1918 and received a hearty reception. Duffy got married in the same year to Maggie Hegarty and the couple were to have seven children and twenty-four grandchildren.

James Duffy was born in the home of his mother, Catherine Doogan, in the township of Thorr, Gweedore, County Donegal, on 17 November 1889. When he was a few months old he was brought to stay with his father, Peter Duffy, at Bonagee, Letterkenny. He was the couple's third son. Later James attended primary school at Drumlodge, near Letterkenny.

Duffy's father was employed in seasonal work such as agriculture and fishing. James, too, took to fishing. However, he sought a living in Scotland and settled in Glasgow, where he worked in the John Brown Shipyard. He was there when war broke out and joined the Army on 1 December 1914. He was then posted to the 6th (Service) Battalion, the Royal Inniskilling Fusiliers, who had been formed in Omagh in August. They were part of 31st Infantry Brigade, 10th (Irish) Division, which was the first complete Irish division to serve with the British Army. The regiments were drawn from Ireland's four provinces. Early training was carried out in the Dublin area. In May 1915 the division left for Basingstoke in Hampshire and embarked for the Mediterranean in July, arriving at Mudros on 7 August 1915. The division later served in Gallipoli, landing at 'C' Beach south of Suvla Bay. Duffy, acting as a stretcher-bearer, saved many lives. On 24 October the battalion moved to Salonika and took part in the actions on 7 and 8 December at Kosturino and, later, at Karajakois. They moved to Alexandria, Egypt, in September 1917 to prepare for their role in the invasion of Palestine. On 1 November the 6th Inniskillings captured Abu Irgeig and took part in the Third Battle of Gaza, which, under the command of Gen. Allenby, was a huge success. The 31st Brigade also took part in the capture of Sheria. Duffy was involved in the operations during the rest of the year, culminating with his winning of the VC two days after Christmas Day.

Duffy was demobilised in 1919 and was never to have regular employment again.

In November 1929 he attended the House of Lords' VC Dinner. In 1934 he took part in the Armistice Day ceremonies in Londonderry, probably as an official guest. In 1938 a report in the *Derry People* of 3 September stated that Duffy lived in a four-roomed cottage at Bonagee, 'for which he pays a weekly rent of 2*s* 6*d* out of a disability pension of 13/6 weekly, awarded him for malaria and rheumatism. As well as his pension he receives a yearly grant of £10 from the fund for necessitous VCs.' The report also mentions that he missed several invitations to royal functions such as garden parties, through the non-arrival of letters of invitation incorrectly addressed. If he could find employment, Duffy worked as a casual labourer on the roads or helped to bring in the harvest. When he was ill he had to be sent to Leopardstown Hospital, Dublin. He received a weekly grant of 25*s* provided from a fund set up by a wealthy American for distressed VC winners. Duffy was also assisted by the British Legion.

In 1956 Duffy was invited to Dublin's Festival of Remembrance and met up with three other holders of the VC: Gen. Sir Carton de Wiart, J.E. Woodall and John Moyney, accompanied by Sir A. Clutterbuck, the British Ambassador. In the same year he attended the VC centenary celebrations in London. Two years later he was also a special guest at a dinner held in Dublin to commemorate the memory of the six Irish regiments disbanded in 1922.

In the *People's Press* of 11 April 1969, Duffy was quoted as saying the following when questioned about his deed:

> I cannot remember how many times I made the journey. Some soldiers died after medical treatment, some died in my arms, but I know that at least two men lived. My bandages were riddled with bullets, and one even

> cut through my shirt. Shells exploded all around me. I went on. I didn't care if they got me, because all my friends were dead or dying.

Duffy was said to be 'of a very quiet disposition and very reluctant to speak of his heroic action. He was inclined to "Play down" his award, and would prefer to speak generally of life in the army. He was very popular with all creeds and classes.'

During one of his regular summer holidays in Ireland, Earl Mountbatten, who was later murdered by the IRA in 1979, paid Duffy a visit.

Duffy died at Drumany, near Bonagee, after a long illness on 7 April 1969 and was buried at Conwel Cemetery. His wife predeceased him in 1944. The inscription on his grave is 'Sacred Heart of Jesus Have Mercy on his soul'. Duffy's military funeral was organised by Maj. George Shields, Chairman of the Belfast branch of the Royal Inniskilling Fusiliers Regimental Association, who had served with Duffy at Corval Hill in 1917. He worked in tandem with Archdeacon Louis Crooks of Raphoe, who had become a good friend of Duffy. He was the last remaining Northern Irish holder of the VC in the First World War. On the day of his funeral, a Requiem Mass was celebrated in St Eunan's Cathedral, Letterkenny, and later shops and offices in the town of Letterkenny closed and the majority of the population lined the route of the cortège. Lorries stood empty as their drivers left their vehicles and stood with their heads bowed in respect. 'The only sound was the clink of medals of the old soldiers.' The procession began at Duffy's cottage when his coffin was passed through the small sitting-room window. He was carried by eight pallbearers dressed in mufti, who were members of the Royal Irish Rangers under their warrant officer, CSM William O' Neill. A pipe major, James Creggan, led the parade playing *The Flowers of the Forest*.

The ½-mile procession halted at the cemetery after a 2-mile drive. After a short service Duffy was laid to rest beside his wife, Margaret. The *Last Post* and *Reveille* were sounded at the graveside by L/Cpl J. Maxwell and several wreaths were laid at the grave.

Duffy had bequeathed his VC and medals to the Museum of the Royal Inniskilling Fusiliers about twenty years before his death. In the Lummis file in the National Army Museum, there is a letter from a Niall McGinley dated 15 August 1988. He talks of the 'downside of winning a VC' and how it could ruin your life. The winning of the VC probably only brought misery to Duffy's life because money was always scarce. Pressures from the family to encourage Duffy to sell his VC to the highest bidder might have caused a great schism in the family.

If this observation is true then Duffy always found keeping his head above water a considerable problem, as employment was no more than seasonal at best. As Duffy had served in the British Army and won a VC he came to the notice of the IRA who kidnapped him in 1921.

Duffy left five surviving sons and a daughter. In 1997, Hugh ('Hugo') died and was buried in the same grave as his parents. There are portraits of the two men with the VC between them and 'Rest in peace' has been added to the inscription on the gravestone.

Duffy's name is commemorated on the regimental plaque displayed at St Anne's Cathedral, Belfast. On 10 July 2007 a stone bench was unveiled in Letterkenny Park to his memory, which also has a memorial garden.

Duffy's decorations also included the 1914–15 Star, BWM, VM (1914–19), King George VI Coronation Medal (1937) and Queen Elizabeth II Coronation Medal (1953), which are held by the Royal Inniskilling Fusiliers Museum in the castle at Enniskillen, Northern Ireland.

H. WHITFIELD

Burj-el-Lisane, near Tel, Asur, 10 March 1918

After Jerusalem had fallen on 9 December 1917, the Allies possibly thought that the campaign in Palestine and Syria was almost all over, and for the next few weeks they made further advances north and north-west of the Holy City.

After Gen. Allenby's very successful campaign in Palestine, his sights would have been trained on progress towards the towns of Damascus and Aleppo to the north. However, during the early part of 1918, events in France on the Western Front played a major factor in what was to happen next in Palestine, Jordan and Syria. Owing to the German success in France in the spring of 1918, Allenby was forced to reduce his force as a result of urgent calls for more divisions to serve on the Western Front. He was to lose the 52nd (Lowland) and 74th (Yeomanry) Divisions in April, along with nine Yeomanry regiments. Indian troops were brought in to replace them. So in early 1918 any plans of advance were scaled down, leaving the first priority to make an offensive towards the ancient walled city of Jericho to the north of the Dead Sea.

As a preliminary to this advance, the 53rd (Welsh) Division on the right of the line, 20–25 miles north-west of Jerusalem, relieved the 60th (London) Division on the Nablus road, which would allow the 60th

Division to take over the Eastern Front, 3 miles from Jerusalem. The ANZAC Mounted Division was also involved.

After three days of intensive fighting, the 60th Division and the ANZAC Mounted Division captured Jericho on 20 February. The mounted cavalry had played a major role and the ANZAC horsemen swept into the old city on the 21st, driving the Turkish forces in front of them towards the river crossing at Ghoraniyeh before establishing themselves in the Jordan Valley. To the south, the New Zealand Mounted Rifles successfully reached and captured the enemy Dead Sea post at Rujm-el-Bahr; the base was very important as a landing place and would allow communications to be opened with the Northern Operations of the Sherifian Army when they were in the Kerak area.

The fighting in the Jordan Valley was already proving to be much more suited to cavalry than infantry action. Both XXth Corps and XXIst Corps had been very successful in the operations to the north after Jerusalem had been taken in early December 1917, and they were soon to push up to a line where they would remain until September 1918. However, three more VCs were to be gained by the British Army

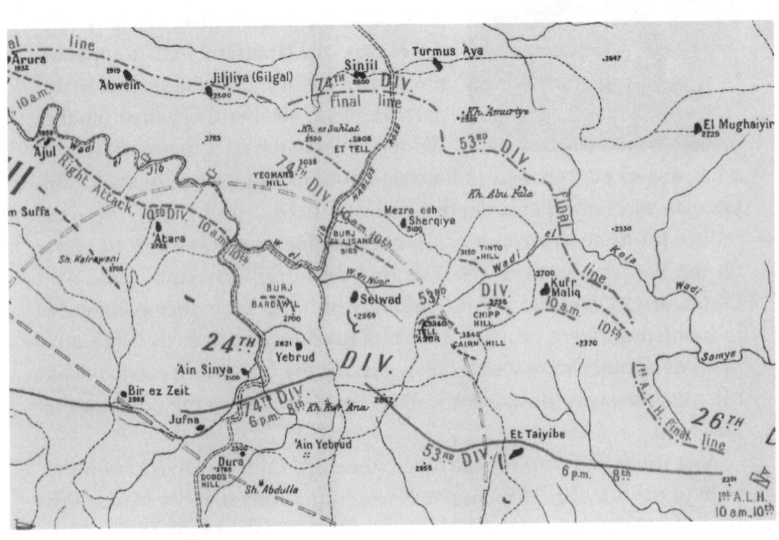

Selwad and Burj-el-Lisane, 10 March 1918.

before September, and the first one of 1918 was awarded to Pte Harold Whitfield on 10 March. He was a member of the 10th King's Shropshire Light Infantry, 231st Infantry Brigade, 74th (Yeomanry) Division. His brigade had recently been attached to the 60th Division.

This division was formed in Egypt in early 1917 and in August 1917 became part of XX Corps, taking part in the attack against Beersheba on 31 October. During the winter months it was involved in hill fighting. On 8 March 1918 the division moved towards the Jerusalem–Nablus road, with the 53rd Division on the right and the 10th (Irish) Division on the left. On the following day, 231st Brigade attacked the hostile defences of the village of Selwad. The 10th King's Shropshire Light Infantry cleared the village, capturing five officers and twenty-three other ranks. But, on its way towards Burj-el-Lisane, it was delayed when having to cross a deep wadi and became very exposed when both flanks were unguarded. On their right, two attempts by the 230th Brigade on Yebrud had been unsuccessful.

However, early on the following morning the 231st Brigade stormed the precipitous ridge of Burj-el-Lisane and the battalion moved across what was very steep and difficult ground towards the slopes of the ridge, whose summit was reached by 6 a.m. and the enemy ejected from his positions. The battalion then managed to defend it against three heavy counter-attacks, and at one point the left flank of the position was in considerable danger. It was during this action that Pte Harold Whitfield won the VC when he managed to knock out an enemy machine-gun team.

At the same time the 230th Brigade was making up for their lack of success the previous day when after heavy fighting they captured Yebrud and Burj Bardawil. The brigade then proceeded to advance 2 miles despite strong enemy resistance. On the 11th the 231st Brigade captured Sheikh Selim, while the 230th occupied a ridge overlooking Sinjil.

These were the last operations by the 74th (Yeomanry) Division in Palestine, and they left for France a few weeks later, arriving in Marseilles on 7 May.

The citation for Whitfield's VC was published in the *London Gazette* nearly nine weeks later on 8 May, two days before he was promoted to sergeant:

> Harold Whitfield, No. 230199, Private, 10th Yeomanry Battn. King's Shropshire Light Infantry. For most conspicuous bravery, initiative and absolute disregard of personal safety. During the first and heaviest of three counter-attacks made by the enemy on the position which had just been captured by his battalion, Private Whitfield, single-handed, charged and captured a Lewis gun which was harassing his company at short range. He bayoneted or shot the whole gun team, and turning the gun on the enemy, drove them back with heavy casualties, thereby completely restoring the whole situation in his part of the line. Later he organized and led a bombing attack on the enemy who had established themselves in an advanced position close to our lines, and from which they were enfilading his company. He drove the enemy back with great loss, and by establishing his party in their position saved many lives, and materially assisted in the defeat of the counter-attack.

On 4 March the writer Siegfried Sassoon was posted to the 25th Royal Welsh Fusiliers, who were part of the same brigade as the 10th King's Shropshire Light Infantry (231st), and in his diaries he described the ceremony when Whitfield was presented with his VC ribbon. As will be seen, Sassoon is very bitter at this time, although he didn't take part in the operations to capture Burj-el-Lisane.

In his diary, Sassoon wrote that, in the afternoon on 20 May, a part of 231st Brigade formed a hollow square:

> ... on a green hillside above the red-roofed village [Cauchy south of Lillers], snug among its trees. The Brigadier stalked on to the scene, and the Divisional General followed, receiving the salute of flashing bayonets, a small forest of them.... The General ... 'speaking loud and distinct, though rather fast, said that he had never been more honoured and proud and pleased etc than to-day, when he had come (like a dear, middle-aged turkey-cock) to do honour to one of the most gallant men he had ever known.' ... He read out and descanted on the exploits which had won Harold Whitfield (10th King's Shropshire Light Infantry) the V.C. Nothing was finer in the whole history of the British Army (the rest of the Brigade, of course, say that Whitfield's deeds were very much exaggerated, but the K.S.L.I. are pleased and proud). Whitfield had captured a machine-gun-post single-handed, shot and bayoneted the whole team (they were Turks

> – probably harmless conscripts – but possibly Bosches or Austrians). He had killed immense numbers of the enemy, and redeemed the situation on his battalion front. The General then called for 'Corporal Whitfield', and a clumsily built, squat figure in a round steel helmet ran out of the front rank of his Company, stopped, and saluted. He did not look a heroic figure. The General then pinned something on his breast (after dropping the pin, which a Brigade Major quickly recovered from the long grass). In a loud voice the General wished a long and happy life to wear it, and wrung him by the hand; and the little Corporal turned and was escaping to the shelter of the bayonet-forest; but was recalled, to stand out there beside the General, who called for the General Salute; 'to do honour to Whitfield'. 'Present-Arms!' Everyone saluted the stumpy little soldier, including the Generals. Three cheers were then given for Whitfield. And he escaped.
>
> It was an absurd show; not dignified in any way; not impressive, because one suspected that a lot of the men realised that it was only a 'stunt' (like Campbell's lecture) to raise the morale of the troops. The man who 'voluntarily supplies blood for transfusion to a comrade' does not – technically – perform an act of gallantry. But one who, in a spirit of animal excitement and over-strain, kills a certain number of Turks is acclaimed by his comrades, and made a fool of by the Mayor and Corporation when he goes on leave, shakes hands with George V and sees his face on the front pages of the gutter-press illustrated papers. The whole thing is childish – not manly – although the man and the deed are intrinsically fine things. The Army is kept going by 'stunts' like these. General Maurice is the man who should stand out to be honoured and acclaimed by his comrades.

Sassoon also wrote about Whitfield in a similar style in his book *Sherston's Progress,* where he becomes 'Corporal Whiteway'. In a recently published biography of Sassoon, Whitfield, as noted in the index, has incorrectly been elevated to the rank of captain!

Soon after the announcement of Whitfield's VC was published in the *London Gazette* of 8 May 1918, a special Oswestry Town Council meeting took place at the Guildhall on 16 May. The meeting was convened in order to discuss what steps should be taken by the council in recognition of the distinction on the borough which Whitfield's VC had brought. It was understood that Whitfield would soon be home for a few days and any arrangements needed to be made quickly. An illuminated album was one of the proposals, a civic welcome another, which duly took place in the town a few weeks later. Whitfield had many relatives in the area and was now a sergeant. On 23 May he arrived at the local station on the last train from Paddington and was met at the Great Western station by the Mayor and members of the town council, together with other dignitaries. Although no band or car had been laid on because of the short notice, the parish church bells rang out a greeting and a large crowd hastened to the station approaches. After the official greetings, he was asked how he felt and replied: 'Oh all right, like; got a bit of a cold, and am a bit hoarse.' Further cheers broke out after he emerged into Station Road and he was then swept up and borne shoulder-high to the Guildhall. After the procession reached the Guildhall, the Mayor then made a speech about the deep appreciation that the borough owed to their Oswestry boy. Many of Whitfield's relatives were present.

After the Mayor's address, a Maj. Felton of the Shropshire Yeomanry made a supporting speech in which he claimed Whitfield for the Yeomanry, knowing full well that he had been serving with the King's Shropshire Light Infantry at the time that he won the first regimental VC of the First World War. Then Whitfield was able to reply: 'I thank you for the welcome you have given me. All I can say is I did my whack like a Shropshireman, as Shropshiremen have always done' [loud applause].

The evening went on with Whitfield the centre of a group of relatives and friends, and it was 11 p.m. before he could escape and return home to Pool Far with his aunt and several other relatives.

Whitfield had been promoted from private to sergeant in the field by Sir Douglas Haig:

> He is one of the 'King's Sergeants' – a term with which military men are familiar, as indicating the holder of a rank which possesses peculiar privileges beyond other non-coms of a similar rank otherwise conferred.

During a three-day tour of the West Riding, the King took part in an investiture held at Becketts Park, Leeds. On 31 May the ceremony took place on the steps leading up to the Orthopaedic Hospital:

> ... and the King and Queen were surrounded by a great square of wounded soldiers, nurses, and other spectators. Three Victoria Crosses were presented, but unhappily two of them could only be handed to the next-of-kin. Sergeant Whitfield, of the Shropshire Light Infantry, received his decoration personally.... The remaining two Victoria Crosses were given by the King to the widows of Acting Lieutenant-Colonel William Herbert Anderson, Highland Light Infantry, and Private Walter Mills, Manchester Regiment.

Both widows brought young children with them to receive their father's posthumous medal. While Whitfield stood to attention, his citation was read out by Sir John Maxwell.

In early June 1918 Whitfield was guest of the evening at a concert arranged by the local Conservative Club. A few days later another ceremony took place at Caeglas Park, at which he was honoured by a civic reception. The ceremony took place in front of a huge and enthusiastic crowd, which included Lord Harlech, colonel of the Shropshire Yeomanry, and Lady Harlech, together with Gen. Montgomery, local dignitaries and friends and relatives of Harold Whitfield. The Mayor and Lord Harlech made speeches and the latter hoped that Whitfield would be returning to the ranks of the Shropshire Yeomanry after the war. Gen. Montgomery then spoke before the official presentation was made by the town clerk.

On 20 June 1918, before he returned to active service, Whitfield was also given a token of appreciation at the Boar's Head pub by some of his former colleagues in the Yeomanry.

While Whitfield was in England, his battalion had arrived in France on 7 May 1918, and on 10 July it took over trenches at St Floris, south of La Lys Canal. On 22 August it managed to cross the canal, but was later pushed back to where it had been previously. At the end of August the battalion moved down to the Somme, and on 2 September took part in the attack at Moislains. Five days later it helped to capture the village of Villers Fauçon. Later it took part in the Battle of Épehy in the general advance, and on 28 September moved to La Vallee, near Choques, and five days later took over positions at Herlies. In early November it helped to drive the enemy out of Tournai. On Armistice Day it found itself at Ostiches.

Harold Whitfield, one of at least six sons, was born in Oswestry, Shropshire, on 11 June 1886. Born in Willow Street, he was a son of John and Katherine Whitfield. John used to run the Five Bells public house in the town where Harold was born. It appears that he was brought up by a Miss Edwards, an aunt at Pool Farm, Middleton, Oswestry. At some point, possibly from 1888, John Whitfield had served in the Yeomanry, and father and son later trained together after Harold had enlisted with them in 1908.

The 1/1st Shropshire Yeomanry were part of the Welsh Border Mounted Brigade on the outbreak of war, and on 4 September became part of the 1st Mounted Division in East Anglia and carried out training at Flixton, close to Bungay on the Norfolk–Suffolk border. On 25 October they moved to Lowestoft, before returning to Flixton at the end of the year. In August 1915 they left for Benacre, south of Kessingland, and on 21 October moved to Gorleston. In November they were made into a dismounted unit and sailed for Egypt on 4 March 1916, arriving at Alexandria on 14 March. At Cairo on 2 March 1917, together with the Cheshire Yeomanry, they were shortly to be incorporated into 10th King's Shropshire Light Infantry, 231st Brigade, 74th Division.

On 4 July 1920 at the Oswestry Conservative Club, a ceremony and concert took place. This time it was the occasion of the unveiling of two portraits of Brig. Gen. John V. Campbell VC and Sgt Harold Whitfield VC by the local Conservative MP's wife, Mrs Bridgeman. The two pictures screened by the Union Jack were unveiled, followed by singing by the assembled company of 'God Save The King'. Speeches were made by Mrs Bridgeman and Gen. Montgomery, and brief replies came from Gen. Campbell and Sgt Whitfield, who was accompanied by his aunt and his sister, Katie.

In mid-June 1925 Harold Whitfield married Miss Mary Tomley, daughter of Mr and Mrs J. Tomley of Middleston, Oswestry. The service took place at Holy Trinity Church, Oswestry, and after the ceremony the couple left the church under an archway of swords held by B Squadron of the Shropshire Yeomanry. Later the reception was held in a marquee at the bride's home. The couple then left for their honeymoon in London. It is interesting to note that in 1921 Whitfield was a tenant running a mixed farm at Drenewydd Farm, Whittington, one of Lord Harlech's farms, and Harlech presented the couple with a canteen of cutlery as a wedding present. In March 1927 Whitfield was attacked by a bull and his right hand was damaged. The Whitfields had one daughter. Sadly Mary died of cancer after only four years of marriage. Harold then had a housekeeper at Drenewydd Farm, Rose Mary Scoltock, fifteen years his junior. The couple married on 15 November 1929 and were to have seven daughters and two sons.

Whitfield retired from the Shropshire Yeomanry in 1936 after twenty-eight years' service and was given the honorary rank of sergeant major.

Whitfield was too old to take an active part in the Second World War, but kept on with his farming. However, he gave up the tenancy in 1943 when the business no longer paid and instead took a job with the Express Dairy at Whittington. The family home was now Uplands, Oakhurst Road, Oswestry.

In early 1956 he was ill, so spent some time in Oswestry and District Hospital; he now lived at 55 Lloyd Street. He was, however, well enough to attend the VC centenary commemorations in London in June 1956, travelling to London on 25 June with his wife and 19-year-old son, John, and he was given a civic send-off. A week later they were welcomed back by the Mayor at Oswestry station. The Express Dairy sponsored the whole trip and also laid on a chauffeur-driven car which took the Whitfields not only to all the VC events but also for a day out at Windsor Castle. Apart from the Hyde Park Review and a Garden Party at Marlborough House, they were fêted by actors and actresses at a special performance given for the VCs and their wives at the Lyceum Theatre.

Later in the year, together with a VC from the Second World War, G.H. Eardley, Whitfield took the salute at a passing out ceremony of King's Shropshire Light Infantry recruits in Shrewsbury. The two also presented medals for the best shots and other achievements.

On Sunday 16 December 1956, when cycling home to 55 Lloyd Street, Oswestry, on the Whittington Road from his work at Whittington Express Dairies, Whitfield was severely injured in a traffic accident and taken to Oswestry and District Hospital. It was about

6.45 p.m. on a damp and windy night and it appears from witnesses that his bicycle might have been blown to the centre of the road where a Park Hall Garrison Police Landrover, travelling at about 25mph, was unable to avoid hitting him; Whitfield was flung over the handlebars, sustaining severe injuries, including a fractured skull. He never regained consciousness and died three days later on Wednesday 19 December. Two other holders of the VC, Cecil Knox and Arthur Sutherland, also died in traffic accidents.

Whitfield was given a full military funeral and buried at Oswestry General Cemetery on Saturday 30 December, Plot W, Grave 26. His first wife shares the grave. A Union Jack was draped over the coffin and a firing party was supplied by the King's Shropshire Light Infantry, who fired volleys of shots over the grave; a bugler, also from the regiment, sounded the *Last Post*.

A very large number of friends, members of the family and representatives of many organisations attended the service, including Lt Col W.H. Wilberforce, who represented the 64th Training Regiment, Royal Artillery, Capt. J.B. Gross, representing the regiment, and the Chief Constable of Shropshire. Apart from his widow, Rose, he was survived by his children Marjorie, Rosemary, Dorothy, Betty, Margaret, Jean, John and Reginald.

Whitfield's will was made public at the end of June 1957 and, surprisingly considering he was employed as a dairy charge hand, he left £18,354. However, this did not reflect the true picture as his family would only receive a £15,000 legacy from his brother, John, a prosperous company director, after his brother's wife had died. He left his medals to his son, John, and then to any son that John might have and, failing that, the medals would pass to John's younger brother Reginald. An inscribed gold watch given to him in 1918 by the Shropshire Yeomanry was given to Reginald and the furniture, together with a small annuity, to his widow Rose. On her death, Rose was buried in the same grave as her husband and his first wife, Mary.

The Regimental Museum at Shrewsbury Castle has a fine collection of items relating to Harold Whitfield, which were presented by Rose on 2 May 1961. The items include medals, a Trooper's Sword, a Short Magazine Lee Enfield rifle, a Trooper's full dress helmet, a Sam Browne belt, some spurs and medal ribbons for his seven medals. The rifle and bayonet were the ones he used in the VC action.

As for the VC itself, the family placed it in a bank for safekeeping, but a bank clerk employed in the Midland Bank, Oswestry, stole it from the bank vaults in 1977 and sold it to a dealer in London for £2,000. The dealer became suspicious and the family were able to retrieve the precious medal. The bank clerk meanwhile was given 200 hours' community service.

In April 2000 Whitfield's VC was finally presented to the Regimental Museum, The Castle, Shrewsbury, by Sheila and John Whitfield at a ceremony at the castle. It was the 'icing on the cake' of the Whitfield VC display at the museum. The medals were later taken out of the museum to be worn by John at a Remembrance Day service held at Oswestry in November 2000. Harold's other medals kept in the Regimental Museum are the BWM, VM (1914–19), Territorial Force War Medal (1914–19), Territorial Efficiency Medal (1921), King George VI Coronation Medal (1937) and Queen Elizabeth II Coronation Medal (1953).

In recent years a plaque to Whitfield's memory has been set up at the Five Bells Public House in Willow Street, Oswestry.

K. Rana

El Kefr, 10 April 1918

A month after Pte Whitfield won his VC at Burj-el-Lisane, the same honour was won by an Indian Rifleman, Karanbahadur Rana, serving with the Gurkha Rifles of the Indian Army.

The 75th Division, with the 232nd, 233rd and 234th Brigades, a mixture of Territorial and three Indian battalions, came into existence in Egypt in June 1917 and was part of XXI Corps. At the end of October, on the day that the town of Beersheba was captured, the division was concentrated in the Mansura area, a few miles to the south-east of the coastal town of Gaza. A week later, on the day of the fall of Gaza itself, the 232nd Brigade captured a position known as the 'Labyrinth' and 'Ali Muntar', and by 1.30 p.m. occupied the 'Quarry' and 'Delilah's Neck'. A few days later the brigade, co-operating with the 52nd (Lowland) Division, captured Burkah and Brown Hill. On the 19th the brigade made further progress when capturing Amwas and Latron, and pushed on through strong opposition as well as hilly terrain to reach within 1 mile of Saris. On the 20th the brigade, after enveloping Saris, attacked and overcame the last defences of Kuryet-el-Enab. Two days later it captured Kustil, and on the 22nd was caught up with heavy counter-attacks around El Jib. They were relieved two days later by a brigade of the 60th Division.

A few months later, in April 1918, the 2nd Battalion of the 3rd Queen Alexandra's Own Gurkha Rifles, 232nd Infantry Brigade, 75th Division, was involved in attacking a German-held position on

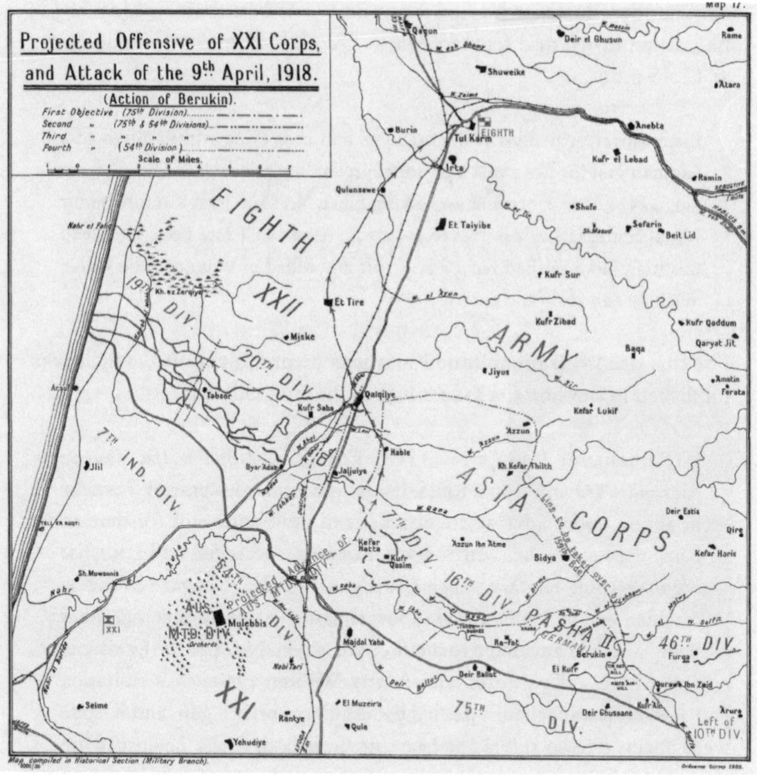

El Kefr, 10 April 1918.

the top of a rocky slope at El Kefr, which was covered in scrub and of great assistance to the defenders. Any attempted advance would also be quite visible to the enemy.

Karanbahadur Rana was No. 2 in a Lewis gun section in B Company, who were suffering heavy losses, including their commander, from heavy German machine-gun fire. In addition, the No. 1 in the Lewis gun team had been killed. Making the decision that the German machine-gun which was causing all this havoc had to be dealt with, Karanbahadur Rana set about the task. He not only knocked out the machine-gun, but also managed to rescue Lt Barter, his company commander. Barter, who had won the VC at Festubert in May 1915, had fallen down and feigned death. Quoting from the brigade diary, at 12.45 p.m:

> Lieut Barter turned up at the ridge; he had been lying within 30yds of a German gun for five and a half hours pretending to be dead. The machine gun was put out of action by a Lewis gunner, No 4146 Rfm Karanbahadur Rana, enabling Lieut Barter to get away. After No 1 had been shot dead this man No 2 pushed No 1's body off and killed or wounded the whole machine gun crew and escort.

For this deed Karanbahadur Rana was awarded the VC, which was published in the *London Gazette* of 21 June as follows:

> Karanbahadur Rana, No. 4146, Rifleman, 2/3rd Battn. Queen Alexandra's Own Gurkha Rifles. For most conspicuous bravery, resource in action under adverse conditions, and utter contempt for danger. During an attack he, with a few other men, succeeded under intense fire in creeping forward with a Lewis gun, in order to engage an enemy machine gun which had caused severe casualties to officers and other ranks who had attempted to put it out of action. No. 1 of the Lewis gun opened fire, and was shot immediately. Without a moment's hesitation Rifleman Karanbahadur pushed the dead man off the gun, and in spite of bombs thrown at him and heavy fire from both flanks, he opened fire and knocked out the enemy machine-gun crew; then, switching his fire on to the enemy bombers and riflemen in front of him, he silenced their fire. He kept his gun in action and showed the greatest coolness in removing defects which on two occasions prevented the gun from firing. During the remainder of the day he did magnificent work, and when a withdrawal was ordered he assisted with covering fire until the enemy were close on him; he displayed throughout a very high standard of valour and devotion to duty.

In September 1918 Queen Alexandra, widow of King Edward VII, sent Rana a signed photograph of herself via the colonel of the regiment.

Karanbahadur Rana was born in Mangalthan, Gulmi, Litung, Baghlung (Bag Lung) District in Nepal on 20 or 21 December 1891. He was a Rana of the Magar clan and probably joined the 2/3rd Gurkha Rifles of the Indian Army in 1908 at the age of 16.

After the war, in August 1919 Karanbahadur came to England to take part in the procession of Indian troops through London on 2 August. They were also received by the King at Buckingham Palace and an investiture was held when he was personally decorated by the King-Emperor. The King then addressed his Indian soldiers:

> It is with feelings of pride and gratification that I welcome here in my home this representative contingent of British and Indian officers and men of my Army in India, and I am especially glad that this meeting should take place when we are celebrating peace after victory. I deeply regret that unavoidable circumstances prevented your joining the troops of the Empire and of our Allies in the Victory Procession on 19 July. I thank the British troops for their magnificent services in the field. I gratefully recognize the prompt and cheerful response of the Territorials to their country's call, their patient endurance of a prolonged separation from their homes, and the sacrifices they made in giving up their occupations in civil life. When temporary trouble arose in India they, in common with their comrades from Mesopotamia, who were on their way home, of their free will remained at their posts (though home-coming was at hand). The exemplary conduct of all has filled me and their countrymen with admiration. I heartily thank all my Indian soldiers for their loyal devotion to me and to my Empire, for their sufferings, cheerfully borne, in the various campaigns in which they have served in lands and climates so different from their own. At times their hearts must have been sad at the long separation from their homes; but they have fought and died bravely. They have rivalled the deeds of their ancestors; they have established new and glorious traditions which they can hand on to their children for ever. I am glad to see among you representatives of the Imperial Service Troops, and I thank the Princes of the native States of India and their subjects for their noble response to the call made by me for the defence of the Empire and for the cause in which the Allies have fought and conquered. I know you will all unite with me in gratitude to God for the victory we have achieved. I trust you will enjoy your visit to England. May you return in safety, and take with you to your homes and villages my personal message of thanks and goodwill.

Karanbahadur left the Indian Army in the mid-1930s and unfortunately not much has been recorded about his life after the First World War, although the following information was published in *Weekend* on 14–20 July 1971:

> The former rifleman, who had lost an eye in the war is always at home in Litung in Nepal ... he is a wizened man of 80 with one eye and he doesn't go far these days from the dark of his tiny mud hut. But as he sits among the chickens and pigs that share his home Karanbahadur can recall the time when his home was the toast of the pink-gin sipping colonels who were around when the rifleman's conspicuous bravery and utter contempt for danger won him the Victoria Cross.

On 25 July 1973 Karanbahadur Rana died in his home village of Litung at the age of 82 and was buried at Bharse, Gilmi, Litung.

Later his VC and six other decorations were obtained from one of his sons by a representative of the Gurkha Museum, and they arrived at the museum on 1 November 1974. They included the BWM, VM (1914–19), India General Service medal (1908–36) with one clasp ('Waziristan 1919–21'), King George V Silver Jubilee Medal (1935), King George VI Coronation Medal (1937) and Queen Elizabeth II Coronation Medal (1953). The Gurkha Museum is in Winchester, Hampshire.

R.E. CRUICKSHANK

North of Shunet Nimrin, East of Jordan, 1 May 1918

Three weeks after the Gurkha Rifleman Karanbahadur Rana won the VC in the fighting at El Kefr, Pte Robert Cruickshank gained his VC to the east of the River Jordan. It was on 1 May 1918 when he was serving with D Company of the 2/14th (County of London) Battalion, The London Regiment (London Scottish), 179th Infantry Brigade, 60th (London) Division, during the battle of the second crossing of the River Jordan.

The 179th Brigade had returned to Bethany in Palestine on 9 April 1918 when they were ordered northwards to relieve one of the brigades of the 10th (Irish) Division to the north of Jerusalem on the Wadi Gharib. Soon afterwards, the 60th Division relieved the whole of the 10th Division. Having earlier retired, the Turkish Army had by now received reinforcements, who crossed the Jordan at Jisr-ed-Damieh. The enemy then reoccupied the Shunet Nimrin position, which, according to the divisional history, was of considerable strength. But the Allies then planned a raid that was intended to cut off the Turkish force.

The 179th and 180th Infantry Brigades, together with troops of the Desert Mounted Corps, were given this task, which began at 2 a.m. on 30 April. The 180th Brigade was to the right and the 179th on the left against the position of El Haud, which had been already attacked previously without success. The foothills were reached at dawn and the divisional history noted:

> ... it was soon evident that very serious opposition was to be encountered.... The Scottish, with the Westminsters, on their left, in spite of a very heavy machine-gun and rifle fire gained the position on Spectacle Hill, taking seventy-six prisoners; but the enemy's fire was too heavy to permit of any further advance.

Attempts at an advance were continued and:

> ... the fighting throughout had been desperate, and the troops had done all that was humanly possible in the face of the heavy casualties sustained, which taxed to the utmost the powers of the stretcher bearers, who excelled themselves in their heroic efforts to succour the wounded...

The London Scottish had lost thirty-three men killed and 140 wounded, nearly half their strength.

It was during this desperate and ultimately unsuccessful advance that Pte Robert Cruickshank of the 2/14th (County of London) Battalion, The London Regiment (London Scottish), gained the VC. Bernard Blaser described what happened in his book *Kilts Across the Jordan*:

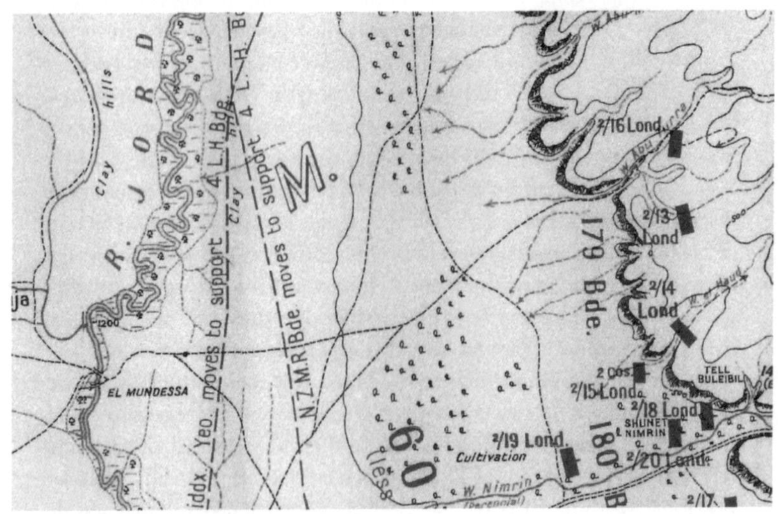

Wadi-el-Haud, east of Jordan, 1 May 1918.

> Again we tried to advance, but our endeavours were useless. In one instance the platoons had to cross a ridge, and advance up the wadi on the opposite side. They reached the ridge, but as soon as they attempted to proceed a murderous fire was opened upon them. Those who were left of the right platoon, only half of their original number succeeded in reaching the bottom, where they were comparatively safe, but the other platoon was confronted by a precipice down which it was impossible to climb.

Slowly the numbers of the platoon were reduced until there were only ten men surviving from an original thirty, including a lance corporal who called for a volunteer to take a message back to Company HQ:

> It was a job attended by the utmost danger, for no sooner did a man move from his little bit of cover than sure enough he attracted fire from the ever-watchful Turks. Although it meant running the gauntlet, with but a faint hope of getting through alive, one man, Private Cruickshank, offered to take that chance. Both sides of the ridge were exposed to the enemy, but Cruickshank chose that down which the remnants of the other platoon had gone earlier. As soon as he moved he was greeted with a shower of bullets, one hitting him in the arm. With as much haste as the rocky nature of the ground would permit he began the descent, but fell wounded in the thigh. Getting up again, undaunted, he hobbled on, but fell an easy target to that merciless fire, and with some half-dozen more bullet wounds in his leg he lay for a few seconds panting. It would have been fatal to have lain there long, so realising this he began to roll. Over and over he went, bumping against stones and boulders, but never stopping till he reached the bottom. All the while the Turks, in their determination to destroy him, kept up a hot fire, but he was mercifully saved from further wounds. By a piece of amazing good fortune he alighted among several men of the other platoon, all wounded, who were sheltering behind a large rock. By dint of much squeezing into one corner they made room for him, and there they remained all the day until a party of stretcher bearers came along and carried them back to safety. For his gallantry and self-sacrifice Cruickshank won the Victoria Cross, this being the second awarded to the Battalion.

The London Scottish and the Queen's Westminsters were relieved after dark by the Civil Service Rifles and Kensingtons.

Robert Cruickshank's VC was published in the *London Gazette* of 21 June 1918 as follows:

> No. 511828, Robert Edward Cruickshank, Private, 2/14th Battn. London Regt. (London Scottish) (Territorial Forces). For most conspicuous bravery and devotion to duty in attack. The platoon to which Private Cruickshank belonged came under very heavy rifle and machine-gun fire at short range, and was led down a steep bank into a wadi; most of the men being hit before they reached the bottom. Immediately after reaching the bottom of the wadi the officer in command was shot dead, and the Sergeant who then took over command sent a runner back to Company Headquarters asking for support, but was mortally wounded almost immediately after; the Sergeant having been killed in the meantime, the only remaining N.C.O. (a Lance-Corporal), believing the first messenger to have been killed, called for a volunteer to take a second message back. Private Cruickshank immediately responded and rushed up the slope, but was hit and rolled back into the wadi bottom. He again rose and rushed up the slope, but being again wounded, rolled back into the wadi. After his wounds had been dressed he rushed a third time up the slope and again fell badly wounded. Being now unable to stand, he rolled himself back amid a hail of bullets. His wounds were now of such a nature as to preclude him making any further attempt, and he lay all day in a dangerous position, being sniped at and again wounded where he lay. He displayed the utmost valour and endurance, and was cheerful and uncomplaining throughout.

Pte Cruickshank was presented with his VC by the King in the ballroom of Buckingham Palace on 24 October 1918.

Robert Edward Cruickshank was the first of five children and was born in Winnipeg, Manitoba, Canada, on 17 June 1888. His Scottish forebears came from Sutherland. Three years after his birth, his family left Canada for England and Robert was educated at Central Foundation School, Cowper Street, London. He later attended Bancroft's School, Woodford Green, Essex. In 1908–11 he served in the City of London Yeomanry (Rough Riders) and had also been an assistant scoutmaster.

Robert joined the services on 9 November 1915 and began with the RFC before transferring at his own request to 2/14th London Scottish (County of London) Battalion, The London Regiment, in France in the second half of 1916. He took part in the Battle of the Somme and was wounded at Leuze Wood on 10 September. After being invalided back to England, he recovered and went back to the 3rd Battalion before joining the 2nd Battalion in Salonika in February 1917. According to the *London Scottish Regimental Gazette* of October 1961, he was a member of what became known as 'G.N. Smith's draft' when the battalion was based at Katerini. The battalion consisted of 200 men, many of whom were former 1st Battalion men who had served in France, including perhaps Cpl C.W. Train, the battalion's first VC. Cruickshank then served in Egypt and Palestine in 1917–18. Robert's sibling brother, Percy, died in France in early April 1917 and was buried in Duisans British Cemetery, Etrun. He was a sapper serving with the Canadian railway troops.

Soon after the war was over, Lt Gen. Sir Robert Baden-Powell was present at a fête at Wood Green, Tottenham, at which Pte Cruickshank was presented with a gold watch by Messrs Lipton, who he had worked for a few years before the war. The fête was held in aid of a fund and he was presented with a £200 War Bond and a cheque for £50. In addition, he had also worked for Lever Brothers Ltd for a time and was presented with a £100 War Bond by Lord Leverhulme.

Cruickshank was discharged on 5 February 1919 and a few weeks later married Miss Gwendoline May Mansell of Bush Hill Park, London, on 22 March. In the following year he attended the Buckingham Palace VC Garden Party on 26 June 1920 and the Cenotaph and Westminster Abbey services on 11 November. He also attended the November 1929 House of Lords' VC Dinner, the June 1946 VE Parade and dinner, the June 1956 VC centenary celebrations in Hyde Park and the first two dinners of the VC/GC Association.

Cruickshank worked as an agent for Lever Brothers of Port Sunlight and in the late 1920s probably lived in the southern area. During the Second World War he became a member of the 5th Leicestershire Home Guard, attaining the rank of major and company commander until they were disbanded. He was chairman of Essex County Committee of the British Legion. He retired from work after thirty-nine years on 17 June 1953. He was a regular attendant of 2nd Battalion regimental reunions and other functions at HQ.

Cruickshank was also actively involved in local government and local affairs; he was chairman of the parish council in Glen Parva for thirteen years and a member of the Leicester Association of Parish Councils, of which 'he was chairman for ten years and president for two years'. He was also chairman of the Leicester Old People's Welfare Association, chairman of Glen Parva Parish War Memorial Committee and a member of the Leicester Rural Community Council, the Leicester Playing Fields Association, the Leicester and Rutland Rural Industries Committee, a school manager, a member of the Local Library Committee and chairman of the Local National Savings Committee. After his death, members of Glen Parva parish council stood and paid silent tribute to their former colleague.

Cruickshank had suffered a stroke on 17 August 1961 at home, which deprived him of movement down his left side, and, although he partially recovered, he died a few days later on the 30th at 13 Cork Lane, Glen Hills, Glen Parva, Leicester. His funeral took place on 1 September at Gilroes Crematorium and the London Scottish Regiment was represented. His ashes were laid to rest in the Garden of Remembrance on the north side of nearby All Saints churchyard, Blaby. His name is also included in a Book of Remembrance. His widow, Gwen, later moved from No. 13 Cork Lane to No. 10. The couple had no children and she died at the age of 103.

After his death, Cruickshank's miniature medals were passed to his niece and they included the VC, BWM, VM (1914–19), Defence Medal (1939–45), War Medal (1939–45), King George VI Coronation Medal (1937) and Queen Elizabeth II Coronation Medal (1953). His decorations were presented by his widow to the London Scottish on 1 October 1962 and they can be seen by appointment at the Regimental Museum in Horseferry Road, London, together with those of Charles Train. After the presentation ceremony, the Queen Mother's personal piper played *Delaspee*. In 2006 a plaque was unveiled in Bancroft's School in Woodford Green.

S. NEEDHAM

Kufr Qasim, 10/11 September 1918

Ever since Gen. Allenby's force had been severely depleted in April 1918 by the call for more divisions in France and the Western Front, his hands had been tied with regard to any grand schemes for a further advance and he could only conduct limited or local actions. It is true that Indian troops were brought in from the Mesopotamian Front to make up the shortfall in numbers, but these men needed to be trained and to acclimatise to the new conditions. In addition, to conduct a successful campaign during the stifling summer heat in the scorching Jordan Valley was asking the impossible of both man and horse. The daily temperature was usually well over 100°F and this was often accompanied by hot winds that drove choking clouds of dust up and down the river valley, which was also 1,200ft below sea level.

The Turkish Army did make a strong attack in July, but they later became encircled by troops of the Australian and Indian cavalry. There was a sense that the Turkish troops, who were surviving in very poor conditions, by now really wanted to throw in the towel as they were no longer strong enough to repel any future Allied advance. On the other hand, Gen. Allenby's troops had been rested and reorganised, and were keen to finally drive the enemy out of Palestine.

In view of the British Army's 'quiet summer', it is hardly surprising that no VCs were gained in the period between 1 May, when Pte Cruickshank gained his, and the second week of September when Pte Needham of the 1/5th Bedfords won his.

On 8 September 1918 the 1/5th Bedfords (TF), 162nd Infantry Brigade, 54th (East Anglian) Division began to relieve the 1/5th (TF) Essex in the line, which was completed by noon on the following day. Two hours later, the artillery bombarded Bureid Ridge and a patrol was sent out, which was met with a warm reception from the Turkish defenders. During the patrol, Lt D.F.P. Spurgeon of the London Regiment was killed and at 11.30 p.m. a second patrol was sent out, but failed to find the lieutenant's body. The following day was quiet, but during the succeeding night the Allies bombarded Bureid Ridge once more, as well as Kh Ummel Bureid, and the infantry moved forward in the darkness. The Allied shells were going too far over the ridge and did not affect the Turkish defenders in their elevated positions.

Capt. Yarde of the Bedfords then pushed three parties forward, consisting of three officers and fifty other ranks, in an attack which managed to reach the first objective. After a fairly heavy enemy barrage the British patrols had become virtually isolated. However, 2/Lt Hope managed to lead his patrol forward with the aim of making a reconnaissance to Kh Ummel Bureid. One hundred and fifty yards

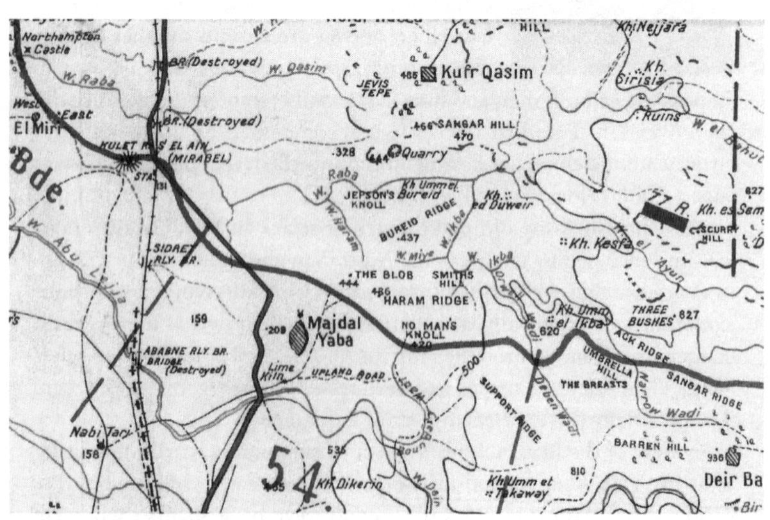

Kufr Qasim, 10/11 September 1918.

from their objective, the small patrol was driven back by heavy fire and groups of the enemy who were now moving up either side of the wadis.

The enemy made several efforts to regain the ridge and, despite the assistance of two machine-guns firing from the banks of the Wadi Rabah, they were successfully driven off. However, at 1.30 p.m., after an enemy barrage, a Turkish force of some 150 men launched an attack on three sides. The battalion history noted:

> The Turks came on throwing bombs, firing their rifles and calling on the name of Allah. The Yellow Devils stood to it, however, and beat them back with rifle and Lewis gun fire, and those who survived the bullets were dealt with by bombs at close range.
>
> At one stage of the operations on Bureid Ridge one of Capt. Yarde's patrols suddenly bumped into a very much stronger Turkish patrol and, when our men were getting demoralised owing to casualties, Private S. Needham, who was a miner from Hull, saved the situation and won the Victoria Cross. He charged the enemy single-handed and, fighting like one possessed, accounted for many Turks. His berserk fury created such a diversion, in the darkness and confusion that, for the moment, the enemy were checked and themselves gave way before him. His comrades were unanimous in thinking that Private Needham's action enabled them to get away, otherwise they would all have been surrounded and cut off. Had this happened the valuable information which Captain Yarde brought back would not have been available for further operations.

After a brief pause in the fighting, the Turkish forces made a more successful attack and finally the Bedfords had to extricate themselves to avoid annihilation:

> By a ruse of vehement cheering, each party covered the retirement of the next ... the enemy, immediately the cheering burst out, threw themselves on the ground and fired high.

Two men from the Bedfords had been killed and twenty-three wounded. As for the enemy, at least fifteen men had been killed and, owing to Needham's actions, probably more. One very important piece of information which the patrols had discovered was that the Bureid Ridge was virtually a double ridge, with the main part of the enemy force on the second level. Armed with this knowledge the 54th Division commenced the beginning of what was to be the final advance a few days later.

Needham's VC was published in the *London Gazette* of 30 October and it is very unlikely that he ever knew about the award as he died of wounds on 4 November:

> On the night of 10–11 Sept. 1918 near [Kufr Qasim], Palestine, one of our strong patrols was attacked by enemy in considerable force, supported by heavy and field artillery, also machine-gun fire. At a critical moment, when the patrol had been overcome by superior numbers, forced back and thrown into confusion, Private Needham showed extraordinary bravery. A fresh body of enemy were coming on when he ran back, faced alone and fired rapidly at about 40 Turks at only 30yds' range. His action checked the enemy, and just gave the patrol commander time to get together his men after the shaking they had in the first encounter. Even then, had he not been ordered back, it is thought Private Needham would have remained where he was and deliberately sacrificed his life to save his comrades. The patrol had twenty-five casualties out of a total of fifty, but successfully got back all their wounded, and it was only by the action of individuals, of which this one is the most outstanding of all, that the whole lot were not cut off by the enemy and either killed or made prisoners. Apart from what he actually effected in holding up the enemy single-handed, Private Needham's example was of greatest value at a critical moment, when men were somewhat shaken, owing to enemy swarming round them, and the fact of this man standing up to the enemy by himself did more than anything to instil confidence in the men, and undoubtedly saved a critical situation.

A few days after the surrender of the Turkish Army in Syria on 31 October, Pte Needham died on 4 November 1918 at Kufr Qasim of wounds received in action, and was buried at Kantara War Memorial Cemetery, Row E, Grave 181, about 27 miles from Port Said on the east bank of the Suez Canal, Egypt.

Samuel Needham was born on 16 August 1885 at Great Limber, North Lincolnshire, west of Grimsby. He was the son of Septimus and Mary (née Quickfall) of Little Limber Grange, Brocklesby, and was orphaned when only 10 years old when his parents died of typhoid fever in February and March 1896 respectively. Septimus was only in his mid-50s and he and Mary were buried in Scartho Road Cemetery, Grimsby. At that time the family lived at 38 Lord Street, Grimsby, and Septimus was 'a carriage owner and driver'. He had previously been an agricultural labourer.

Samuel was baptised two days after his birth and his father, who at that time worked as a groom, registered his son's name on 25 September at Caistor. He was educated at the Macaulay Street schools and later worked for Lord Yarborough on his estate at Brocklesby, and also for the Duke of Westminster. In 1918 one of his six sisters lived at Waltham and was Sir Alec Black's housekeeper. Black was a local steamship owner and benefactor from Great Grimsby who lived at Bargate in 1918.

From records outstanding it appears clear that the family moved to Grimsby between September 1885 and February 1896. Samuel might 'possibly' have worked in Hull as a miner, as it was from there that he enlisted in the Army Service Corps on 14 December 1914; his number was TS/5023.

Needham was transferred after twenty months' service to the Bedfordshire Regiment in mid-1916 and left for Egypt in January 1917. His new service number was 30982. He served in the Palestine Campaign in 1917–18 and, like others, had no leave during his service.

His VC was presented to one of his six sisters by the King at Buckingham Palace on 13 February 1919. In 1956 Mrs Baron, a sister, presented her brother's VC to the Bedfordshire and Hertfordshire Regiment at a special ceremony. Three VC winners also attended: Col T.E. Adlam, Mr A.A. Burt and Mr C.A. Cox. The VC is at present in the Regimental Museum in Luton and his other medals would have included the 1914–15 Star, BWM and VM (1914–19).

The Church of St Peter, Great Limber, has a pamphlet on the life of Samual Needham for sale and he is remembered in Grimsby Cemetery in Scartho Road, where the CWGC have set up a Visitor's Information Panel.

B. Singh

West bank of the River Jordan, 23 September 1918

Ressaidar Badlu Singh of the 14th (Murray's Jat) Lancers, Indian Army, was attached to the 29th Lancers, which was part of 11th Cavalry Brigade, 4th Cavalry Division. On 8 August 1918 this division returned from Ras Deiran, where it had been on leave, and was going to resume patrol duties in the valley of the River Jordan.

On 18 September the division, concentrating in orange groves, was preparing for an advance into Samaria, and on the 19th passed through the village on its way northwards to the Kakon–Liktera switch line. The front of the force was attacked by Turkish troops, but later the position was attacked on horseback and 250 prisoners taken. The 11th Cavalry Brigade then occupied positions at Tel-ed-Dhrur. On the 20th Lejjun was occupied in the early morning, and by 4.30 p.m. the 10th Cavalry Brigade had reached Beisan. A total of 800 prisoners were captured en route. On the 21st they captured 158 more prisoners as a result of a moonlight charge.

At 8 a.m. on 23 September the 11th Cavalry Brigade intercepted a large and retreating party of the Turkish Seventh Army, which was attempting to retreat across the Jordan at the ford at Makhadet Abu Naj, 6 miles to the south of Beisan. They were assisted by machine-guns, but the ford was not actually captured until midday. The 29th Lancers, 11th Cavalry Brigade, captured twenty-five machine-guns on the west side of the river, while the 35th Jacob's Horse broke up the column on the east bank.

The advance of the regiment was then held up at the village of Khan-es-Sumariveh by a large Turkish force, with rifle and machine-gun fire impeding progress of C Squadron. The enemy were in positions to the south-east between the village and the river.

Capt. Jackson MC, with A and D Squadrons, was sent to deal with the threatening situation; a personal reconnaissance revealed that a large body of Turkish troops was trying to escape across a ford in the south-east of the village. They were being protected by a rearguard, which had also been the group firing on C Squadron and had established machine-gun positions on the ford on both sides of the Jordan. After leaving A Squadron in order to try and work round the enemy's right flank, Jackson established positions for his Hotchkiss guns and took D Squadron, and the men who were left, on a wide encircling movement round the left flank of the enemy, and then charged them from the rear.

It was during the course of this action that Badlu Singh noticed the enemy machine-gun posts causing such fearful casualties. He must

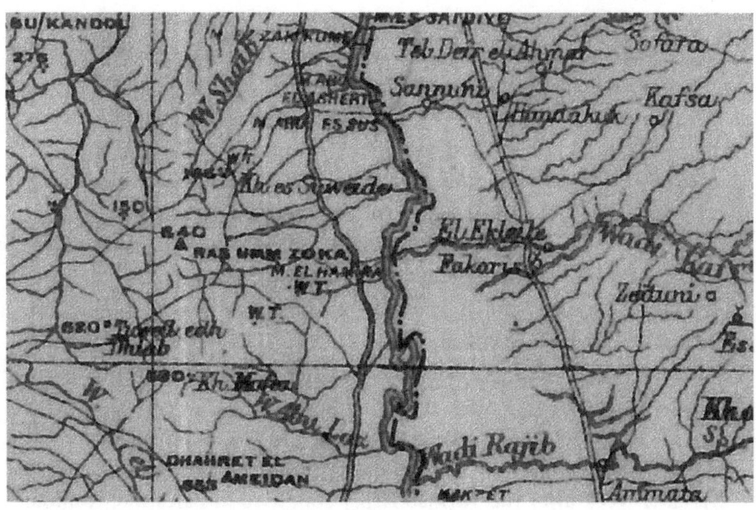

West bank of the Jordan, 23 September 1918.

also have been aware of 200 supporting enemy infantry. Despite these overwhelming odds, he immediately collected six men and charged the offending enemy position. His predictable death had not, however, been in vain. The regiment captured up to 1,000 prisoners and eight machine-guns, a tally largely assisted by the actions of the gallant Badlu Singh.

Later in the day, D Squadron returned to brigade reserve and was sent to assist C Squadron, which reported a large party of Turks moving from the south who surrendered without a fight. Many prisoners and supplies were captured, including a Turkish divisional general, fifty Germans, 2,325 Turkish troops and twenty-one machine-guns.

After Ressaidar Badlu Singh died of wounds in action, he was cremated where he fell on the west bank of the river. The citation for his VC was published in the *London Gazette* of 27 November 1918 and the *Gazette of India* (No. 263) of 31 January 1919 as follows:

> Badlu Singh, Ressaidar, late 14th Lancers, Indian Army, attached 29th Lancers. For most conspicuous bravery and self-sacrifice on the morning of 23rd Sept. 1918, when his squadron charged a strong enemy position on the west bank of the River Jordan, between the river and Khan-es-Sumariveh Village. On nearing the position Ressaidar Badlu Singh realized the squadron was suffering casualties from a small hill (Khanes Hill) on the left front occupied by machine guns and 200 infantry. Without the slightest hesitation he collected six other ranks and with the greatest dash and utter disregard of danger charged and captured the position, thereby saving very heavy casualties to the squadron. He was mortally wounded on the very top of the hill when capturing one of the machine guns single-handed, but all the machine guns and infantry had surrendered to him before he died. His valour and initiative were of the highest order.

Ressaidar Badlu Singh, together with seven other ranks, was killed and seventeen others wounded. His VC was the last to be won in Palestine before the Turkish Armistice on 31 October 1918, and the last to be awarded to a member of the Indian Army during the First World War.

By 25 September Palestine was completely in Allied hands after British troops occupied Haifa and Acre and got as far as the Sea of Galilee. General Allenby's forces then continued northwards through Syria. A week after the Turkish Army collapsed in Palestine, Amman in Jordan was captured and Damascus, south-east of Beirut in Syria, also fell to the British and control was handed over to the French to supervise. During the remainder of October the advance continued towards Aleppo in northern Syria, which was captured on 26 October. Five days later the Turkish Army signed an armistice and agreed to leave the country in mid-December. By now the Turkish Army was finished and the 600-year rule of the Ottoman Empire was at an end.

Over 2 million men served at one time with the Allied forces in the Middle East between 1914 and 1918, of whom 163,000 had become casualties.

Badlu Singh was born in November 1876 in Dhakla Village, near Jhaijar, Rohtak District, Punjab, India. He enrolled in the 14th (Murray's Jat) Lancers on 10 September 1895. The Lancers had been raised by Gen. Murray of the United Province Police in 1858, and on the outbreak of war were entirely composed of Hindu Jats. Badlu Singh was promoted to lance dafadar on 16 October 1908, dafadar on 1 August 1909, jemadar on 5 January 1915 and, finally, ressaidar on 9 January 1917. He served on the North-West Frontier from 18 September to 25 October 1915 and during this time would have taken part in a small Mohmand war: 'The Regiment charging the enemy together with the British 21st Lancers on September 5th, 1915 – a charge made through high crops, and one the subject of much discussion at the time.' During this action at Hafiz Kor, Shoeing-Smith Charles Hull gained the VC. The 14th Lancers were later in France from 16 May 1916 to 18 March 1918. They had previously supplied reinforcements to the 6th Cavalry Division until the end of the war. In 1919 Syria passed into French control and France and Great Britain proceeded to carve up the oil-rich countries in the Middle East for themselves. Kings Faisal and Hussain, together with the help of T.E. Lawrence, had encouraged an Arab revolt against Turkish forces in Arabia. After the war was over these promises were broken and subsequent support for a separate Jewish state within the borders of Palestine intensified. It was with the Balfour Declaration and Sykes–Picot Pact that many of the seeds of the subsequent troubles in the Middle East were sown.

Badlu Singh's VC was presented to his son, Chotan Singh, in India in 1919, possibly from the hands of the Viceroy. Badlu Singh's widow, two sons and a daughter survived him. His name was commemorated in the Indian Army listings on the panels of the Heliopolis Memorial at the Heliopolis War Cemetery, Port Tewfik, Cairo.

An Indian Army Order dated 8 July 1920 noted that Chotan Singh was awarded a special grant of land of the annual cash value of Rs 400. His father's VC was sold at Sothebys on 26 January 1972 and bought by Spinks for £1,550. It was sold again on 28 November 1995 and the notional price was from between £18,000–£22,000. It was sold to a private collector for £32,000 and is now part of the Lord Ashcroft Collection in the Imperial War Museum. His other medals would have been the BWM and VM.

SALONIKA

H.W. Lewis

Macukovo, near Seres,
22/23 October 1916

By the terms of the Treaty of Bucharest of August 1913, Macedonia, which in effect had been under Turkish control for 500 years, was divided up between Serbia to the north-west, Austria, supported by Bulgaria, to the north-east, Greece to the south, and Albania and Montenegro to the west. The main territorial prize was the Vardar river valley, which linked Europe with the strategically vital port of Salonika at the head of the Aegean Sea.

In August 1914 Greece decided initially to watch developments and remain neutral. By no means could the Greeks be relied upon by the Allies for military assistance, as one moment they sided with the Central Powers and the next with the Allies.

Bulgaria was also going to await developments, while Turkey sided with the Austro-German Central Powers before having to deal with an attempted Allied invasion of their country at Gallipoli in the Dardanelles. By October 1915 Bulgaria had abandoned its policy of neutrality and had thrown in its lot with the Central Powers, and together with Austria and Germany invaded Serbia, inflicting a crushing defeat. Serbia was now effectively out of the war and what was left of the Serbian Army was forced to struggle through mountainous Albania to safety on the island of Corfu.

After Bulgaria's success against Serbia, the Allies declared war on them and sent a force to Salonika. This force included the 11th

Welsh Regiment, 67th Infantry Brigade, 22nd Division, which left Marseilles under the command of Maj. (T/Lt Col) A. Victor Cowley on 27/28 October bound for Salonika where it arrived on 8 November. As part of the Mediterranean Expeditionary Force under the command of Gen. Sir Bryan Mahon, their mission was to prepare for an expected attack by German and Bulgarian forces under the leadership of Gen. von Falkenhayn. Soon the total Allied army was represented by troops from Britain, France, Italy, Russia, Serbia, India and China, and was under overall command of the French Gen. Sarrail. With a force of this size it became vital for the Allies to try to keep Greece from becoming permanently committed to the German cause, as 150,000 Allied troops might then become prisoners of war overnight and the whole mission in Salonika would be at an end.

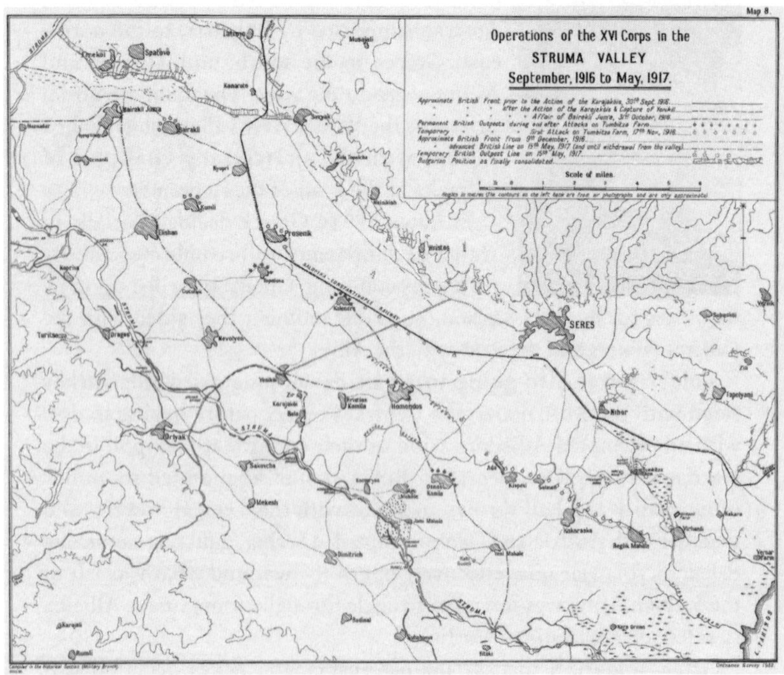

Struma Valley, September 1916 to May 1917.

Initially the 11th Welsh Regiment or 'Pals' were greeted at the port of Salonika with sunshine, and the troops were excited to be well away from the mud and trenches of the Western Front. The port was a town of many factions and groupings, and included Turkish, Greek and Levantine quarters. Not surprisingly, German spies abounded and busied themselves noting down all troop movements in and out of the port. Eastern-bound railway journeys were available daily, which reached Constantinople, the capital of Turkey.

It was hardly surprising that the Allied forces were not very popular locally, although their presence would undoubtedly have boosted the local economy. However, disillusion soon put paid to any idea that the 'Pals' might have had a 'cushy time' when they left the picturesque and polyglot port and departed for the Macedonian Front, marching 8 miles out from the town to spend their first night in a bleak and bare moorland landscape. No camp had been prepared for them, but a few bell tents were set up a few weeks later. Established here, they carried out a daily programme of training, marching and running. Conditions were very poor and the temperature often dropped to below freezing.

The landscape was bare, mountainous and populated with poverty-ridden villages. Worse than the landscape itself was the climate. It was continuously windy, boiling hot in summer, freezing cold in winter, with only a briefly tolerable period in the spring. The heat, lack of fresh water, the overbearing presence of flies and dust, topped up with little to do in a military sense, contributed to an attitude of complete boredom and a feeling of having been forgotten by those in authority back home in Great Britain.

It was during this period that the famous 'Birdcage' was constructed not only to protect the Allied army from a German advance from Serbia, but also an attack from Bulgaria, and to make Salonika impregnable. All four British divisions were involved in the essential navvying work required for these defences.

In mid-April 1916, Col Cowley, an extremely unpopular disciplinarian, was suddenly recalled to Britain for 'health reasons' and the 'Pals' were delighted to now be under the command of the more sympathetic Lt Col H.J. Wingate.

By the following August malaria had taken a considerable toll on the 'Pals' and their numbers had dwindled to about 600 men. Malaria continued to be a curse until a few months before the end of the war.

In May 1916 the British divisions were taken over by Gen. Milne. At the end of the summer the 22nd Division took over the frontline from the French to the south-west of Lake Dorian, where they were looked down upon by an enemy who had built up an impregnable defensive line in the mountains. The width of no man's land ranged from 5,000yd to 200yd when close to the lake.

In September an Allied offensive was planned on the left flank of the British positions at Macukovo, near Seres, east of the River Vardar; an attack which would include French, Russian and Serbian troops. It was on the night of 22 October after a period of very heavy rain that about 100 of the 'Pals' made their first raid as a battalion, for which they carried out special training against the Dorsale heights. The raiding party, which was to bring back prisoners and the evidence of what forces they were facing, had to move up the sides of a steep ravine during an advance which took three hours. Gaps in the wire had been made by the Allied artillery, but a stream of enemy red warning lights confused the Welsh Battalion for a time and they became pinned down for forty minutes by murderous shell, rifle and machine-gun fire and suffered casualties. Fearing they would be cut down, orders were given to advance the 120yd across the flattened wire entanglements, despite the artillery not having lifted off the frontline, in order to take advantage of the confusion the artillery was causing the enemy in their frontline trenches. However, the barrage did lift in time and the raid was deemed a success with the killing of thirty-four Germans and the capture of sixteen prisoners. D party, to which Pte Lewis belonged, was to attack the enemy communication trenches between trenches four and five. Like the others he was equipped with 70lb of ammunition and a Mills Bomb, in addition to his usual rifle, bayonet and wire cutters. The 'Pals' had some casualties of their own – six killed and thirty-three wounded – including Pte Hubert Lewis, who, on hearing a cry from the trench which he had just left, and despite his two wounds, returned to find a badly burned Lt Edgar Harold Holmes Turner.

Taking the officer on his shoulder, Lewis helped the lieutenant out of danger and then proceeded to do similar work for other wounded men; in the process he was wounded a third time. After the 'Pals' retired they were pursued by Bulgarian artillery. Lewis collapsed with exhaustion and was taken to the advance dressing station in Smol Church. A month later, at No. 2 Convalescent Depot, Salonika, he was visited by Sgt J. Nicholls, a friend who had won a DCM in the Dorsale Raid, and he was unable to prevent himself from blurting out that Lewis had been recommended for the VC for outstanding valour. It was published in the *London Gazette* of 15 December 1916. Sadly Lt Turner did not live long and died of his wounds on the 23rd:

> Herbert [Hubert] William Lewis. No. 16224. Private. 11th Battn. Welch Regt. For most conspicuous bravery and devotion during a raid. On reaching the enemy trenches Private Lewis was twice wounded, but refused to be attended to, and showed great gallantry in searching enemy dug-outs. He was again wounded, and again refused attendance. At this point three of the enemy were observed to be approaching, and Private Lewis immediately attacked them single-handed, capturing all. Subsequently, during the retirement, he went to the assistance of a wounded man, and under heavy shell and rifle fire brought him to our lines, on reaching which he collapsed. Private Lewis showed throughout brilliant example of courage, endurance, and devotion to duty.

On the announcement of the award of the VC to a local man, there was great excitement both in Milford and throughout Pembrokeshire. In December Lewis was sent home on leave and given a great welcome when he reached Cardiff station. Later he had to face the press at a meeting arranged in the Grand Hotel, where he spoke of his colleagues from the Cardiff 'Pals' serving with him in the Balkans:

> Believe me ... they are the finest body of soldiers serving in the British Army. I have soldiered overseas with them ever since the autumn of 1915. Naturally, we are all very glad to be home again. I joined the Welch Regiment as a raw recruit, and I am proud of the fact that I have not disgraced the honour and proud record of the Regiment.

He later corrected his entry in the *London Gazette* and said that he could only remember being wounded twice and not three times!

Lewis was presented with a gold watch by the people of Milford Haven and a gold wristwatch from Haverfordwest. He was also presented with a silver cigarette case from Milford Haven and a

National School Bible from the local Wesleyan Sunday School and St Katherine's Church. He was later decorated by the King at Buckingham Palace on 5 February and the King told him: 'Really, I am proud of you.' By mid-February the private was back on the Balkan Front.

It was to be another two years before a second VC was won on the Salonika Front, this time by Lt Col Daniel Burges. Burges was in command of the 7th South Wales Borderers in a disastrous attack against the impregnable Grand Couronne on 18 September 1918, in which the 11th Welsh took part with 'Stokey' Lewis acting as orderly to Lt D. Guthrie Morgan.

Morgan was wounded a third time during the war when a machine-gun bullet damaged his thigh and Lewis lay down by his side. Morgan told his orderly to take his map and papers 'and get out of here', but Lewis dragged his wounded officer until he could hand him over to stretcher-bearers.

Hubert William Lewis, the second son of Adrian and Sarah Lewis (née Broome), one of at least four children, was born in Robert Street, Milford Haven, Pembrokeshire (later Dyfed), Wales, on 1 May 1896. His father was a brass moulder and fitter at Milford Haven Docks and the family later moved to Dartmouth Terrace. Hubert was educated at the National School, Milford Haven, and was known as 'Stokey'. He left school at the age of 13 when he began work at the local fish market as a packer. He also played football for the local Milford Stars team. In early September 1914 he attended a recruiting meeting, and on the 4th enlisted in the 11th (S) Battalion the Welch Regiment (Cardiff Pals) Commercial who were formed in Cardiff in the same month.

The following day Lewis left his hometown together with seventy-five volunteers in Kitchener's New Army and was then part of a group of forty-six men who were sent to the depot of the Welch Regiment at Maindy Barracks in order to join the newly formed Cardiff 'Pals'. They left the barracks on 14 September as part of 67th Brigade, 22nd Division, and moved for training to Lewes, close to the South Downs, where they were given their main meal in the local prison and slept in beds set up in the County Hall. Later they moved to Eastbourne,

Hastings and Seaford, before finishing training at Aldershot, where they were inspected by the King and Lord Kitchener before sailing for France from Southampton on 5 September 1915, arriving in Boulogne the following day. On the 10th Lewis was attached to the machine-gun section of the 9th Border Regiment, the Divisional Pioneer Battalion, for trench duty familiarisation with the 1st Devon Regiment. For a few days they were billeted at Suzanne on the Somme. A few days later, after Bulgaria entered the war on the side of the Central Powers, it was decided that the 22nd Division should be sent to Greece. On 27 October their commanding officer, Col F. Russell Parkinson, who had trained them in southern England, was deemed to be too old for service in Macedonia; a decision which not only saddened him but also 'his boys', who thought of him as a sort of favourite uncle. Lewis arrived in Salonika on 8 November and was to serve there until the end of the war, during which time he was wounded twice, including being gassed. He was a private in rank, but served as an acting corporal.

Lewis was the third member of the Welch Regiment to win the VC in the First World War and was later promoted to acting corporal and demobilised with the rank of lance corporal on 16 April 1919, having finally left the Balkans on 27 February. He returned to Milford Haven and worked as a fish merchant in the fish market with his cousin, Billy Brown. The business failed in the early 1920s, so he took a succession of occasional jobs, which included helping with the early morning fish catches. Later he found a more permanent position in a Milford ice factory, where he worked unloading ice from lorries. He became the company's foreman at the Milford fish market, a position he held for forty-three years. He was known as V.C. Lewis.

In June 1920 Lewis attended the first of many VC functions, the Garden Party at Buckingham Palace. Four months later, on 9 October, he married Edith Eveline Etherington in Haverfordwest; the couple were to have three sons, Vernon, Edward and Arthur. On 3 September 1921, Lewis was invited to unveil the Pembrokeshire County War Memorial at Haverfordwest, the Dale Village War Memorial on 19 June 1923 and the Milford Haven War Memorial on 24 April 1924. In November 1929 he attended the House of Lords' VC Dinner. In January 1936 he represented his local British Legion branch at the funeral of King George V. Two years later, at a British Legion dinner, he was presented with a set of miniature medals from the Pembroke Dock Branch as a token of admiration. In June 1940, already a member of the Home Guard, he was approached by an officer and invited to join a resistance group set up in order to repel German invaders.

After his service in the Second World War, Lewis was awarded a Certificate for Good Service. His eldest son, Vernon, was killed when on a Lancaster Pathfinder mission on 24 August 1943 and was buried in Berlin; his name is included on the Second World War listing on the Milford Haven War Memorial. Lewis received his son's posthumous Distinguished Flying Medal (DFM) from King George VI on 14 May 1946, and a few weeks later he was back in London attending the 1946 VE Parade and the dinner at The Dorchester. He also attended the Hyde Park VC centenary celebrations on 26 June 1956, the second reunion of the VC/GC Association in July 1960 and five other functions until his last in July 1968 when he was 72. Lewis was a great friend of Ivor Rees VC and they often attended functions together. In April 1961 Lewis took part in a moving ceremony in Milford Haven as a result of certain ex-gunners in Milford Haven agreeing to transfer to the Welsh Regiment in order to re-establish a Pembrokeshire company.

In 1964 Lewis was invited to the premiere of the film *Zulu* starring Michael Caine and Stanley Baker, and he had tea with Michael Caine after the showing of the film. He was accompanied by two other VC holders, Ivor Rees VC and E.T. Chapman VC. Five years later, Edith Lewis died on 4 July 1969 and she was buried in St Katherine's Cemetery, Milford Haven, Section H, Grave 111.

Four years later, the Pembrokeshire County War Memorial at Haverfordwest, which commemorates 3,000 men who gave their lives in the First World War, was moved from Salutation Square Roundabout to a new site near the County Hall. The memorial to the eighty-eight men from the Second World War has also been moved to a position near the First World War memorial. Lewis attended the re-dedication service.

'Stokey' lived in a semi-detached house on a council estate, 26 Prioryville, Milford Haven. Being an end house it overlooked Milford Haven Grammar School sportsfield where 'Stokey' used to watch the sports taking place there. He died at his home on 22 February 1977, the last First World War VC holder from Wales to die. His funeral was held three days later at St Katherine's Church and he was buried next to his wife in Milford Cemetery. The Welsh Regiment was well represented at the service and provided a bearer party from the 4th Battalion of the Royal Regiment of Wales (formerly the Welsh Regiment), who bore the coffin draped in a Union Jack to the grave. The *Last Post* and *Reveille* were sounded. The service was attended by a large number of ex-servicemen and representatives from service organisations in Pembrokeshire and other parts of Wales. The large cortège was led from St Katherine's Church to the cemetery by police and army vehicles. Lewis was survived by one son, Edward.

In 1987 Milford Haven organised a Festivities Week and 'Stokey' Lewis was honoured twice. First, a watercolour portrait of him by Sidney Vaughan was displayed in the local Arts Club's annual exhibition in the town hall. Secondly, the local Rotary Club presented a silver shield with a replica of his VC on it, as well as an inscription emblazoned with the words 'For True Grit', in his memory. The shield, which also showed the Welsh Regiment badge, was to be awarded to the Pembrokeshire Army Cadet who showed 'a "Stokey" Lewis-type of determination in his training'.

In the following year a memorial to 'Stokey' in the form of a sundial was dedicated in the Memorial Gardens, Milford Haven, and in the same year the North Road Primary School created a special exhibit of pictures made of cardboard and paint of Lewis winning his VC in Salonika. His surviving son, Edward, visited the school exhibition with a warrant officer from the Royal Regiment of Wales. Finally, his name is also included on the Haverfordwest War Memorial and there is a Lewis display at Milford Haven Museum.

Lewis's decorations appeared in a Sotheby's sale held at Billingshurst on 30 November/1 December 1993 and they were purchased for £26,450 by Mr A. Abrahams from Cardiff. With the medals were original papers including 'the Warrant for the French M. M., Certificate for the 1937 Coronation Medal, and several items appertaining to the VC'. Apart from his VC and MM, his other medals included the 1914/15 Star, BWM, VM (1914–19), King George VI Coronation Medal (1937) and Queen Elizabeth II Coronation Medal (1953). They were later acquired by Lord Ashcroft and are part of his VC collection in the Imperial War Museum.

D.BURGES

Jumeaux in the Balkans, 18 September 1918

In August 1915 the French Gen. Sarrail arrived as commander of the French section of the Allied force in Salonika, and five months later, in January 1916, he became the commander-in-chief of the Allied forces. He seems to have achieved little apart from gaining a reputation for being a great intriguer and left the Salonika Front at the end of 1917 after being replaced by Gen. Guillaumat. From then on the organisation and co-operation between the Allied forces began to considerably improve. The Balkan Front had suddenly become more important as a result of the collapse of the Russian Army, the Italian defeat at Caporetto and the deteriorating situation on the Western Front. In Greece, the vacillating King Constantine was replaced by the Prime Minister Venizelos, who was outwardly more sympathetic to the Allied cause and allowed the Greek Army to take part in the operations on the Macedonian Front, which began in the spring of 1918. In June, a few months later, Gen. Guillaumat was replaced by Gen. Franchet d'Espèrey, who then proceeded to devise a plan with the aim of using British and Greek forces to contain the Bulgarian Army on the Macedonian (Doiran) Front on a hilly landscape between Lake Doiran and the River Vardar. This move would prevent the Bulgarians from taking on the Serbian Army to the west, where they were to advance over the peaks of the Moglenitza Range. It appears that the French general was not really concerned with the consequences of such an attempt, as long as it would tie up the Bulgarian Army, who boasted two divisions, making it twice as large as the British force that would be used.

During the three years in which British troops had served in Salonika, they not only had to cope with an extreme climate, malaria and dysentery, but since early September 1918 they were also attacked by Spanish influenza and, in effect, were constantly at half strength. By the end of the frontal fighting in September, there were very few men left who were really fit for active service.

It was on 18 September, during the initial actions on the Doiran Front, when the second VC was won in the Salonika Campaign by T/Lt Col Daniel Burges of the Gloucestershire Regiment, who was attached to and in command of the 7th (S) South Wales Borderers at Jumeaux.

Three days before, after a period of intensive training, the battalion had moved up close to the frontline at Tortoise Camp, where HQ and D Company remained while A and B Companies were on the southern slopes and C Company in Elbow Camp. Tortoise Camp was shelled on

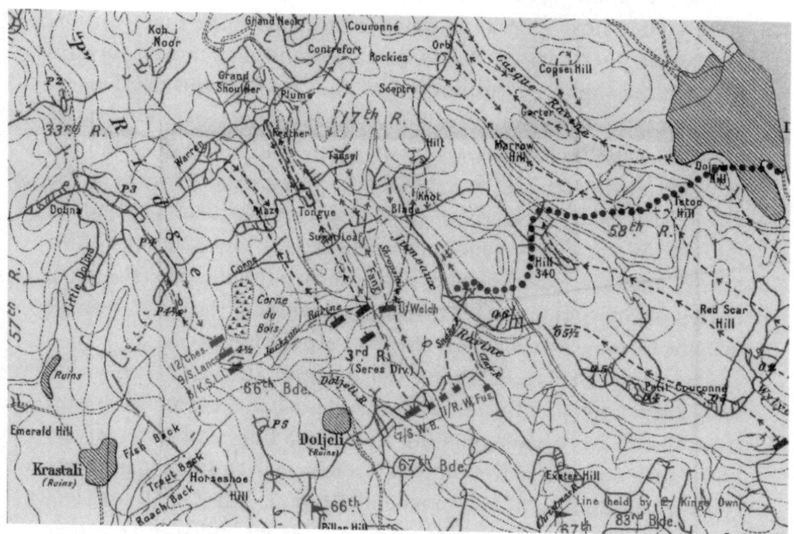

Jumeaux, 18 September 1918.

the 16th, but suffered no casualties. On the 17th it was the turn of A and B Companies to be shelled, which resulted in six deaths and twenty men being wounded.

From 15 September the Allied barrage had come down on the whole of the Macedonian frontline, and on the evening of the 17th a gas bombardment also began. The barrage lifted at 5.05 a.m. on the 18th and the infantry attack against Grand Couronne began three minutes later. It turned out to be a very hot day and the position to be captured was 2,000ft high and strongly defended by concrete and barbed wire 100yd thick. In addition, the Bulgarian Army had turned the lesser hills of the 'Hilt', the 'Tassel', the 'Knot' (part of the second objective) and the 'Sceptre', the 'Blade' and the 'Tongue' into very strong machine-gun positions. The enemy lines in terraces were also well provided with dug-outs and belts of thick wire. Any uphill attack could be seen from a distance and during the Allied advance the defenders looked loftily down upon their British attackers, who were already weakened and now suffering from machine-gunfire, heat and the effects of lingering gas, especially in the ravines. Many men wore gas masks, which added further to their discomfort.

The 7th South Wales Borderers, a left-flanking battalion led by Col Burges DSO through a haze, managed to reach their first position, the 'Sugar Loaf', with very few casualties and then moved forward through the slippery scrub, capturing the 'Tongue' and the 'Feather Hills' and stopping just short on the slopes of Grand Couronne, known as the 'Rockies'. However, their two right-hand flanking battalions, the 11th Welch and 11th Royal Welsh Fusiliers, together with the 3rd Greek Regiment, had not been allowed to enjoy the same success and the 11th Welsh suffered enormous casualties at the small hills of the 'Tassel' and the 'Knot' on the slopes of the Grand Couronne when beaten off by counter-attacks. To the left of the 67th Welsh Brigade line, the Greeks had a similarly dreadful experience.

The Borderers had no choice but to retire after reaching within 250yd of the summit. By now the earlier haze had lifted and they were cut to pieces by machine-gun fire from three sides and suffered very heavy casualties. Fifty-five other ranks managed to survive and were collected together at 'SP1' by a wounded officer, 2/Lt F.A. Stephenson. Col Burges was reported missing as well as wounded, three other officers were evacuated to a field ambulance and the remaining six officers were missing with 100 other ranks killed.

The Borderers held on to 'SP1' from 10 p.m. on the 18th until the night of the 20th, when now, under the command of Maj. W.W. Humphreys, they moved into Exeter Camp. All the men were suffering from the effects of gas poisoning from British shells which had been used during the advance. It was another disastrous day on the 19th when fighting continued in an attempt to contain the Bulgarian Army from attacking the advancing Serbian Army.

On the 22nd Maj. Humphreys renewed an attempt using 100 men and moved up the Grand Couronne, only to find that the Bulgarian enemy had left and that various dumps were being destroyed. On the following day the battalion, acting as the 67th Brigade's advance guard, moved forward as far as 1½ miles south-east of Cerniste, where it camped for the night. On the 24th Humphreys, together with two other officers, was sent to hospital, which left Capt. W. Parry in command of the battalion. On the next day the advance continued as far as Blaga Planina, where they rested before moving down the northern bank of Lake Doiran on the morning of the 28th.

Overall the Allies had advanced very quickly through the rugged terrain, and a gap opened up in the Bulgarians' line and led to their retreat. The cavalry entered Strumitsa and Kosturino, and hostilities against the Bulgarian Army ceased at 12 p.m. on the 30th, followed by much rejoicing among the men. In effect, this victory was the beginning of the end for the supporters of the Central Powers. Austria, who had fought with the Bulgarians, had been deserted by the German Army, most of whom were required for duty on the Western Front. The two countries missed out on the spoils of victory and Serbia, having been carved up by its neighbours, regained the lands that had been seized prior to the war. It was Germany who had fared best out of the whole Balkans Campaign by contriving to tie up 300,000 Allied troops for three years, thus preventing them from being involved in other more important theatres of war.

So highly did Franchet d'Espèrey think of the efforts and gallantry of the 7th South Wales Borderers at Doiran on 18 September that he awarded the battalion the *Croix de Guerre*. The citation read as follows:

> A Battalion animated by a remarkable spirit and a lofty sense of duty. On 18th September 1918 under the energetic leadership of Lt.-Col. Burges, it attacked the enemy's positions, climbing a steep slope under a hail of shells and the fire of trench mortars and machine guns. In spite of heavy losses it pressed on with no thought but to reach the enemy and thereby gave proof of its tenacity and offensive spirit, and formed an example of self-sacrifice worthy of the highest praise.

After Burges was taken prisoner, he was removed to a Bulgarian hospital with a gangrenous leg. His VC was published in the *London Gazette* of 14 December 1918 as follows:

> Daniel Burges, Major (Temporary Lieut-Colonel), D.S.O., Gloucestershire Regt., Commanding 7th Battn. South Wales Borderers. For most conspicuous bravery, skilful leading and devotion to duty in the operations at Jumeaux (Balkans) on 18 Sept. 1918. His valuable reconnaissance of the enemy first-line trenches enabled him to bring his battalion without casualties [to] the assembly point, and from thence he maintained direction with great skill, though every known landmark was completely obscured by smoke and dust. When still some distance from its objective, the battalion came under severe machine-gun fire, which caused casualties amongst company leaders. Lieut.-Colonel Burges, though himself wounded, quite regardless of his own safety, kept moving to and fro through his command, encouraging his men and assisting them to maintain formation and direction. Finally, as they neared the enemy's position, he led them forward through a decimating fire until he was again hit twice and fell unconscious. His coolness and courage were most marked throughout, and afforded magnificent example to all ranks.

A few weeks later, on 16 January 1919, a letter from him was read out at a battalion parade:

> Please thank all ranks of the glorious 7th for the congratulatory cablegram sent to me; the greatest pleasure of all that I have experienced is the appreciation of my great Honour by the splendid men who won it for me.

A newspaper reported:

> Probably the most striking feature of the Despatch is the allusion made to the heroic work of the 7th Battn. of the South Wales Borderers during their attack between 'Pip' Ridge and Grand Couronne. This battalion (a new service battalion of the old 24th Foot) was commanded by Lieut.-Colonel D. Burges, D.S.O., who was taken prisoner by the Bulgars during the attack, but was abandoned in a dug-out with one of his legs severely shattered. The gallant commanding officer gained his VC during this fight, out of which the 7th SWB came with only nineteen unwounded men and one wounded officer. It is another stirring episode in the great fighting career of the SWB and reflects the standard of the new armies. Equally commendable was the fight made by another battalion of this famous Regiment by the 8th SWB, commanded by Lt Col R.C. Dobbs, D.S.O.

A popular music-hall song of the time began 'If you don't want to fight, go to Salonika'. In many ways the conditions that the army had to operate in over a period of three years in Salonika, plus the desperate and often one-sided fighting that took place in 1916 and 1918, made a complete nonsense of the popular ballad.

Daniel Burges was born in Bloomsbury on 1 July 1873, the son of Daniel Travers Burges, Town Clerk of Bristol, and Alice Sarah, eldest daughter of Benjamin Travers of Cape Colony. The family home in Bristol at this time was the Council House, Corn Street, Bristol, and Daniel had three younger brothers. Daniel was educated at Winchester and, deciding to make the Army his career, he attended RMA Camberley and passed into the Army on 21 October 1893 when commissioned as a second lieutenant. He was posted to the 2nd Gloucestershire Regiment on 24 November 1894. On 8 July 1897 he was promoted to lieutenant. He took part in the Boer War in 1899–1902, serving with the 6th Division under Gen. Kelly-Kenny, up until the occupation of Bloemfontein. He commanded the Mounted Signallers Company, Army HQ, until 31 July 1900, and was signalling officer successively to Col Hickman's Column, Gen. Plumer's Column, chief staff officer to Col Viall's Column and, finally, signalling officer to Gen. W. Kitchener until the end of the war.

Burges was awarded the Queen's Medal with four clasps, and the King's Medal with two clasps. He was promoted to captain on 25 October 1903. Two years later he married Katharine Blanche, second daughter of Capt. Edmund Fortescue, Rifle Brigade, at St Bartholomew's, Southsea, on 5 October 1905. He joined the 1st Glosters two months later on 4 December, remaining with the battalion until 1908 when he served with the Punjab Volunteer Rifles until 1913. He then returned to the 1st Glosters for a few months as a staff officer.

When stationed in England, Burges commanded the 3rd (Special Reserve) Battalion, Gloucestershire Regiment, at Bristol on the outbreak of the Great War, and subsequently served as a company commander in the 2nd Battalion in Flanders until wounded during the Second Battle of Ypres, 9 May 1915. His name was Mentioned in Despatches in the *London Gazette* on 12 June 1915 and he was promoted to major on 1 September 1915.

Burges was later appointed commanding officer of the 10th (S) Battalion East Yorkshire Regiment in Egypt, and also when they were in France from 9 November 1915 to 30 June 1916. Four months later he was made instructor at the Senior Officers' School at Aldershot, a post he held until March 1917, when he was transferred to the 2nd Battalion Gloucestershire Regiment, with whom he served in Macedonia on the Struma Front in July and August 1917. He was Mentioned in French General Orders, Salonika, November 1917.

On 18 September 1917 he was given the temporary rank of lieutenant colonel and took command of the 7th (S) Battalion South Wales Borderers on the Doiran Front, which he held for a year until 18 September 1918. During this period he was created a Companion of the Distinguished Service Order, which was announced in the *London Gazette* of 3 June 1918 as follows:

> His Majesty the King has been graciously pleased, on the occasion of His Majesty's Birthday, to approve of the undermentioned rewards for distinguished service in connection with military operations in Salonika. Dated 3rd June 1918. Awarded the Distinguished Service Order: – MID 11 June 1918.

After the announcement of his VC, which came on 14 December 1918, Burges was decorated by the King in the ballroom of Buckingham Palace on the 21st and was presented with his DSO at the same time. He was Mentioned in Despatches three times: 12 June 1915, 11 June 1918 and 21 January 1919. He was awarded the brevet of lieutenant colonel on 1 January 1919.

Burges had been in hospital from November 1918 to February 1919. In June 1920 Burges attended the VC Garden Party at Buckingham Palace and the Cenotaph and Unknown Warrior services on 11 November in the same year. According to his obituary in *The Times*:

> After a period at the War Office as Inspector of Quartermaster-General's services, he became Commandant of the Military Detention Barracks at Cologne, and later held a similar appointment at Colchester.

In 1921 he lived at 5 Chantry House, Eccleston Street, and then, from 1923 in the Tower of London. After going on retired pay he was appointed Major of the Tower and Resident Governor. In November 1929 he attended the House of Lords' VC Dinner.

His first wife, Katharine, died in 1931, and in the following year he married Mrs Florence Wray Taylor of Rathfarnham, Dublin, on 1 January 1932 at St James's, Piccadilly. Through this marriage he acquired a step-son. After holding the post at the Tower for ten years, Burges retired with his new wife to Bristol and he fully entered into the life of the city; in 1933 he was made president of the Society of Bristolians and in 1936 master of the Society of Merchant Venturers in Bristol. He also became director of the Gloucestershire Branch of the Red Cross.

Burges regularly attended Salonika reunions and was often guest of honour at such gatherings. In 1935 he took the salute at a British Legion parade organised by the Bristol Filton Branch. He was always ready to attend any commemorative functions and regularly took part in the wreath-laying ceremony of the South Wales Borderers in Bristol.

Dan Burges died at his home, Hyde Lodge, in Bristol on 24 October 1946, aged 73, and was cremated five days later at the Arnos Vale Crematorium, where a plaque to his memory was set up in 2006. The unveiling took place on 24 October, sixty years to the day of his death.

There are also plans to create a memorial garden in the grounds of Arno Vale.

There are also portraits of Burges both in the Imperial War Museum and the Soldiers of Gloucestershire Museum in Gloucester. His decorations, apart from the South African medals, VC and DSO, included the *Croix de Guerre* with oak leaves, Greek Military Cross (2nd Class), the 1914–15 Star, BWM, VM (1914–19) and MiD Oakleaf, and King George VI Coronation Medal (1937). They are not publicly held.

Sources

The sources used in the preparation of this book include the following:

The Lummis VC files at the National Army Museum, London
The Victoria Cross files at the Imperial War Museum, London
The National Archives at Kew, Surrey (TNA)
Regimental Museums and Archives
The London Gazette 1914–1920 (HMSO)
Stand To! and *Bulletin* are journals published by the Western Front Association. The Victoria Cross Society also publish a regular journal.

AFRICA

J.F.P. Butler

Clifford, H., *The Gold Coast Regiment in the East African Campaign* (Murray, 1920)
Hordern, C., *Military Operations in East Africa August 1914–September 1916* (HMSO, 1941), vol. 1
The King's Royal Rifle Corps Chronicle

W.T. Dartnell

TNA WO39/33566 W. Dartnell
TNA WO95/3140 WD MI Company
TNA WO95/5339 War Diary 2nd Bn Loyal North Lancs
Boyd, W., *An Ice Cream War* (Hamish Hamilton, 1982)
Darlington, L., *Firefight at Maktau* (Medals News, September 2001)
Kelleher, J., *'Elegant Extracts' – The Royal Fusiliers Recipients of the VC* (The Royal Fusiliers Association, London 2010)

Patience, K., Lieutenant Wilbur Taylor Dartnell, 'An East African Victoria Cross'. *The Journal of the Victoria Cross Society*, vol. 7, p. 28–30, October 2005

Patience, K., *When Bravery Pays*, July 1978

Uys, I., *For Valour* (Uys Publishers, Johannesburg, 1973)

W.A. Bloomfield

TNA WO95/5347 War Diary 2nd South African Mounted Brigade

Uys, I., *For Valour* (Uys Publishers, Johannesburg, 1973)

F.C. Booth

Uys, I., *For Valour* (Uys Publishers, Johannesburg, 1973)

INDIA

E. Jotham

Butler, Ruth and Gilbert, Don, *For Valour: Kidderminster's Four V.C.s* (no date (nd))

Hodson, R.V.E., *The Story and Gallantry of The North West Frontier 1849–1947*, part 16 (nd)

Lovell, N., *V.C.s of Bromsgrove School* (Bromsgrove School Enterprises)

Lovell, Nick, 'Captain Eustace Jotham V.C. Portrait of an Edwardian officer', *The Journal of the Victoria Cross Society*, vol. 4, pp. 33–7, March 2004

C. Hull

Hodson, R.V.E., *Frontier Heroes: How Can a Man Die Better?* (nd)

——, *The Story of Gallantry of the North West Frontier 1849–1947*, part 16 (nd)

The White Lancer and the Vedette (nd)

ITALY

Edmunds, J.E. and Davies, H.R., *Military Operations: Italy 1915–1919* (HMSO, 1949)

Gladden, N., *Across the Piave* (HMSO, 1971)

Wilks, J. and Wilks, E., *The British Army in Italy 1917–1918* (Leo Cooper, 1998)

C.E. Hudson

TNA WO95/4230 23rd Division
TNA WO95/4235 68th Infantry Brigade
TNA WO95/4240 War Diary 11th Sherwood Foresters
TNA WO339/27827 Captain E.H.B. Edward Brittain MC
Derby City Libraries
Berry, P. and Bostridge, M., *Vera Brittain: A life* (Chatto & Windus, 1995)
Brittain, V., *Honourable Estate: A Novel of Transition* (Macmillan, 1936)
Two Lives, 1892–1992: The Memoirs of Charles Edward Hudson, VC, CB, DSO, M.C. and Miles Matthew Lee Hudson (privately published, 1992)

J.S. Youll

TNA WO95/4230 23rd Division
TNA WO95/4235 68th Infantry Brigade
TNA WO95/4236 11th Northumberland Fusiliers
Durham County Council
Spinks Prospectus (nd)
Gladden, N., *Across the Piave* (HMSO, 1971)

W. McNally

TNA WO95/4230 23rd Division
TNA WO95/4235 68th Infantry Brigade
TNA WO95/2184 8th Yorkshire Regiment
TNA WO/363 W/1662 'Burnt File'
Gordons Catalogue, May 1993
The Green Howards Regimental Museum
Liddle, P., interview with W. McNally, December 1968, tape 1669, ref GS 1809 (Special Collections, Leeds University Library)
Chapman, R., *Beyond Their Duty: Heroes of the Green Howards* (Friends of the Green Howards, 2001)

W. Wood

Campion, David, 'The Unknown Warrior', *Bulletin* June/July 2011, no. 90

TNA WO95/4230 23rd Division

TNA WO95/4235 68th Infantry Brigade

TNA WO95/4236 10th Northumberland Fusiliers

Railway Magazine, Nov./Dec. 1943 issue (Ian Allen, Ltd)

MESOPOTAMIA

Anglesey, The Marquess of, *A History of the British Cavalry*, vol. 6: *1914–1918 Mesopotamia* (Leo Cooper, 1995)

Barker, A., *The Neglected War: Mesopotamia, 1914–1918* (Faber, 1967)

Braddon, R., *The Siege* (Cape, 1969)

Moberly, F.J., *Official History of the War: Military Operations – The Campaign in Mesopotamia, 4 vols* (HMSO, 1923–1927)

Report of the Mesopotamia Commission (HMSO, 1917)

G.G.M. Wheeler

TNA WO95/5085 6th Indian Cavalry

TNA WO95/5086 7th Hariana Lancers

Bedford Modern School

Nunn, W., *Tigris Gunboats: A Narrative of the Royal Navy Co-operation with the Military Forces in Mesopotamia* (Melrose, 1932)

Victor comic, 3 August 1974 (D.C. Thomson)

C. Singh

TNA WO95/5127 7th (Indian) Division

TNA WO95/5139 1/9th Bhopal Infantry

Lala

TNA WO95/5127 7th (Indian) Division

TNA WO95/5138 21st Brigade

Candler, E., *The Sepoy* (John Murray, 1919)

Younghusband, G., *A Soldier's Memoirs in Peace and War* (Dutton, 1925)

J.A. Sinton

TNA WO95/5073 3 (Indian) Corps DDMS, Dec. 1915–Mar. 1917
Lindsay, S., 'Merseyside Heroes' (unpublished MS)
Biographical Memoirs of Fellows of the Royal Society, vol. 2 (The Royal Society, 1956)

G. Stringer

TNA WO95/5108 The 1st Manchesters

A. Buchanan

TNA WO95/5161 4th South Wales Borderers
South Wales Borderers (Fact Sheet 17 August 2001)
TNA WO95/5160 40th Infantry Brigade
TNA WO95/5147 13th Division
'Army and Legion Honour Coleford's Hero' (October 1987)
'English Heroes' (*This England*, Spring 1986)
Hart, C., *Coleford: The History of a West Country Forest Town* (Alan Sutton, 1983)
Jones, The Revd Cyril H., *Recollections of Angus Buchanan*

S.W. Ware

Queen's Own Highlanders Museum

W.R.F. Addison

TNA WO95/5147
Coins and Medal News (June 1983)
Cranbrook's Chaplain V.C. (nd)
Eastern Daily Press, 13 September 1958, 'Gift to Norfolk V.C. Rector'
Eastern Daily Press, 19 February 1983, 'The Padres were brave'
'East Anglian V.C.s', *Eastern Daily Press*, nd
'Tribute to a Quiet Country Parson, V.C.', *Eastern Daily Press*, 22 January 1962
'Coltishall's V.C. Rector to Retire', *Eastern Daily Press*, 26 July 1958

J.H. Finn

TNA WO95/5147 13th (Indian) Division
TNA WO95/5160 40th Infantry Brigade
TNA WO95/5161 4th South Wales Borderers
Bodmin Town Museum
Diary kept by James Finn for 1916 (Bodmin Town Museum)
Long, L.E., *An Old Cornish Town: Bygone Bodmin in Essay & Anecdote* (Bodmin Books Ltd, 1975)
South Wales Borderers
'The Roll-Call of Heroes: The Royal Investiture in Hyde Park' (*Sunday Pictorial*, 3 June 1917)

E.K. Myles

TNA WO95/5147 13th (Indian) Division
TNA WO95/5157 39th Brigade
TNA WO95/5159 9th Worcesters
The Boys' Brigade Gazette, 1 November 1916
'Lieut. Edgar Kinghorn Myles, V.C.' (Supplement to the *East Ham Secondary School Magazine*) (n.d.)
Page, B.J. and Pewsey, S., *Most Conspicuous Bravery: The Life of Edgar Kinghorn Myles V.C. A Forgotten Essex War Hero* (Troy Novant Press, 1995)
Spinks Prospectus April 1961
The Echo and Mail, 29 September 1918, 'V.C. for East Ham Scholarship Boy'
'V.C. to be Leyton's Air Raid Officer', *Leytonstone Express*, 22 January 1938

S. Khan

TNA WO95/5094 3rd (Lahore) (Indian) Division Jan. 1916–June 1916
TNA WO95/5105 7th Indian Brigade
TNA WO95/5107 89th Punjab Regiment
Khan Bahadur, Colonel Sardar Ashgar Ali, *Our Heroes of the Great War* (nd)

E.E.D. Henderson

TNA WO95/5147 13th (Indian) Division
TNA WO95/5157 39th Brigade
TNA WO95/5159 9th Royal Warwicks
The Stafford Knot (April 1970)

R.E. Phillips

Black Country Bugle (nd)
TNA WO95/5147 13th (Indian) Division
TNA WO95/5159 9th Royal Warwicks
Slim, Field Marshal Sir William, *Unofficial History* (Cassell, 1959)

T. Steele

TNA WO95/5127 7th (Indian) Division
TNA WO95/5136 19th Infantry Brigade
TNA WO95/5137 1/Seaforth Highlanders
Army Records Centre, Hayes, Middlesex
Census for 1891 and 1901
Oldham Chronicle, 9 June 1917
Oldham Evening Chronicle, 20 June 1956 and 30 June 1978
The Standard, 11 June 1917

G.C. Wheeler

TNA WO95/5163 14th (Indian) Division
TNA WO95/5180 2/9th Gurkha Rifles
'New Memorial to gallant soldier' (*The Advertiser & Times*, 11 September 1999)
Military History Society Bulletin (November 1999)

J. Readitt

TNA WO95/5147 13th (Indian) Division
TNA WO95/5155 38th Brigade
TNA WO95/5156 6th South Lancashires
Spinks Prospectus (Spring 2000)

J. White

TNA WO95/5147 13th (Indian) Division

TNA WO95/5155 38th Brigade

Dobkin, M., *More Tales of Manchester Jewry* (Manchester, Neil Richardson, 1994)

Victor comic (D.C. Thomson, nd)

O.A. Reid

TNA WO95/5147 13th (Indian) Division

TNA WO95/5155 38th Brigade

TNA WO95/5156 6th Loyal North Lancashires

Monick, S., *Johannesburg's Tribute to Valour: Captain Oswald Austin Reid's Presentation Sword* (n.d.)

Uys, I., *For Valour* (Uys Publishers, Johannesburg, 1973)

C. Melvin

TNA WO95/5128 7th (Indian) Division

The Black Watch and the Victoria Cross (nd)

'This Was the Great War', *Dundee Courier*, 11 November 1936

J.R.N. Graham

Begg, R.C., *Surgery on Trestles: A Saga of Suffering and Triumph* (Jarrold & Sons, 1967)

Daily Telegraph, 9 December 1980

Thin Red Line (Argyll & Sutherland Highlanders, nd)

The Times, 9 December 1980

PALESTINE

A Brief Record of the Advance of the Egyptian Expeditionary Force under the Command of General Sir Edmund H.H. Allenby, 2nd edn (HMSO, 1919)

Anglesey, The Marquess of, *A History of the British Cavalry, Volume 5: 1914–1919 Egypt, Palestine & Syria* (Leo Cooper, 1994)

Brice, A., *The Last Crusade: The Palestine Campaign in the First World War* (Murray, 2002)

Bullock, D., *Allenby's War: The Palestine–Arabian Campaigns 1916–1918* (Blandford Press, 1988)
Falls, C., *Armageddon 1918* (Weidenfeld & Nicolson, 1964)
Gardner, B., *Allenby* (Cassell, 1965)
James, L., *Imperial Warrior: The Life and Times of Field-Marshal Viscount Allenby 1861–1936* (Weidenfeld & Nicolson, 1993)
MacMunn, Sir G.F. and Falls, C., *Military Operations: Egypt and Palestine,* 2 vols (HMSO, 1928–30)
Wavell, A.P., *The Palestine Campaigns* (Constable, 1931)

J.M. Craig

TNA WO95/4607 1/5 Royal Scots Fusiliers (RSF)
TNA WO95/459 52 Lowland Division
The Morrisonian Club

A.M. Lafone

TNA WO374/40344 Major A.M. Lafone
TNA WO 95 4504 4th Cavalry Division
TNA WO 95/4507 1/1 London Mounted Brigade
TNA WO95/4507 1/1 County of London Yeomanry
Lindsay, S., 'Merseyside Heroes' (unpublished manuscript)

J. Collins

TNA WO95/4673 74th Yeomanry Division
TNA WO95/4679 231st Infantry Brigade

J.F. Russell

TNA WO95/4614 53rd (Welsh) Division
TNA WO95/4625 158th Infantry Brigade
Journal of the Royal Army Medical Corps, pp. 126–8 (1996)

A.D. Borton

TNA WO374/7727 A.D. Borton
TNA WO/95 4660 60th London Division
TNA WO95/4671 181st Brigade
TNA WO/4671 2/22 London Regiment
Best, Brian, '"Bosky" Borton VC: The Prodigal Son', The *Journal of the Victoria Cross Society*, vol. 6, pp. 28–32, March 2005

Pearse, Bowen, *Magnificent Survivor Arthur Drummond Borton, VC, DSO, CMG, 1883–1933* (Kent Heroes, 2002)
Slater, G., *My Warrior Sons: The Borton Family Diary, 1914–1918* (Peter Davies, 1973)

S.H.P. Boughey

TNA WO374/7847 S.H.P. Boughey
TNA WO95/4607 155th Brigade
TNA WO95/4607 1/4 Royal Scots Fusiliers
Education, Leisure and Cultural Services (Blackpool Borough Council)
Smith, David, 'Stanley Boughey: Blackpool's First VC', *The Journal of the Victoria Cross Society*, vol. 5, pp. 36–7, October 2004
Spinks Prospectus, 10 December 1986

C.W. Train

TNA WO95/4660 60th London Division
TNA WO95/4667 179th Infantry Brigade
TNA WO95/4668 2/14 London Regiment
TNA Burnt File Missorts
The London Scottish Regimental HQ
The London Scottish Regimental Gazette (Sept. 1918 and June 1965)
Blaser, B., *Kilts Across the Jordan* (Witherby, 1926)

J.A. Christie

TNA WO363/c 538 Burnt File
TNA WO95/4654 54th Division
TNA WO95/4652 162nd Infantry Brigade
TNA/WO95/4654 XI London Regiment
'English Heroes' (*This England*, Winter 1984)
The Railway Gazette, 31 January 1919

J. Duffy

TNA WO95/4567 10th Irish Division
TNA WO95/4585 31st Infantry Brigade
TNA WO95/4585 6th Royal Inniskilling Fusiliers
Rodgers, Francis O'N., 'An Irish V.C. (Battle Lines)', *Journal of the Somme Association* (1998)
The Royal Inniskilling Fusiliers Regimental Museum

H. Whitfield

TNA WO95/4673 74th Division
TNA WO95/4679 231st Infantry Brigade
TNA WO95/4679 10th Shropshire Light Infantry
The Oswestry Library, Shropshire County Council
John Whitfield
Hart-Davies, R. (ed. and intro.), *Siegfried Sassoon Diaries, 1915–1918*, pp. 253–4 (Faber & Faber, 1983)

Karanbahadur Rana

TNA WO95/4680 75th Division
TNA WO95/4689 232nd Infantry Brigade
The Gurkha Museum

R.E. Cruickshank

TNA WO95/4660 60th London Division
TNA WO95/4671 181st Brigade
Blaser, B., *Kilts Across the Jordan* (Witherby, 1926)
London Scottish Regimental Gazette (October 1961)

S. Needham

TNA WO95/4637 54th East Anglia Division
TNA WO95/4653 1/5th Bedfordshire
Bedfordshire County Council
The Wasp (Journal of the 16th Foot) (1956)

Badlu Singh

The Gurkha Museum
Khan Bahadur Col. Sardar Asghar Ali, *Our Heroes of the Great War* (The Times Press, 1922)
Spinks Prospectus 1995

SALONIKA

Falls, C., *Military Operations Macedonia, 2 vols* (HMSO, 1933–35)
Owen, H. Collinson, *Salonika and After: The Sideshow that Ended the War* (H. Collinson Owen, 1919)
Palmer, A., *The Gardeners of Salonika* (Deutsch, 1965)
Wood, W.T. and Mann, A.J., *The Salonika Front* (Black, 1920)

H.W. Lewis

TNA WO95/4857 11th Welsh Regiment
TNA WO363 L 535 Microfilm
Cooper, K. and Davies, J.E., *The Cardiff Pals* (Militaire Cymraeg, Cardiff 1998)
Ireland, W., *The Story of Stokey Lewis* (1986)

D. Burges

TNA WO95/4841 23rd Division
TNA WO95/4856 67th Brigade
TNA WO95/4857 7th (S) The South Wales Borderers
Chapman, G., *Vain Glory* (Cassell, 1937)

Bibliography

The following list of published sources used in the preparation of this book does not include the many unit histories that were consulted.

Arthur, M., *Symbol of Courage: Men Behind the Medal* (Pan, 2005)

Ashcroft, M., *Victoria Cross Heroes*, revised edition (Headline/Review, 2007)

Australian Dictionary of Biography

Bailey, Roderick, *Forgotten Voices of the Victoria Cross* (Ebury Press, 2010)

Bancroft, J. W., *Devotion to Duty: Tributes to a Region's V. C.* (Aim High Publications, Manchester, 1990)

Bancroft, J.W., *The Victoria Cross Roll of Honour* (Aim High Productions, Manchester, 1989)

Bean, C.E.W., *The Official History of Australia in the War of 1914–1918*, vol. 6: *The A. I. F. in France during the Allied Offensive 1918* (University of Queensland Press, 1983)

Brazier, K., *The Complete Victoria Cross: A Full Chronological Record of all Holders of Britain's Highest Award for Gallantry* (Pen & Sword, Barnsley, 2010)

Canadian War Records, *Thirty Canadian VCs, 1918* (Skeffington, Canada, 1919)

Chapman, R., *Beyond Their Duty: Heroes of the Green Howards* (The Green Howards Museum, Richmond, Yorkshire, 2001)

Clark, B., *The Victoria Cross: A Register of Awards to Irish-born Officers and Men* (The Irish Sword, 1986)

Deeds that Thrilled the Empire: True Stories of the Most Glorious Acts of Heroism of the Empire's Soldiers and Sailors During the Great War (Hutchinson, London, nd)

De la Billiere, P., *Supreme Courage: Heroic Stories from 150 Years of the VC* (Abacus, 2005)

Denman, T., *Ireland's Unknown Soldiers: The 16th (Irish) Division in the Great War, 1914–1918* (Irish Academic Press, Dublin, 1992)

Doherty, R. and Truesdale, D., *Irish Winners of the Victoria Cross* (Four Courts Press, Dublin, 2000)

Gilbert, M., *First World War Atlas* (Weidenfeld & Nicolson, 1970)

Gliddon, G. (ed.), *VCs Handbook:* The Western Front 1914–1918 (Sutton Publishing, Stroud, 2005)

Harvey, D., *Monuments to Courage: Victoria Cross Headstones & Memorials* (D. Harvey, 1999)

James, E.A., *British Regiments 1914–1918* (Samson Books, 1978)

Lindsay, S., '*Merseyside Heroes*' (unpublished manuscript)

The London Gazette, 1916–1920

McCrery, N., *For Conspicuous Gallantry: A Brief History of the Recipients of the Victoria Cross from Nottinghamshire and Derbyshire* (J. H. Hall & Sons, Derby, 1990)

Moberley, F.J., *Military Operations: Togoland and the Cameroons, 1914–1916* (HMSO, 1931)

Murphy, James, *Liverpool VCs* (Pen & Sword Military, Barnsley, 2008)

Napier, G., *The Sapper VCs: The Story of Valour in the Royal Engineers and its Associated Corps* (The Stationery Office, London, 1998)

Nicholson, G.W.L.N., *Canadian Expeditionary Force 1914–1919* (Queen's Printer, Ottawa, 1962)

Official History of the Great War Military Operations Maps on CD-Rom: Other Theatres 1914–19 (Imperial War Museum/Naval & Military Press)

O'Moore, Creagh, General Sir, Humphris, E.M. and Miss, E., *The VC and DSO*, vol. 1, 1924

Pillinger, D. and Staunton, A., *Victoria Cross Presentations and Locations* (D. Pillinger and A. Staunton, Maidenhead, 2000)

The Register of the Victoria Cross (This England Books, 1988)

Ross, Graham, *Scotland's Forgotten Valour* (Maclean Press, 1995)

Shannon, S.D., *Beyond Praise: The Durham Light Infantrymen who were Awarded the Victoria Cross* (County Durham Books, Durham, 1998)

Smith, M., *Award for Valour: A History of the Victoria Cross and the Evolution of British Heroism* (Palgrave Macmillan, 2008)

Smyth, Sir John, *VC: The Story of the Victoria Cross* (Frederick Muller, 1963)

Staunton, A., *Victoria Cross: Australia's Finest and the Battles they Fought* (Hardie Grant Books, Victoria, 2005)

Stewart, Iain, VC website: www.victoriacross.org.uk

Wigmore, L. and Harding, B., *They Dared Mightily*, second edition revised by Williams, J. and Staunton, A. (Australian War Memorial, Canberra, 1986)

Williams, W. Alister, *Heart of a Dragon: The VCs of Wales and the Welsh Regiments, 1914–1982* (New Edition Bridge Books, Wrexham, 2008)

INDEX

Individuals

Places (in text order)

Burial Locations